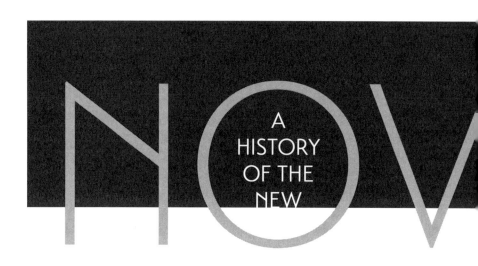

A
HISTORY
OF THE
NEW

MICHAEL NORTH

THE UNIVERSITY OF CHICAGO PRESS

Chicago and London

MICHAEL NORTH *is*
professor of English
at the University of
California, Los Angeles
and the author of
Henry Green and
the Writing of His
Generation *(1984);*
The Final Sculpture:
Public Monuments and
Modern Poets *(1985);*
The Political Aesthetics
of Yeats, Eliot, and
Pound *(1991);* The
Dialect of Modernism:
Race, Language, and
Twentieth-Century
Literature *(1994);*
Reading 1922: A Return
to the Scene of the
Modern *(1999);* Camera
Works: Photography
and the Twentieth-
Century Word *(2005);*
and Machine-Age
Comedy *(2009), and*
the editor of The Waste
Land: A Norton Critical
Edition *(2001).*

The University of Chicago Press, Chicago 60637
The University of Chicago Press, Ltd., London
© 2013 by The University of Chicago
All rights reserved. Published 2013.
Printed in the United States of America

22 21 20 19 18 17 16 15 14 13 1 2 3 4 5

ISBN-13: 978-0-226-07787-1   (cloth)
ISBN-13: 978-0-226-07790-1   (e-book)
DOI: 10.7208/chicago/9780226077901.001.0001

Library of Congress
Cataloging-in-Publication Data
North, Michael, 1951– author.
    Novelty : a history of the new / Michael North.
        pages ; cm
    Includes bibliographical references and index.
    ISBN 978-0-226-07787-1 (hardcover : alkaline
    paper)—ISBN 978-0-226-07790-1 (e-book)
    1. New and old.   2. Evolution.   I. Title.
    B105.N4N67 2013
    001—dc23

                                        2013005365

♾ This paper meets the requirements of
ANSI/NISO Z39.48–1992 (Permanence of Paper).

CONTENTS

INTRODUCTION

The state of being recent, unfamiliar, or different from the past is actually a little difficult to talk about in itself, since modern English is peculiarly deficient in respectable terms for the new. *Newness* can suffice in a pinch, but it seems both awkward and fussy. *Novel* has a slightly pejorative sense when used as an adjective, and a very restricted meaning when used as a noun. And *novelty* has a very shady reputation, redolent of dime stores, corny songs, and practical jokes. What does it mean, that the most common terms for the new are so hard to use? How does the quality that makes a new shirt or a new friend such a positive experience turn into something almost sinister in the abstract? That quality, of being different from what has gone before, is clearly of great importance to us, though we find it difficult and even embarrassing to give it a name. But the linguistic awkwardness in finding a good descriptive term for the new is almost certainly the effect of a deeper difficulty in coming up with a definition of it. Perhaps there would be a better noun than *novelty*, one above suspicion, if English speakers were more certain about what they mean when they call something new. Filling in that blank, giving the term *novelty* something more certain to stand for, is the purpose of this book.

Right now, at a time when most first-run movies seem to be either remakes or sequels, when the popular new singers are all expert mimics of some vocal style of the past, when period nostalgia progresses through the decades faster than time itself and threatens to catch up with the present, the status of novelty as a value would not seem to be particularly high. Indeed, a consumer marketing firm determined as long ago as 1991 that "newness used to have a cachet all by itself. It doesn't anymore."[1] In the art world, indifference to the new has been a popular pose at least since the 1960s, when Robert Smithson decreed, "Nothing is new, neither is anything old."[2] In fact, the whole distinction between modernist art and that which followed in the 1960s, a distinction that once seemed so epochal, was based on an apparent disagreement about the very possibility of the new and about the desirability of associated qualities such as originality and autonomy. All of these were blown away like so much dust, it seemed, when Andy Warhol promoted some Campbell's Soup cans from the supermarket to the art gallery.

Desire for the new, however, seems to be a fairly durable human quality, and interest in it persists even now, after its role in the worlds of art and fashion has been exposed and debunked. The computer and consumer electronics industries, before all others, keep the topic of innovation current and popular, even as the movie industry tears through its old comic books looking for heroes, and a considerable amount of academic research is aimed at defining innovative business strategies so that they can be imitated. Innovation is also a concern in the sciences, especially biology, where the nature of evolutionary novelty is one of the main points of contention between developmentalists and traditional molecular biologists. Emergent evolution, briefly fashionable a century ago, has been revived by such disputes and is now seriously considered an explanation for the new not just in biology but also in physics, in systems theory, and in the work of contemporary theorists such as Manuel De Landa.[3] Certain strains of continental philosophy, especially those following from the work of Gilles Deleuze and Alain Badiou, get much of their polemical punch from the claim that these thinkers can adequately explain how the world generates genuine novelty.[4] Of course, very little obvious overlap exists between this sort of philosophy and the study of commercial innovation, though Deleuze was concerned enough about the apparent similarities between his work and the "disciplines of communication" to ward them off with a blast of sarcasm.[5] Such antipathies aside, the problems and possibilities of novelty now receive a considerable amount of attention from a number of different disciplines.

Despite this interest, however, there is considerable diffidence about defining the nature of the new as such. For example, contemporary study of innovation in business begins with an article of faith laid down by the economist Joseph Schumpeter: "The fundamental impulse that sets and keeps the capitalist engine in motion comes from the consumer's goods, the new methods of production or transportation, the new markets, the new forms of industrial organization that capitalist enterprise creates."[6] Though Schumpeter seems quite insistent about the necessity of the new, and though innovation studies in sociology, anthropology, social psychology, and communications have such an ingrained bias in favor of novelty that it threatens to become a shibboleth, "similar to 'motherhood' and 'patriotism,'"[7] the basic term in the field still seems to have been left more or less alone, untouched by close examination. The standard text on the diffusion of innovation defines an innovation as "an idea, practice, or object that is perceived as new by an individual or other unit of adoption." And it declares forthrightly that "it matters little, so far as human behavior is concerned, whether or not an idea is 'objectively' new as measured by the lapse of time since its first use or discovery."[8] Novelty is supposed to be an ontological possibility, since there is a "first use or discovery," but its objective status is mysterious enough to be protected by scare quotes.

To innovate is, in Latin at any rate, to renew or to reform, not to start over afresh, though it has acquired in English usage the implication of introducing something new to a particular environment. In this sense, however, "diffusion of innovation" is something of a redundancy, since an innovation is by definition something that has become new by being moved to a place unfamiliar with it. Diffusion, that is to say, is itself tantamount to innovation. But one problem with this definition is that diffusion also assumes acceptance and thus the dissipation of novelty. Even in its reduced form as innovation, then, actual novelty only exists at the very crest of the wave, in the time, however short, between introduction and acceptance. Since the novelty in question is purely subjective in nature, dependent on its relative unfamiliarity to a new audience, it tends to evaporate almost at the very instant it is recognized.

Innovation is therefore a term that compacts within itself the whole hopeless treadmill of capitalist advance that had been decried even before Marx, powered by a double bind in which novelty is both necessary and impossible at the same time.[9] In such a system, oddly enough, the novel can persist only insofar as it meets with resistance and doesn't diffuse. This is one reason why the avant-garde is often considered a necessary adjunct to the settled order it supposedly opposes, why sociologies of innovation in the arts strongly resemble sociologies of commercial innovation. The economist David Galenson's intriguing project, for example, attempts to quantify and compare the relative importance of major modern artists, using novelty as the definitive characteristic of accomplishment. As he shows with abundant quotations, this was the standard often applied by the artists themselves. To take just one example from many, Joris-Karl Huysmans praises Edgar Degas as "a painter who derived from and resembled no other, who brought with him a totally new artistic flavor, as well as totally new skills."[10] However, whatever Huysmans may have had in mind, the "totally new" is a quality that proves very hard to capture.

In fact, Galenson passes over the new itself, restricting the term *novelty* to obvious, startling developments with little staying power, to concentrate on *innovation*, which he defines as "a change in existing practice that becomes widely adopted by other artists."[11] An innovation is a novelty that sticks—a difference, as the anthropologist Gregory Bateson would have it, that makes a difference. This, then, is Galenson's version of the paradox visible in the sociology of diffusion, since it seems to make innovation almost the opposite of novelty, insofar as the importance of an innovation comes to depend on its acceptance and durability and not on its difference. As Galenson's own evidence shows, artists resisted this double bind with just as much commitment as they proclaimed the new. Like a member of a medieval craft guild jealous of its secrets, Georges Seurat tried to prevent others from appropriating his techniques: "The more of us there are, the less originality we will have, and the day when everyone practices this technique, it will no longer have any value and people will look for something new as is already happening."[12] Innovation, defined as a widely accepted change, thus turns out to be the enemy of the new, even as it stands for the necessity of the new.

The trouble in such cases seems to come from the paradoxical relation between relative and absolute novelty, since the relative is not actually a modest version of the absolute but rather the antithesis of it. To say that everything is new to someone somewhere is to make novelty a routine fact of existence, part of the steady state of the universe. A genuine novelty, in the sciences at any rate, is a major disturbance in the universe, a development like consciousness or life itself. Novelty of this kind is the stock-in-trade of evolutionary biology, and evolution itself is the most widely accepted account of novelty in the absolute sense. And yet, there is still considerable controversy among biologists about what should count as an evolutionary novelty, and there is a great deal of troubled introspection in the field about its standards and methods of defining the new. Popular accounts such as the biochemist Nick Lane's *Life Ascending* dramatize evolution as a series of splendid "inventions" such as eyesight or sex,[13] but practicing biologists have warned for some time that such developments are far too general to be considered discrete evolutionary novelties. They are, as the paleornithologist Joel Cracraft puts it, "typological constructs . . . and as such are limited in what they can tell us about the processes actually responsible for the origin and maintenance of evolutionary novelties."[14] That is to say, something like eyesight is not a single "invention" at all but a bundle of genetic changes and developmental adaptations, one that can differ as dramatically from species to species as the eye of the octopus differs from that of the chimpanzee. But the problem left by Cracraft's skepticism is how to find an evolutionary innovation that is not a "typological construct," and where, in the complex relation between discrete genetic change and gross phenotypic appearance, to find the defining hallmarks of the new.

Novelty, in short, is at once an indispensable concept and a serious problem, not just in one but in a number of different disciplines. Given this situation, it makes sense to assume a fairly well-developed tradition of commentary on the concept, a continuing discussion of it in the abstract, apart from the practical definitions applied in particular fields. But it doesn't take much looking to discover that there isn't any such tradition, no standard text, no omnibus history. Though novelty is not itself by any means new, being one of the very first ideas to trouble the consciousness of humankind, it seems almost to have no past, as if it arose from nothing every time it occurred. Of course, novelty as such has been discussed any number of times between Parmenides and Whitehead, and some of these discussions look back over past attempts before beginning their own. Philosophical accounts of the new became especially self-conscious, not oddly, around the beginning of the twentieth century, when William James and Henri Bergson added their considerable efforts to those of Whitehead. But these are really additions to the history of the new and not accounts of it, except insofar as all three philosophers identify novelty as one of the great unsolved problems in modern thought.

Clearly, novelty subtends modernity itself, and so the lack of any solid notion of what the new might mean threatens the validity of common concepts of the modern. Here, the chief symptom is the prevalence of Ezra Pound's famous slogan, Make It New, the ubiquity of which signifies both the centrality of the concept and the absence of any real attention to it. A good recent example is offered by the scholar and critic Jed Rasula's very capable survey of modernist demands for the new, a survey he calls simply "Make It New."[15] Like many of those who have reused Pound's perennially useful slogan, Rasula puzzles briefly over the "it," which seems to be such a pointed reference and yet remains so vague. Surprisingly, though, he does not wonder at all about the real gist of the slogan, the "new," which to him "seems concrete and unambiguous."[16] Then, since the most important part of the slogan does not require definition, writer after writer can be brought forward to say his or her piece about the immediate necessity of novelty without anyone pausing to wonder what is meant by that term.

Rasula can hardly be blamed for not defining what is taken so wholly for granted by his sources. As the literary theorist and critic Terry Eagleton comments in a review of a recent collection of artists' manifestos, "Nothing is more typical of these activists than a mindless celebration of novelty—a brash conviction that an absolutely new epoch is breaking around them. . . . How one would set about identifying absolute novelty is a logical problem that did not detain them."[17] Of a group of avant-garde composers working later in the century, the philosopher Stanley Cavell once observed, "There is, first, an obsession with *new-ness* itself. . . . None, that I recall, raises the issue as a problem to be investigated, but as the cause of hope or despair or fury or elation."[18] In these first-hand accounts of the work of modernism, what is perhaps the most important distinguishing quality of that movement is left unexamined and undefined.

Novelty, in short, is a crucial and yet vague term in the sciences, the social sciences, and the arts, so that defining it is an inherently interdisciplinary task, beyond the interests and ambitions of any particular field. Perhaps it is not so odd, then, that so little is to be found in the scholarship on novelty as such. For the same reason, we are steadily less likely, every year, to get a general account of the concept, as the work of sociology, philosophy, biology, and aesthetics advances, becoming ever more daunting to the nonspecialist. To anyone foolish enough to approach the problem on so broad a front, however, it soon becomes apparent that there is a considerable consistency, not in definitions of the new, which are always very hard to come by, but in the models that have been applied to the problem. The simple fact that very few of these exist, that serious workers in every field have come back to the same few methods of conceptualizing the new, makes it possible to attempt its history.

What follows, then, is not a comprehensive account of everything said on the subject of novelty, or even of the best that was said, but rather a basic history of the conceptual models that have made it possible to think about what seems an unthinkable problem. That there is something necessary about these models is suggested by the fact that their basic shapes were established before Plato and have not varied much since. The purpose of the first chapter of this study is therefore to show how there came to be but two ways around philosophy's foundational skepticism about the very possibility of novelty. One of these, recurrence, has the advantage of seeming to have the sanction of nature but the disadvantage of not seeming to offer any real novelty. The other, recombination, seems to offer unlimited novelty, but only if unprecedented relations between existing elements can be considered truly new entities. Despite the equivocal nature of these models, between them they can account for virtually every one of the major ways in which novelty has been conceptualized in European history—reformation, renaissance, revolution, invention—and it is the purpose of the second chapter to describe, in fairly summary fashion, the development and differentiation of these and the political and intellectual implications of the differences between them.

Modern experimental science originally based its account of the universe on a revived version of ancient atomism, and thus, by its lights, recombination explained the creativity of nature as it also described the nature of scientific investigation itself. Later, in the twentieth century,

Thomas Kuhn demoted this sort of science, suggesting that significant advances and discoveries arrive as total revolutions in the way science is done. But science itself, in the form of evolutionary biology, had already worked out a highly sophisticated symbiosis between recurrence and recombination, the genesis of which is the subject of the third chapter. It seems very telling that the most influential modern model of creative change should itself have been invented as a subtle combination of two ancient precursors. Evolution, imagined even by Darwin as a revolution in human thought, advanced beyond such models from the past mainly by consuming them, producing a new hybrid with significant advantages derived from all its antecedents.

Another purpose of the third chapter is to show how evolution made novelty fundamental to nature and thus sparked renewed interest in it as a scientific and philosophical issue, without definitively settling any of the basic controversies that had dogged discussions since the pre-Socratics. Later biologists called on a wide range of other disciplines in order to address what turned out to be one of the main open questions left behind by Darwin—the actual nature of evolutionary novelty, and it is the purpose of chapter 4 to show how probability, statistical mechanics, and information theory came together not just to inform late twentieth-century biology but also to offer a model of the new that would become influential all across the information age. Cybernetics, systems theory, and information processing seemed like such new disciplines when they arrived in the 1950s and 1960s, in part because they appropriated the new as their raw material and because they promised, somewhat paradoxically, to make the production of the new automatic and certain.

The issue in all these cases is the nature of ontological novelty, which is surely the most daunting version of the problem, since the very laws of physics seemed for so many years to rule the truly new out of the question. Turning to epistemological novelty would seem to make things a good deal easier, since it must be true that everyone has new ideas and new experiences every day. Relative and subjective novelty of this kind must be common and thus easy to define. It is the general burden of the last three chapters, however, that this is not the case. As far back as Plato's *Meno*, in fact, philosophers have been troubled by a homely paradox: how can I find out what I want to know unless I already know it well enough to identify it? In the *Meno*, the argument is openly eristic, and it is meant to be swept aside by the resolution that we already know what is important, so that learning is really recollection.[19] Plato resolves the issue, in other words, by showing that there is no such thing as a new idea. Modern scientific inquiry would be neither necessary nor possible if such were really the case, but some modern philosophers of science have also believed that preconceptions have an inevitably primary role in scientific research. According to the most influential account of modern scientific discovery, in fact, "particular laboratory manipulations presuppose a world already perceptually and conceptually divided in a certain way."[20] If so, then it would seem that a new idea would be just as hard to come by as a brand-new lump of matter.

It is not surprising, then, that influential modern explanations of new ideas in the sciences should follow very closely ancient models of novelty in the physical world. Chapter 5 follows this resemblance in the influential work of Thomas Kuhn, which is, despite its overt reliance on the trope of revolution, a virtual anthology of old models of the new. Kuhn's particular way of arranging recombination and recurrence into a self-sustaining cycle owes an obvious debt to Darwin, but it also bears a strong resemblance to the project of cybernetics, which reached the height of its fame at about the time Kuhn published his masterwork. Thus the chapter will take up a number of intriguing similarities between Kuhn and Norbert Wiener, particularly the ways they attempt to account for scientific discovery and advance within a system of knowledge that is self-sustaining and thus to some extent impervious to change.

In their different ways, Kuhn and Wiener try to explain how a system might arrive at a point where the new is both routine and revolutionary. At this same time, critics of modernist art and literature were facing a similar puzzle: how to handle the transformation of modernism into a settled fact of contemporary life. Could there be, they wondered, a tradition of the new? The first step toward answering this question is to determine what modernists meant by the new, and this is not by any means a simple task. As chapter 6 will show, writers and artists of the early part of the twentieth century held a wild variety of positions on the subject of novelty, some of them strongly negative. Even those in favor of the new as such had a great many different ways of describing their ideal.

In fact, it seems that the only reason there is any order at all to the ca-
cophony of modernist statements in this respect is that the range of available models of novelty had already been circumscribed by history. Modernism, in other words, does not have its own theory of the new, in part
because there is no one theory of the new universally subscribed to by
modern artists and writers. Even the apparent simplicity of Make It New
can be opened up to reveal a series of layers, telling the history of novelty
back to its beginnings.

One of the most interesting things to be discovered by a serious examination of Pound's slogan is that it was not a slogan until the late 1950s
and early 1960s. The phrase that is now universally taken to summarize
the ambitions of modernist artists and writers was quite obscure until
the literary scholar and critic Hugh Kenner gave it some prominence
in the *Hudson Review*. It became so notorious, not because it summa-
rized the ambitions of the modernists themselves, but rather because it
helped critics and scholars to talk about a quality that was then under
serious debate. The contest joined in the 1960s between the essayist and
visual art critic Clement Greenberg and the artists responsible for Pop,
minimalism, and conceptual art was very largely fought out over the
issue of novelty. A great deal of the struggle within Greenberg's criticism
itself is over the difference between the necessary novelty of modernist
art and the apparently spurious novelty of the art that followed. Chapter 7 is about this contrast, between the tradition of the new as it came to
be defined by Greenberg, Stanley Cavell, and the modernist art critic and
art historian Michael Fried and what Greenberg damned as the "Novelty
Art" of the movements of the 1960s, movements that are still commonly
lumped together under the damning title of the "neo-avant-garde."[21]

Partly by coincidence, the tradition of the new established and defended by Greenberg and Cavell very strongly resembles the circular pattern of upheaval and reintegration discovered in the sciences by Kuhn
and Wiener. Some of this similarity might also be explained by the example of evolution, discernible in the distance behind both models, and
some more of it may be due to the friendship between Kuhn and Cavell.
The intellectual part of that friendship was based on a mutual interest in
the problems and possibilities presented by the later Wittgenstein, especially by the tacit forms of life that Kuhn came to call paradigms. On one

hand, the shared linguistic conventions that Wittgenstein explored are flexible and open-ended, and thus they seem to present the possibility of infinite novelty. On the other hand, there is no such thing as thought outside a paradigm, and no way to check the authority of a paradigm from a vantage point beyond it. The result is a newness that always remains circumscribed within the limits of the old.

The conclusion will reconsider this paradox in light of the history of the new in general. That history may also be able to shed some light on the disturbing fact that so many twentieth-century prophets of innovation, in the sciences as well as the arts, have come to be seen as repressive traditionalists. Is it the passage of time that makes a radical thinker like Kuhn seem an apologist for the status quo? Were the great modernists secretly conservative all the time, even when they were making their innovations? Perhaps there is something in the structure of novelty itself that might account for the fact that change and continuity lie so close together in twentieth-century art and thought. Or perhaps there is a tension within our ideas about the new that results in a pattern of constantly frustrated expectations. If so, then it may be possible to untangle our expectations by investigating their history and thus to come to a better estimation of the possibilities and impossibilities of the new.

HOW NEWNESS
COMES INTO THE
WORLD

PART I

1

NEWNESS COMES INTO THE WORLD

THE PATHOS OF THE NEW

As Saladin Chamcha and Gibreel Farishta fall from the exploded remains of the airliner *Bostan*, the narrator of Salman Rushdie's *Satanic Verses* poses what turns out to be the abiding question of that novel: "How does newness come into the world?"[1] It is a pertinent question for these two, who need to sprout wings very quickly or suffer annihilation on the beach below; and it becomes even more relevant after their miraculous survival, as they undergo a series of fantastic transformations. It is also a typically modern question, not just in the value it places on the new but also in the confidence with which it assumes that novelty exists. In his haste to ask *how* newness comes into the world, the narrator neglects to establish that it does come. But the peculiar way he asks this question about novelty actually casts some doubt on its status. Newness is expected to "come into the world," apparently from some point outside it, as if there were some other sector, not the world as we know it, with a reservoir of novelty that periodically "leaks" into our space, to take a memorably odd metaphor from William James.[2] The metaphor implies that novelty doesn't belong in the world at all, and that once here, stray droplets of it must soon dry up and cease to be new.

Rushdie's narrator and his characters ultimately spend some time worrying about novelty, sifting through authorities from Lucretius to Darwin, without really clarifying—much less answering—the original question. In its earnest demand for something new, its blithe assumption that a store of novelty exists somewhere, and its utter, contradictory vagueness about the nature and status of that source, Rushdie's question fairly represents the attitude of modernity toward what is usually considered its most definitive attribute. Whenever it is supposed to start, modernity is always marked off from whatever comes before by the conversion of the new from a relative term into an absolute value. At some point, the ordinary, trivial freshness of the passing moment becomes the *novum*, the new in itself, and the present becomes the *Neuzeit*, a time not just radically different from all others but better because of its difference.[3] Before novelty could become "the essence of modernity," it had to be essentialized itself, a host of novel effects and stylistic surprises, natural wonders and scientific discoveries, inventions and innovations gathered up into one abstract category explaining and exalting them all.[4] In this respect, "Make It New" stands first on the command line of the modern program because it converts everything into a format that modernity can use. In its vagueness, Pound's motto dictates something grander and more abstract than the transformation of "it" into a new version of itself. Enlisting every particular in a single, all-inclusive category, the slogan makes everything into the one thing that matters: the new.

How much sense does it make, though, to want everything to be new absolutely, once and for all? It seems an especially feckless ambition when even the ordinary claims of any relative novelty are so easy to dispute. In merely empirical terms, the boasts of any period or movement to have effected "an absolute beginning" are easily disproved, so that the breakpoint of the modern is pushed farther and farther back until the Renaissance becomes the "early modern" and the stretch of temporal wasteland once known as the Dark Ages is revealed in its turn as a series of preparatory renewals.[5] If George Boas is right and "what we call 'periods' are simply the names of the influential innovations which have occurred constantly in . . . history," then every period is vulnerable to the inevitable disputation of its novelty and thus to the loss of its conceptual distinctness.[6] The fact that "Make It New" is itself an ancient saying and not a coinage of 1914 is one of the best examples of the apparently inevitable priority of the past over the pretensions of the present, and the resulting paradox of an old saw commanding the new might then stand for the uneasy condition of any modernity that bases its claims on lack of precedent.[7]

If the relative newness of every period, every movement, school, or trend is open to dispute, if any particular novelty is always subject to the inevitable evidence that discoveries are preceded and innovations anticipated, then what of the category itself? Are these historical difficulties evidence of a more general problem in the concept of novelty as such? Even in the abstract, of course, novelty depends on something prior, on the very continuity it claims to violate.[8] If what distinguishes new things is their difference from what existed before, then it does not seem possible to establish novelty as such, without reference to a past that did not contain it.[9] As Josiah Royce argued some time ago, this means that the newness of any new particular cannot be apprehended in the particular itself, nor can it be generalized as an abstraction. The apparent novelty of any particular moment, he says, "is neither to be adequately expressed through any of our processes of classifying objects, nor yet . . . to be adequately presented to us by any datum of sense or of feeling. For a sensory datum or an immediate feeling does not immediately show you that it is unique in its own kind."[10] If Royce is right, then perhaps problems in defining the modern, whenever it occurs, begin in a more fundamental problem with the concept of novelty in general, as distinct from any particular new thing.

And yet, for several centuries the new has floated in front of scientists and artists, a goal quite separate from particular discoveries, inventions, or artworks. Hannah Arendt dates this desire for absolute novelty to the Enlightenment, especially to revolutionists in France and America, who insisted that "they saw things never seen before, thought thoughts never thought before."[11] Arendt refers in two books to this "strange pathos of novelty," a phrase as strange as the feeling it describes. For *pathos* can mean "passion," which is apparently what Karl Jaspers had in mind when he coined the phrase *Pathos des Neuen*.[12] But Arendt not only uses *pathos* in this sense but extends it to "the enormous pathos we find in the American and French Revolutions, this ever-repeated insistence that nothing comparable in grandeur and significance had ever happened in the whole recorded history of mankind."[13] What is so strange, even apparently to Arendt herself, is the sense of suffering the term *pathos* brings to this vaunting claim of absolute originality.

Arendt's phrase implies that the hopes of the new are always disappointed and pretensions to absolute novelty brought low by their inevitably relative realization. But the phrase may also imply something like the opposite, that the relative enjoyment afforded by any minimally different experience is negated by an unappeasable hunger for the absolutely new. For the new, as an ideal, is inherently unapproachable, its essential quality of not having been before ruined as soon as it is realized. Utopian desire, which is aimed at an ever-receding future, can apparently be strengthened by unending deferral, but the passion for novelty, which depends on the present not being the past, is made pathetic by the passage of a second. Making it new may therefore be a sure way of making it self-contradictory and therefore ultimately dissatisfying and disappointing.

The "pathos of novelty" thus conflicts with a much more common notion: the *frisson nouveau* that Theodor Adorno dates to Victor Hugo, in which historical and social changes promise an inexhaustible sequence of unprecedented sensations, new thrills. For Adorno as well as Arendt, though, the passage from the relative, new thrills, to the absolute, the thrill of the new, inflates and imperils the experience of novelty, giving it a kind of pathos. As he puts it in *Aesthetic Theory*, "The new is the longing for the new, not the new itself. This is the curse of everything new."[14] If, as he suggests elsewhere in the same text, it is "the cryptic inaccessibility of the new"[15] that constitutes its appeal, then every actual instance of the new is a violation of its category and thus an emotional disappointment. The passion for the new is a feeling that always keels over into suffering, since it is a desire motivated by its own unrealizability.

For Adorno, then, the new "is a blind spot, as empty as perfect thisness."[16] What attracts explorers, scientists, and artists to the new, however, is an obtuse desire to stare into this blind spot—not to find some new thing, some merely temporary innovation, but to find novelty in all its abstractness. This is impossible, since, as Adorno says, consciousness "can dream *of* the new, but it cannot dream the new itself."[17] Nonetheless, he admits, it is the necessary abstractness of the new itself that pulls individual acts, discoveries, and works of art out of their degraded status as instrumental entities and makes them instances of freedom. Without the impossible goad of novelty as such, that is to say, there would not be any of the incidental novelties that distinguish a progressive life from blank, eternal continuity. Though there seems to be an absolute disjunction between relative and absolute novelty, the latter seems to be at least the psychological precondition of the former.

Novelty, then, is "ontological nonsense. Something *is*, although and because it is *not* what was before."[18] It may also be experiential nonsense, if Royce is right to insist that the quality of not having been before is not really perceptible in the thing itself. Philosophers of science from the time of Pierre Duhem have also argued that conceptual novelty presents a paradox, that major changes in scientific thought must actually precede the empirical evidence that ostensibly supports them.[19] Some philosophers have been just as wary of logical novelty, on the traditional argument that if a logical connection is to hold, then the conclusion is already implied by the premises preceding it.[20] Perhaps this is why so few attempts have been made to formulate a rigorous definition of novelty, why it features so rarely in philosophical discussions, where it tends to tag along as an adjunct to the larger and graver problems of time or change. But if it cannot be defined or even adequately conceptualized, novelty can apparently be modeled; and the history of philosophy and practice are full of, perhaps even defined by, the structural metaphors that have been applied to the problem.

One of the most hopeless of these is to be found in Adorno, who often represents novelty as a negatively ironic effect of mechanical production: "In its original economic setting, novelty is that characteristic of consumer goods through which they are supposed to set themselves off from the self-same aggregate supply, stimulating consumer decisions subject to the needs of capital."[21] In this, probably the most common model of novelty currently in use, the new is reproduced over and over, like any other manufactured item.[22] The ontological paradoxes of absolute novelty, no longer philosophical inconveniences, are in fact the basis of its utility in the capitalist system, in which every real product is a broken version of one product, the new, which is always on offer but never actually available. Novelty of this kind is automatically self-canceling: the more of it there is, the less it can be novel. But since, in this case as in all others, scarcity drives demand, the absence of the definitively new simply increases its hold on the desires of the consumer.

Whatever aesthetic prestige the new may once have had has been pretty well ground to dust by the influence of this model, which relies on the irrefutable truism that novelty is the ultimate object of every sale, though it cannot in fact be delivered.[23] Yet even Adorno is not exclusively bound to this model, and *Aesthetic Theory* often surprises by the positive treatment it gives to novelty, which so often features there as one of the most transparent lies of the capitalist system. In fact, the mechanical production model is only a recent example of a kind of modeling that has been influential since the very beginning of Western philosophy. Structural metaphors of one kind or another have long helped to mediate between novelty as ontological nonsense and novelty as practical possibility. The basic shapes of the most durable models were laid down at the very beginning, in response to the first declarations of philosophy that novelty is nonsensical.

NOTHING COMES FROM NOTHING

Where novelty is concerned, the common sense of the ages seems to have been expressed for good and all in Ecclesiastes: "What has been is what will be, and what has been done is what will be done; and there is nothing new under the sun. Is there a thing of which it is said, 'See, this is new'? It has been already, in the ages before us" (1:9–10). But Ecclesiastes simply declares that novelty does not exist, not that it is ontologically impossible or logically incoherent. These more extreme judgments were left to philosophy. According to Hans-Georg Gadamer, the dictum *Ex nihilo nihil fit*—nothing comes from nothing—the rule that outlaws all novelty, which must somehow come from that which does not contain it, expresses "the highest principle of our orientation in the world of experience."[24] The truth of this statement may be demonstrated by the appearance of *Ex nihilo nihil fit* at both ends of the history of Western philosophy.

At this end, in Wittgenstein's *Tractatus*, the work that was supposed to finish off Western philosophy as it had been practiced for centuries, is this proposition: "If things can occur in states of affairs, this possibility must be in them from the beginning."[25] On the surface, at least, this seems to be Wittgenstein's version of the ancient philosophical cliché that the effect is implicit in its cause. It appears here in apparent defiance of the skepticism of Hume, who cast doubt on the necessary relation of cause and effect, and against the opposition of pragmatists such as James, who felt that belief in this relation made real novelty impossible.[26] Wittgenstein is not concerned as much with metaphysics as with logic, but in the latter case as well he maintains "there can *never* be surprises."[27] Sweeping away all the old claptrap of the syllogism, with its merely accidental relations, Wittgenstein replaces it with a logical syntax, the validity of which is implicit in very notion of logic itself. Once this structure is in place, "a new possibility cannot be discovered later."[28] Still, the *Tractatus* ends with some famous quasi-mystical hints of a vantage point outside this world, enclosed as it is within its own rules of thought. And it does allow that although objects are "unalterable and subsistent; their configuration is what is changing and unstable."[29] If we cannot actually surprise ourselves with thoughts we are incapable of thinking, that is to say, we may at least rearrange the mental furniture a little to keep ourselves amused.

Such a radical austerity was meant to clear away centuries of philosophical confusion, and thus it may not be pure accident that it strongly resembles the very first steps in that philosophy, before the confusion set in. In fact, Wittgenstein's first step, the proposition "The world is all that is the case,"[30] a step that all by itself seems to rule out the new, had already been taken twenty-five hundred years earlier, when the goddess of wisdom informed Parmenides "that Being is ungenerated and imperishable, entire, unique, unmoved and perfect."[31] On the surface at least, Parmenides' poem is about cosmology, and for him questions about "what is" are questions about the earth, the sun, and the stars.[32] But it was not difficult for Bertrand Russell to read the poem as a treatise on logic, in which being is a property belonging to objects of thought, "to everything that can occur in any proposition, true or false, and to all such propositions themselves."[33] In so doing, he brings the beginnings of Western philosophy into contact with its conclusion and makes Parmenides sound a good deal like Wittgenstein.[34]

Cosmological or logical, the completeness of being makes the imposition of something new quite impossible, for this would violate the law that Parmenides was apparently the first to lay down: nothing comes from nothing, "a thesis which," according to Aristotle, "more than any other, preoccupied and alarmed the earliest philosophers."[35] This thesis can be interpreted as a statement about physical being, that nothing can be created except from preexisting matter; as a statement about cause and effect, that everything must have a cause that already in some sense contains or implies it; or as a statement about epistemology, semantics, or logic, to the effect that creation from nothing is unthinkable, unsayable, or illogical.[36] In any of these cases, the thesis lays down what Alexander Mourelatos calls "a sweeping ban on coming-to-be."[37] But Parmenides was so alarming to other early philosophers because the ban on entirely new things seemed also to outlaw change of any kind. As Simplicius reasoned it out, "if something has changed, what-is has perished and what-was-not has come into existence," and thus the unity and consistency of the universe have been violated.[38] What looks like change to ordinary mortals is therefore either a mistake, since we cannot always sense the underlying consistency of what appears to be different, or an illusion, propagated by the world of opinion, which is denounced at length in the second part of Parmenides' poem.[39]

In chronological priority and in intellectual influence, nothing comes from nothing can be considered the foundational premise of Western philosophy, with a durable prestige based on its uncompromising, if not irrefutable, logic and on the counterintuitive unpleasantness of its implications.[40] Starting from the simplest of all possible premises, that what is, is, Parmenides arrives at a conclusion that seems to call all practical experience into doubt. Generation and change thus became the abiding problem of early Greek philosophy, because Parmenides had ruled out of existence what seems such an obvious fact of everyday life.[41] At the same time, Parmenides' example served to identify philosophy, and with it science and other forms of organized thought, with invariance. The basic distinction laid down in his poem, between the way of truth and the way of opinion, remains for later thinkers what it was for him—the difference between consistency and change. Thus the assumption that invariance is fundamental, while novelty and change are merely epiphenomenal, is itself an invariance that links Parmenides, at the beginning of Western philosophy, to Wittgenstein at the end.[42]

The influence of Parmenides' distinction is especially evident in Plato. In the *Theaetetus*, Socrates confesses to "a kind of reverence . . . for the great leader himself, Parmenides, venerable and awful," a reverence surely based on more than the fact that Parmenides is the only inter-locutor known to have bested him in debate.[43] Parmenides' foundational premises, that what is, is and what is not cannot come to be, were ap-parently so impressive that they established the essential conditions for Plato's ontology. In the *Timaeus*, he defines the real as "that which keeps its own form unchangingly, which has not been brought into being and is not destroyed, which neither receives into itself anything else from anywhere else, nor itself enters into anything else anywhere." What ap-pears to the senses, on the other hand, because it changes all the time, is merely the matter of opinion.[44] Plato does make a minimal concession to the world of experience by admitting that various qualities may be predi-cated of being; but these qualities, such as whiteness or largeness, are themselves immutable essences, each of which has the unchanging dura-bility of Parmenides' singular "is."[45]

Since, according to the *Timaeus*, "the pattern exists from eternity," change is an illusion and novelty a definite impossibility.[46] For Plato, this ontological ban on innovation is both a philosophical necessity and a political convenience. The purpose of government, according to the *Re-public*, is maintenance, and the governors ought to ensure that the good foundations of the state, so long as they are good, should not be upset by change. Even "music and gymnastic should be preserved in their origi-nal form, and no innovation made. . . . When the modes of music change, the fundamental laws of the State always change with them."[47] This is why philosophers should rule, because men in the world of opinion often prize "the newest song which the singers have," while "philosophi-cal minds always love knowledge of a sort which shows them the eternal nature not varying from generation and corruption."[48] In the ideal state, ruled by the ideal rulers, there would be no change, and the very memory of innovation would fade, like a pain that has finally subsided.

Plato thus preserves as much of the awful simplicity of Parmenides' system as he can, though he adds a good many innovations of his own to the original axiom that what is, is. For Aristotle, on the other hand, the axiom, though true enough in the abstract, is just not particularly useful in practice. When he says of Melissus and Parmenides that "we must not suppose they are speaking about nature," he gently sets them aside, like expensive curios.[49] To anyone with an interest in nature and with a constant eye on it, he implies, the notion that nothing changes is a philosophical affectation. The world of appearances may be misleading, but as far as Aristotle is concerned it is not wrong *by definition*, and therefore the changes we see in the natural world "are as 'real' as they appear to be."[50] Still, to say that something changes is tantamount to saying that something persists, for there must be some thing that undergoes the alteration, so "that the being of this matter and the being of 'alteration' stand and fall together."[51] Having admitted this, however, how is Aristotle to avoid the next step, in which all things are but one thing under different alterations, which is the last step before the logical whirlpool opened up by Parmenides?

In the *Physics* and *On Generation and Corruption*, Aristotle spends a good deal of time worrying about this particular step, about the difference between coming-to-be this or that, as in coming to be old, as opposed to coming-to-be in itself, as in being born. The actual existence of the latter, real novelty and not just change, is what must underlie the actual multiplicity of the world, guaranteeing that different things exist in it and not just one thing with different aspects. Even here, though, as Aristotle must admit, "there is *always* something which underlies what comes to be, from which what comes to be comes, for instance animals and plants come from seed."[52] If this is *always* the case, though, then isn't coming-to-be just a simple change after all, and creation just the appearance of differences in some fundamentally undifferentiated stuff? Traditionally, this stuff was called prime matter, and though experts now debate the extent to which and the possible ways in which it actually functioned in Aristotle's system, it served for many centuries as a logical convenience, invisibly guaranteeing that there was *something* at the beginning of every chain of generation.[53]

For the only alternative, apparently, is to find some definitive way around Parmenides' ban on something coming from nothing, while Aristotle never felt free to do more than evade it just a bit: "We also affirm that nothing comes to be without qualification from what is not. Nevertheless, we maintain that a thing may come to be from what is not *in a certain way,* for example, accidentally."[54] Aristotle thus describes a number of cases in which it might be said that something comes from nothing: if the substratum of a thing is imperceptible before a change but perceptible after it; or if one thing entirely loses its qualities and acquires a whole new set. Though the first case seems a matter of appearance, the second does seem to allow for the introduction of new substantial forms.[55] But it is just as hard to imagine how a form might arise, except from prior forms, as it is to imagine matter just popping into existence. Though Aristotle assembles some formidable machinery in the service of saving real change from its demotion to the world of opinion, he still steadies that machinery on a solid, unchanging foundation. Over the centuries, his foundational premises, such as prime matter or its counterpart the first mover, came to constitute traditional authority in philosophy, science, and religion and thus helped to support the inherent antipathy of tradition for the new.

PRE-SOCRATIC SOLUTIONS

All Aristotle's tremendous sophistication seems to show is that it not possible to think a way out of Parmenides' original ruling against novelty and change. In fact, Zeno's mind-bending paradoxes, which seem to show that it is impossible to manage even a single step, were apparently meant to demonstrate the irrefutable unity and consistency of being as taught by Parmenides and the patent absurdity of dividing it into parts, and these continued to trouble philosophers even in modern times.[56] Even disputing Parmenides' conclusions often meant accepting some of his premises, so that he succeeded at least in posing the questions that philosophy was supposed to address. Instead of constructing an entire system in resistance, as Aristotle did, the pre-Socratics generally accommodated themselves, like Plato, to the inevitability of Parmenides' wisdom. In doing so, they established some of the most durable patterns by which the apparent fact of change would be reconciled with the ostensible unity of being.

Empedocles began by accepting all Parmenides' basic assumptions while adding logically incompatible sophistications of his own devising. In a poem much like Parmenides', he taught that being is in fact one, though it has a double beginning, in love and strife, and a quadruple aspect, as earth, air, fire, and water. Beyond this basic repertoire, however, there is nothing, and nothing is ever added to or subtracted from the sum: "Nothing comes into existence or ceases to exist; there is only them. For if they were constantly perishing, they would no longer exist. What might increase this totality? Where might such a thing come from?"[57] All the multifarious things of this world thus arise from the cyclical convergence and dispersal of these basic elements, brought together by love and then dispersed again by strife: "under love we unite into a single ordered whole, Which under strife once again becomes, instead of one many, From which arise all that was and is and will be hereafter."[58]

Empedocles thus establishes two methods of coping with Parmenides' wisdom that were so influential they now seem inevitable. He accommodates himself to the singularity of being by dividing it into a few parts, each of which is just as eternal and unchangeable as the original one, and he preserves the temporal stasis of Parmenides' system by enclosing change within a repetitive cycle. On one hand, then, the unity of being is qualified a little so that its eternity can be preserved, while on the other hand eternity is modulated slightly so that being can be maintained in a unified state.[59] There is always a moment at which unity and temporal consistency converge and the universe is in its most perfect condition, when being is a "single ordered whole"; and for Empedocles this does seem to be an actual moment in historical time and not just a logical phase in the argument. The multiplicity of nature as we know it can therefore be explained by our living in a part of the cycle far removed from the moment of unity. Thus Aristotle, who left an extensive critique of Empedocles, paraphrases him as saying "that the universe is in the same state now under strife as it was before under love."[60]

The idea of cyclical recurrence predates Empedocles, even in Greek philosophy, and it must have been almost universally suggested by the rhythms of the earth and the rest of the solar system.[61] There is, of course, a particularly influential version in the Great Year of Plato's *Timaeus*, and other versions appear throughout Western philosophy and religion, even after Augustine offers what was supposed to be a definitive refutation in *City of God*. These vary widely in the details: some promising perfect repetition, others only cyclical recurrence, some deciding that time itself repeats, others that only events repeat themselves within time.[62] Empedocles offers a particularly spare and internally consistent version of the system, though, the impact of which is apparent in the amount of space Aristotle devotes to disputing it. His version also shows with particular clarity the interestingly double relation of recurrence to the idea of novelty.

It seems fairly clear that for Empedocles, as for Parmenides, the apparent moil of temporal events is not just an illusion but a malign one. What makes new things seem to appear is the action of strife, upsetting and dividing the original unity achieved by love. Thus the tremendous difference between the irrefutable conceptual unity of being and the mess we see all around us is explained as the result of a decline; and novelty must then be seen as a mark of that decline, each innovation nothing but a step away from original bliss. On the other hand, however, on the upswing as it were, the cycle brings back its own beginnings in perfect love, and the first moment recurs, as a new point of origin. What is promised at the end of the cycle, in other words, is the first point of departure, new again. In the hopeless mode, of course, cycles of recurrence promise only the same old over and over again, as in Ecclesiastes; but in their hopeful mode they promise the same novelty, over and over, somehow still new every time.

Though they constitute an essential part of the system of recurrence, Empedocles' four elements, if isolated from his temporal argument, can also point to a different model of novelty. The four elements themselves are a common feature of Greek philosophy, useful insofar as they preserve the basic consistency and completeness of being by dividing it just in four. Of course, once we start dividing, it is hard to stop at four, despite the mystic authority of that number. Plato, who also deployed the four elements when it was convenient, ultimately decomposes these into two sorts of triangles, which then make up everything between them.[63] As the irreducibly basic representation of a plane, the triangle can be thought of as the unit of three-dimensional reality, the building block which in various combinations makes up everything we see. Being, conceived as a schematic sea of triangles, is nearly as implacable as when Parmenides imagined it a single sphere, and yet the triangles can move about and rearrange themselves into the apparently limitless combinations that make up the world. Though the triangles themselves are uniform and unchanging, their rearrangement gives rise to what appears as novelty.

Plato's triangles share many characteristics with the atoms postulated by Democritus and Leucippus in their attempt to square the truth of Parmenides with the facts of observable reality. Parmenides is often understood to have proposed what is called a block universe, a unitary reality with no parts and no spaces and no void into which a part might move even if it did exist. To call this concept counterintuitive seems an understatement, since it bears no resemblance whatever to the world available to human senses. One way of closing the rather prodigious gap between concept and percept is to suggest that the unchanging universe is not available to the senses because it is composed of eternal elements too small to see. These correspond to Parmenides' description of being insofar as they cannot be created, destroyed, or altered. Given a void to move in, something the first atomists justified by the observable fact of motion in the universe, these units make up reality by combining themselves in various configurations. Change does exist, in the form of combination and recombination, though the basic consistency of the universe remains as unaltered as it was in Parmenides' vast and featureless sphere.[64]

Atomists such as Epicurus, who developed the system immortalized by Lucretius in *De rerum natura* (*On the Nature of Things*), believed just as strongly as Parmenides that nothing comes from nothing. As Lucretius rather nervously explains it in his poem, "If things could be created out of nothing, any kind of thing could be produced from any source; nothing would need a seed."[65] Lucretius produces as a cautionary illustration what is actually a rather entertaining word picture of human beings springing from the sea and fish from the ground, the whole of creation squirming with a Bosch-like mixture of plants and animals. But the logical principle of cause and effect, active in the world as the biological principle that like begets like, prevents any such chaos from breaking out. Though the world is but a cloud of particles whirling in the void, its size, shape, consistency, and pattern of development are fixed and eternal:

> At no time was the fund of matter either more solidly packed or more sparse than it is now. It experiences no gains and no losses. Thus the movement of the ultimate particles now is identical to what it has been in ages past, and it will always be so in the future. Things that have been produced will continue to be produced under the same con-

ditions, and each will exist, grow, prosper in its strength, insofar as it is permitted by the ordinances of nature.[66]

On the surface, at least, this universe does not seem any more hospitable to novelty than the block universe of Parmenides, despite its having so many more parts.

In fact, Lucretius seems to limit novelty to an early period of jostling, when the atoms are still sorting themselves out and finding the most viable combinations, as dictated by their various shapes. Without any consciousness of their own or any direction from some greater intelligence, the atoms simply have to bang about, "buffeted and impelled by blows," until they fall into configurations that will last.[67] These, then, constitute the world as we know it. Change in this world is explained by the fact that configurations are always falling apart and being reassembled, as things die and are born again; and it is not at all to be wondered at if, in the incessant business of building the world over and over from the tiniest parts, sports and monsters of various kinds are spun off. Yet new combinations, beyond those established in the first great research and development period of the universe, are not viable, and must die out. Lucretius goes so far as to criticize those mesmerized by the "empty word *novelty*" (*novitatis nomine inani*), who imagine that the world, then or now, could create what it cannot by nature contain.[68]

Given these limitations, it may be hard for modern readers to understand how atomism came to be associated over the centuries with intellectual anarchy, apart from the common misconception that Epicurus sanctioned a godless hedonism. As a philosophy of conduct, Epicureanism actually taught indifference to novelty as to every other aspect of human life: "Obviously a new state of things is bound to please one who is discontented with the old; but when one has suffered no distress in time past, but has led a life of happiness, what could kindle in one a passion for novelty?"[69] What provoked both scientific disdain and moral disapproval down through the ages was the tiny, accidental, and yet indispensable maneuver called the *clinamen*, or swerve. Having conceived of the universe as a constant rain of atoms, all falling through the void in the same direction, Epicurus used the swerve to explain how these parallel lines of descent might ever have met. A random, inexplicable hitch to one side or the other thus became the building block for the building blocks, the very basis of the principle of combination that was to explain all the things in the world.

It was not, however, just a desperate necessity that drove Epicurus to this invention, but also a conviction that a purely deterministic world system contradicted the fact of human freedom. As Lucretius puts it: "If new movement arises from the old in unalterable succession, if there is no atomic swerve to initiate movement that can annul the decrees of destiny and prevent the existence of an endless chain of causation, what is the source of this free will possessed by living creatures all over the earth?"[70] Though it is not clear in Lucretius's account how the existence of random hiccups in the essential elements of the universe can allow the exercise of human will, the constant possibility of the swerve does at least prevent the atoms from settling into a purely deterministic pattern. This thread of novelty woven into the fabric of things reappears in human action, in what Hans Blumenberg calls the human ability "to introduce absolute beginnings into reality."[71] The original imposition of the random, which ensures that there will be things at all and not just atomic mush, reappears whenever human beings make something new.

The most extensive account of pre-Socratic atomism is the entirely negative one of Aristotle, which assembles an impressive and convincing set of objections to all its basic premises. Aristotle could not see how the world could be made up of invisible indivisibles, or why, once one started to divide matter, there should be any particular atomic size at which to stop. In *On the Heavens*, he pointed out that the odd motion Democritus and Leucippus ascribed to their atoms, falling forever in the infinite void, did not resemble anything actually observable in nature or even conceivable under the laws of physics.[72] In the *Physics*, he objected that atoms could not assume toward one another any of the possible arrangements—continuity, contact, or succession—available to actual bodies or objects.[73] Most important of all for this discussion, he did not agree that mere combination could constitute coming-to-be, as opposed to ordinary change.[74] Aristotle did not have the opportunity to pronounce on the *clinamen*, which had been added to the atomic system of Democritus by Epicurus in order to qualify its determinism; but generations of Aristotelians viewed it with horror, having been taught by their master that natural motion was circular, repetitive, and transparently caused.[75]

Most of Aristotle's objections were met, of course, once real atoms could be observed; but the fundamental issue for the history of novelty—whether a new combination of the same old elements can be considered a new thing—remains open to debate. Nonetheless, recombination became, along with recurrence, one of the few influential models capable of slipping some novelty past Parmenides' ban on change. The great historical models of renewal—Christian rebirth, renaissance, and revolution—major sources of what could be considered new in human history, are different versions of recurrence that promise the return in all its pristine glory of some original newness. More recent scientific models, including evolution, currently the most ubiquitous of all, are based on the mechanics of recombination, which derive the new by rearranging preexisting elements. That the pattern underlying these models is so old, that virtually nothing new has happened in the history of novelty since Epicurus, suggests how difficult it has been to justify and explain what is supposed to be the defining value of the modern world.

Since there are two such different methods of squaring the apparent facts of experience with a conceptual ban on real novelty, the change authorized by these models arrives in very different ways. Belief in recurrence is rooted, as Arendt suggests, in the apparent ubiquity of birth and death, in the "idea that men are equipped for the logically paradoxical task of making a new beginning because they are themselves new beginnings and thus beginners."[76] But the force of this analogy is such that it makes each beginning into the same beginning, in the familiar way with which each sunrise is the same sunrise, each spring the same spring. Novelty is necessarily unique and original, but it returns, just as Troy returned in the shape of Rome and Rome in a very different form as the Christian church. Though this rhythm is explicitly natural, the way in which it constantly returns to the same point suggests that the swings in between are illusory, and thus the recurrence model is implicitly idealist. Since change is but an aberrant turn away from or a necessary return to a constant ideal, matter that changes is also mere appearance. When the new does return, though, it occurs as a total, sudden, and even violent change.[77] Everything is replaced, as it must be if there is to be another new beginning.

Recombination produces a very different temporal pattern. Though it was thought to be the principle behind all organic life, recombination since Empedocles has been conceived as a mechanical process.[78] Atoms attach to other atoms because their shapes fit, and they are driven together or whirled apart by physical forces that are constant in the universe. Thus the atomists were or at least are thought to be materialists, with rather more faith than Plato in the actual facts of experience, even though the atoms themselves are too small to see. Because nature works in such tiny units, change, when it occurs, is gradual and piecemeal, and what novelty it produces is incremental and not total. Though it is made up of the same elements over and over, this sort of novelty is also at least potentially new each time, in contrast to the novelty that returns, though Lucretius himself did not seem to believe that the store of reality can be added to in this way. In fact, atomism does such a fine job in principle of accounting for change that it risks losing its grip on consistency. Why the atoms should cohere in any of the recognizable shapes and why they should stay in them—and what's more, repeat them time after time, so that tigers remain tigers and don't usually turn up with wings or propellers—are mysteries the early atomists had to meet with smoke and mirrors.[79]

For rhetorical support in this effort, Lucretius exploited an analogy buried deep in Latin etymology. The same word that is used to designate the basic parts of a physical or mechanical combine, *elementum*, was used first for letters of the alphabet.[80] Lucretius calls his atoms *elementa*, and when he does he takes advantage of the fact that he can simultaneously invoke the authority of language: "Therefore the supposition that, as there are many letters common to many words, so there are many elements common to many things, is preferable to the view that anything can come into being without ultimate particles."[81] As is his wont, Lucretius repeats this point a number of times in his poem—but it is more than a rhetorical effect, because the way in which language derives nearly infinite variety from a small number of repeated elements offers a precedent supporting what might otherwise seem the counterintuitive claims of Epicurean atomism. Even the repetitiveness with which he makes this point, sometimes attributed to incomplete revision, might be considered an implicit illustration of his thesis, as Lucretius calls attention to the poem itself as a combinatorial system that manufactures meaning from the same few basic bits: "Similarly, throughout these verses of mine you see many letters common to many words, even though you must concede that the verses and the words differ both in sense and in resonant sound. Such is the power letters derive from mere alteration of order. But the primary elements have at their disposal several other means of variation to enable them to create the whole multiplicity of things."[82] The very existence of the poem itself, in other words, is a powerful argument for the validity of the Epicurean system.

The pun on *elementum* has a counterpart in ancient Greek, where the word *stoicheion*, for example, can be used for letters and for elements or parts of a whole. Similarly, *sullabē* covers the case of syllables and of complexes or combinations.[83] This etymological parallel between elementary parts and letters is made explicit in philosophy at least as early as Plato's *Theaetetus*, in the course of which Socrates recounts a dream "that the primeval letters or elements out of which you and I and all other things are compounded, have no reason or explanation; you can only name them."[84] In fact, Socrates uses the linguistic analogy to mount a critical discussion with Theaetetus of the problematic relationship between parts and wholes in general. He begins with "the elements or letters," which according to the dream cannot be known, and then moves to "the syllables or combinations of them," which supposedly can be known.[85] But it is hard to see, as Socrates shows, how the syllable can have a property, that of being knowable or any other property, not present in any of its parts. At the same time, however, the syllable must differ in some respect from the sum of its parts, for at the very least the parts must be connected in the right order and not in any other.[86]

The discussion in the *Theaetetus* has nothing explicit to do with the atomists, but the problem of parts and wholes is clearly relevant to their belief that reality is made up of unknowable simples combined in various ways to make new entities. The dream that Socrates recounts presents a more general version of this view, in which language supports the notion that reality is made up of a few simples, rearranged as letters are to make different words.[87] Though Socrates is finally rather rough with this aspect of the dream, Plato himself used the linguistic analogy in those moments when he wanted to represent reality as made up of unchangeable simples.[88] Lucretius thus relies on what had become a philosophical commonplace when he suggests that all the variety of nature might be manufactured, as it were, from a set of parts as limited as the alphabet. He depends on the common experience whereby meaning somehow arises when meaningless letters are brought together to suggest that meaning stems *from* this combination.

Unfortunately, this is just not the way language works. Letters are not logical or semantic simples, building blocks from which we construct larger intellectual combines. As James says, "It is not as if men had first invented letters and made syllables out of them, then made words of the syllables and sentences of the words;—they actually followed the reverse order."[89] Nor is this the logical order in which language works, as if minimal ideas were encoded in each letter, through which we sort to make larger units of sense in the form of words and sentences. However, when Lucretius mistakes spelling for logic, he participates in an ancient and ongoing search for minimal units of signification that runs from the Greeks to the logical atomism of Wittgenstein and Russell.[90] That whole tradition matters in this context because it is so often associated with physical systems of recombination, as, for example, information theory comes to be associated with genetics, and because it shows how language comes to play the authoritative role for such systems that is played by nature in the case of recurrence. Language becomes the prime example of novelty achieved by recombination, partly because it seems to solve some of the logical difficulties arising from that model and partly because it brings a welcome whiff of the spiritual to a model that is otherwise random and mechanical.

All of ancient Europe's most basic notions about novelty are thus to be found within a few steps of Parmenides' original ban on coming-to-be. Trapped between the tautology that what is, is and the logical contradiction that would arise if what is not could also be, the mere facts of everyday experience, to which new things seem to occur all the time, were called into question. For certain philosophers, this apparently meant logical torture, but no evidence exists even as late as Lucretius of any pathos in the lack of novelty. For him, as much as for Plato, a taste for new things is bathetic and trivial. The goal of Empedocles and the pre-Socratic atomists was not to open up intellectual space for innovation but to save the appearances and thus to make philosophy consistent with observable reality. The two major ways in which they did this seem dictated more by logical necessity than by taste or ambition. Parmenides' ice-cold block of a universe is cracked open along one axis, that of time, so that change can occur in cycles, or along the other, that of space, where the atoms rain down variously forever. Without their subtending analogies in human experience, the cycles of nature on one hand and the combinatorial brilliance of language on the other, these models might not have survived to seem inevitable. But they did survive, and between them came to account for most of what the modern world could think about how newness comes into the world.

TWO TRADITIONS OF THE NEW : CYCLES AND COMBINATIONS

CHRISTIAN RENOVATION

It took a very long time for the ancient prejudice against novelty to seem at all constraining, and even when it did, resistance took the form of repetition. Even when the new became a goal, not an impossible anomaly, aspirations toward it were ruled by habits of thinking established at the very beginning of Western philosophy. Renaissance and revolution imply return as much as they do advance, and even as metaphors they are repetitions of much older patterns of cyclical revival. The theory of evolution may have seemed a startling innovation, but it was often received as if it merely repackaged Epicurean ideas of random development. Though there was one great exception to this rule, one very grand addition to the European stock of ideas about the new as established by the time of Lucretius, it had the paradoxical effect of making human novelty even more difficult to justify.

The one idea on which all philosophers from Parmenides to Lucretius agreed, that nothing comes from nothing, is, of course, flatly contradicted by Christian doctrine. As dogma, the belief that God created the universe *ex nihilo* was laid down by the Fourth Lateran Council of 1215, but it had been taught at least as early as the second century CE and was well established by the time of Augustine.[1] Whether it is much older than that is the subject of some debate. Some extrascriptural Jewish works describe creation from formless matter (Wisdom of Solomon

11:17), while others seem to imply creation from nothing (2 Maccabees 7:28).[2] The first lines of Genesis do not seem to make an explicit claim of creation from nothing and thus have inspired a number of different interpretations. Some biblical scholars still consider creation *ex nihilo* a postbiblical addition, inspired partly by the ambition of the early church to ascribe to its god powers denied to all other deities, and partly by its struggles against the Gnostics, the Manicheans, and other heretics who taught that the created world is in some sense inherently evil.[3]

The omnipotent deity defined in these teachings exceeded all other gods in creating matter as well as form, spiritual beings as well as material ones, with the single exception of himself. Besides the absolute priority of the deity, the most important implication of this doctrine is probably that matter, since it was created by God, cannot be inherently bad, and thus the evil in the world is not a constant characteristic of it but the consequence of human acts of free will.[4] In its utter dependence on God for its very existence, the created world also needs constant support, lest it slip back into inexistence and nothingness. Thus for many Christian theologians, *creatio ex nihilo* was necessarily followed by *creatio continua*, in which God sustains the universe, where necessary, with additional acts of creation.

Though the first creation is by definition a unique event, belief in which did have the effect of redrawing the timeline on which Europe mapped its history,[5] it did not necessarily mark the end of novelty in the universe as understood by Christian theology. Divine interventions of various kinds, including acts of special creation, could, and in the minds of many believers did, supplement the first creation. To doubt the possibility of utterly new things, marvels introduced into the world, would be to doubt the omnipotence of God. By the same token, though, human beings, as creations themselves, could not be creators. According to Augustine, parents, farmers, and others who seem to bring things into being simply modify what God originally created.[6] Later theologians agreed that though human beings could participate in creation in various ways, they could not create from nothing.[7] Until the fourteenth century, this seemed a truism, but Scholastic quibbling opened up the possibility that God, who could create anything, could create beings who could create. However, even those radical enough to advance this possibility understood human creativity as a kind of re-creation, an activation of potentialities first invested in the universe by God.[8]

The doctrine of creation *ex nihilo* thus had a more ambiguous effect on the history of the new than might at first be expected. It was in fact difficult to get around the straightforward pronouncement in Genesis that the Creation was finished by the seventh day, which for centuries sanctioned conservative belief that nothing new could ever be added to what God had originally provided. But the constant presence of an omnipotent God certainly seemed to imply that creation could continue, for why should omnipotence be limited to some initial period of activity? Thus scientists as late as Louis Agassiz believed in numerous episodes of special creation, by which new kinds of animals and plants were supplied to fill up gaps in a needy world. In the case of the human species, at least, each individual was also supposed to possess a unique and immortal soul, whose appearance on earth was a novel event. Though such individuals could not create from nothing, their tie to God was sometimes thought to be expressed best by acts of relative creativity.

Christianity, a self-consciously new religion, understood its own novelty in much the same way. The very notion of a new covenant, like the one announced at the Last Supper (Luke 22:20), implies a reference to the old. In fact, Paul's explanation of the new covenant in Hebrews 8:8–12 explicitly relies on the prediction recorded in Jeremiah 31:31, that "the days are coming . . . when I will make a new covenant with the house of Israel." Thus even the new is founded on the authority of the past. There must be something wrong with the old, "for if that first covenant had been faultless, there would have been no occasion for a second" (Hebrews 8:7)—but, on the other hand, the first covenant must have been good in intention and general design, for the second is supposed to replicate its basic form. In Hebrews, Paul develops an elaborate analogy between the repetitive, material sacrifices required for purification under the old system and the single, spiritual sacrifice offered by Christ under the new. The new covenant is not just a revival of the old in a repaired state but a radical improvement, yet it is still aimed at the same goal of restoring a lost oneness with God. As the medievalist and art historian Gerhart Ladner puts it, the early church "conceived of [its] very newness as making possible the *restoration* of that newness which was man's part on the first glorious day of his creation."[9]

The same complex sort of novelty is proposed for the individual believer, who is referred to over and over in the Epistles as a "new man." On the most mundane level, novelty was to be the result of conversion to Christianity, the Jew and the Gentile reconciled, "one new man in place of the two" (Ephesians 2:15). Baptism into the church involves putting off "the old nature with its practices" and putting on "the new nature" (Colossians 3:9–10). But even though conversion and baptism imply a radical transformation, Paul explicitly claims that the new Christian is actually being renewed in the sense of being restored to a truer self. An original perfection, lost with the Fall, is to be regained through Christ. Since perfection is necessarily timeless, this means being reassimilated to an eternal pattern, one that never should have changed in the first place, in the likeness of the God who does not change. But baptism was also imagined as the reenactment of an original novelty, "as a *repetition* as it were of the *creation* of man."[10] Baptism in this sense involved a promise that the same newness could be experienced more than once, that in fact another instance of the same newness awaited the redeemed believer at the end of time.

According to the church, however, this novelty can be even better the second time around. Since the intervention of Christ, time in the created world cannot return to the very same point again, so if it is to return at all it must return to something better. From the time of Tertullian, then, the church began to teach the doctrine of *in melius reformare*, reform to a better state.[11] Christ was held to have opened up the possibility of returning to a paradisal condition even better than that enjoyed by Adam and Eve. As Augustine explains, this is the state Adam would have achieved had he not fallen in sin; but since he did not achieve it, the redeemed Christian soul can return to a perfection even greater than that enjoyed by our first parents.[12] Thus a more radical novelty, one with progressive implications, is derived from a pattern of renewal that otherwise seems to verge on mere repetition.

Medieval scholars divided Christian theology into the work of creation and the work of restoration, with the second being the main concern of the Bible and the more appropriate occupation of the church. Secular inquiry might take as its subject the matter of the Creation, which after all fills up only a page or two at the beginning of the Bible, whereas the church devotes itself to the rest of scripture, which is meant to repair the damage caused by the Fall.[13] Thus the church set aside all the busy work of temporal innovation and seemed to set its sights firmly on the past—but at the same time built into the structure of its doctrine the notion of reform, and even of reform to a better state.[14] As Erasmus put it, "In all my work, my sole object has been to resuscitate the humanities, which lay almost dead and buried among my own people; secondly, to arouse a world . . . to a new zeal for the true religion of the Gospel; and finally to recall to its sources in Holy Scripture the academic theology of our universities."[15] Innovation might be opposed and sanctioned at the same time by the very flexible dictum "'*Non nova, sed nove*' (not the new, but anew)."[16] The transformation of the church into a centralized authority with vast temporal powers was both justified and resisted by appeals to primitive Christianity.[17] In a sense, then, the Reformation simply proposed to accomplish once and for all what the original church was supposed to have taken as its daily concern.

The Christian church thus developed a powerfully ambiguous version of the old cyclical renewal pattern familiar in Europe from the time of the pre-Socratics. Given the influence of Neoplatonism on patristic thought, it is not at all odd that the Christian version should resemble Plato's graph of gradual diversion from and return to the true forms.[18] But Ladner insists that Christian reform differs from classical patterns of renewal in many ways, most especially in requiring particular acts of willpower, exerted in the context of moral freedom.[19] In this version, human beings effect their own renewal, instead of simply suffering an inevitable return; and insofar as they make their own way back to the beginning, they may be said to make themselves new. Of course, this possibility carried grave temptations to pride, which the church was vigilant in opposing, as the doctrine of *in melius reformare* carried with it temptations to improve not just oneself but the church and perhaps even scripture.[20] Revolutionaries within the church, such as Joachim of Fiore, usually began with a simple plan for something like the reform of monastic life, but the implicit backwardness of Christian renewal often seemed to open out toward Revelation and the future instead—to the New Jerusalem of the Apocalypse, and thus to reforms and renewals that would bring Europe back to origins it had never seen before. The idea of Christian reform thus became a reference point for later, more radical, models of novelty by return.

RENAISSANCE

In the years since the historian of art and culture Jacob Burckhardt gave the Italian Renaissance its modern glamour and authority, the term *renaissance* has become an honorific to be used in a very general sense to anoint any concentrated outbreak of artistic activity, regardless of whether it hearkens back to a predecessor. Thus there have been a great many renaissances, just in the last century or so; and these have been matched, in a way, by the discovery of many predecessors to the fifteenth-century movement in Italy, from the Carolingian *renovatio* to the Theodosian Renaissance and even further back to a time when it was common to think of Rome itself as a reborn Troy. Though it is possible to quibble about the credentials of any one of these episodes and to quarrel over priority and precedent, this proliferation of candidates suggests that the very concept of an authentic or original renaissance is a contradiction in terms. By returning over and over, *renaissance* promises constant renewal and yet also confesses that even the idea of renewal itself is always already old.

Renasci, the term most often used in the fifteenth century, has a mundane basis in horticulture, in organic patterns of growth, renewed each year. In Christian Europe, however, it was hardly possible to use *renasci* or like terms in a mundane fashion, and the art historian Erwin Panofsky suggests that *renasci* was used on purpose to suggest a more considerable and far-reaching revival than *renovatio*, "a sense of regeneration too radical and intense to be expressed in any other language than that of Scripture."[21] The *renascimento* thus exploits the well-established Christian idea of spiritual rebirth as novelty recaptured, along with all the paradoxes that concept implies. But the religious prototype was actually fairly simple by comparison, since it proposed return to a single, punctual, and truly unprecedented moment in time. What the Italian Renaissance wanted to revive was somewhat more ambiguous.

Traditionally, there were two candidates, "back to nature" and "back to

the classics"—the first, in Panofsky's account, more prominent in painting and sculpture, the second in architecture.[22] The fourteenth-century
artist and art historian Giorgio Vasari merged these in one totalizing
theory whereby the ancients, since they were closer to the beginning of
things, combined the authority of nature with that of culture. This clever
compromise established the academic practice of studying nature indirectly, in the form perfected by the ancients, who were supposed to have
worked off all the rough edges and removed the purely accidental features that are so distracting in the wild. Aesthetic novelty thus appeared
to generations of students and artists in a curiously mediated form. The
very notion of renaissance was impacted within that of the classic, which
was both original and refined at the same time, and which, by constantly
maintaining its own newness, froze the moment of rebirth.

Squaring the circle in this way also put another twist in Renaissance
ideas about the new. If the ancients were the source of novelty, as closer to
the wellsprings of nature, then the present must be very old. The art critic
Walter Pater taught this timeline to several generations of aesthetes, who
felt themselves sad and tired in comparison to the fresh, white statues,
most of them late Roman copies, to be found in the museums. In the
early years of the Italian Renaissance, Panofsky shows, medieval art and
architecture were considered antiquated but not antique, since the true
art of antiquity was less out of date than works of the recent past. The
modern, at this early stage in its development as a concept, was thus
oddly synonymous with the unfashionable, since modern art had fallen
away so sadly from the natural standards of the Greeks. Soon, though,
Vasari addressed this anomaly, bringing the antique into alignment with
the modern, so that the *maniera moderno* (modern way) could appear at
both ends of history, enclosing the old in the middle.[23] By a process that
was to be well used by aesthetic modernists in the twentieth century,
the modern became new only insofar as it recaptured an original novelty
buried beneath the errors of the immediate past.

Like Christian rebirth and reform, renaissance promises something
much more complicated than respect for precedent and a return to the
past. The power of the new to come back again and again suggests that it
is something of a constant—that it exists, perhaps by definition, outside
historical time. This means, as Panofsky suggests, that for the Renais-

sance there is a sad distance between the ancients and the present, cut off from each other by something more fundamental than the passage of a few years.[24] It also means that when the new does return it must do so totally, universally, even violently. Vasari set the tone when he found the term *renascita* and used it as a collective noun to designate the entire culture of his time. Renovation can be piecemeal, but rebirth is total. When the new is imagined as an ideal, lost like the Platonic Idea within the confusions of the actual world, then its reappearance in the world will always be apocalyptic.

REVOLUTION

Though *revolution* would seem by definition not just total but also violent, the term has been extended in so many directions that it has come to be a synonym for "any sufficiently noticeable change which takes place at an observably faster rate than others."[25] Along with *evolution*, its near homonym, *revolution* has become ordinary and ubiquitous, in apparent mockery of its real significance, "bound up with the notion that the course of history suddenly begins anew, that an entirely new story, a story never known or told before, is about to unfold."[26]

Or perhaps this apparent degradation has simply returned the word to something more like its original, literal meaning, which not only had nothing to do with novelty but implied the very opposite. Literally, of course, a revolution is simply a single complete turn around an axis. As late as the seventeenth century, this was not just its primary but in fact its only meaning: "a full compassing, rounding, turning backe to its first place or point; the accomplishment of a circular course."[27] For most of the world's history, it was useful only in the context of practical geometry, a career ceremonially capped by the title of Copernicus's astronomical treatise: *De revolutionibus orbium coelestium* (*On the Revolutions of the Heavenly Spheres*; 1543).[28] In 1694, the dictionary of the French Academy gave planetary movement as the "real and primary meaning" of the word, implying at least that others had begun to encroach.[29]

In fact, *revolutio* had been used as a figurative term as early as Augustine, who meant by it the same kind of providential return otherwise designated as *reformatio* or *renascita*.[30] At this point, *revolution* was just another term for this circular return to origins, which had itself returned in various forms ever since Empedocles. Thus it came to be applied to periodic occurrences of all kinds, and to cycles, especially in the fates of nations, which had always been seen as going round on fortune's wheel.[31] By their very nature, of course, these figurative uses ruled out the possibility of fundamental change, and of any novelty not already present in the circular course of history. Variation on this particular graph of history was always periodic and repetitive.[32]

Violent changes of government and civil wars were just as common in antiquity as in any other time, but these were not called revolutions; nor did they present to contemporaries any of the features that came to distinguish a revolution from the simple downfall of a regime. The terms used by the Greeks, such as *metabole*, either meant simple change or were tied to cyclical concepts such as *metabole politeion*, the cycle of constitutions, or *anakylosis*, the turning of the wheel of political change.[33] The Romans tended to use terms such as *conversio*, which were just as indicative of cyclical concepts of recurrent political phases.[34] There are apparently cases in Roman history in which the goal of a revolt is described as *res novae*, but the new things anticipated in such cases do not seem to resemble very strongly the new rights and new governmental structures demanded by the classic modern revolutions.[35]

Even these, however, were often justified as restorations or returns. The parliamentary resistance to royal "prerogative" that led to the English Civil War represented itself as repairing the damage done to the "ancient constitution" by the innovations of the king.[36] The Glorious Revolution of 1688, despite its title, was defined even more conservatively, and it became a point of pride for later British historians and politicians that their revolution had led to so little change.[37] This pattern had a strong influence over the American Revolution as well. Colonial resistance phrased itself, particularly in the early days, as a suit for rights withheld, a restoration of ancient protections restored to English subjects in 1688.[38] Even a radical like Thomas Paine, describing the unprecedented nature of the French and American revolutions, identified them as having accomplished "a renovation of the natural order of things."[39]

Paine's phrase suggests that the concept of revolution escapes from its own cycles of repetition and comes to mean something new by first recasting itself as renovation. In this sense of the word *revolution*, circularity returns a system to its starting point not to regain the old but to revive the new. The model for this paradoxical kind of novelty recaptured was the old religious program of reform, which did in fact offer a prototype and even perhaps an incitement to revolt as early as the Middle Ages. By one line of historical reasoning, political revolution in Europe begins with religious schism, with heresy, as it appeared in episodes such as the Münster Anabaptist revolt of 1534. But it is also possible, as the historian Martin Malia suggests, that "the church's own efforts to reform itself tended to generate a millenarian expectation of the reign of the Holy Spirit on earth."[40] Since the church had dedicated itself, in theory at least, to the work of restoration, it legitimated the idea of a new future, based on the original newness of humankind in the past. The influence of this idea is especially prominent in the English Civil War, with its call for a New Jerusalem, a New Man in a New World, all of which are explicitly scriptural.[41] Augustine's equating *revolutio* with *reformatio* thus comes into full effect, and the Christian promise of a novelty that can happen again helps to lift the idea of revolution out of the rut it had worn for itself since ancient times.

Revolution is finally supposed to have lifted its particular kind of novelty free of prototypes and precedents when the Founders put the phrase *novus ordo saeclorum* (a new order of the ages) on the Great Seal of the United States.[42] Hannah Arendt maintains, however, that this was an uncharacteristic gesture from a group of fairly conservative revolutionaries, whose intentions were retrospectively radicalized by the misunderstanding of their French successors. Even these, she insists, had no thoughts of "novelty and newness as such" until their revolution was several steps farther along than anyone had anticipated.[43] Yet this very surprise is definitive, in that the uncontrollable progress of events taught the lesson that the future could not be predicted. Running out of bounds as it did, the French version of 1789 gave a new meaning to revolution, which now opened out into an "unknown future"[44] mainly because the effects of political acts seemed inherently unknowable. The traditional goal of radical reform, the familiar novelty of original rights and freedoms, was supplemented by another kind of novelty, which was itself new insofar as it was free of content.

The French example established revolution as "a force of nature,"[45] one that, unlike celestial mechanics, did not return things to their starting point. The novelty anticipated at the end of this process had the uncanny quality of being both inevitable and unknown. It had all the certainty of planetary revolutions but none of the familiarity. Unsettling as it must have been to acknowledge revolution as an irresistible force, however, accepting it as such also gave it an authority much like that of tradition, which had always justified itself as the necessary consistency of things. Forces of nature are not just irresistible—they are also constant, or at least they were in the nonrelativistic space of the late eighteenth century. Thus it became possible to think of revolution as more than a recurrent phenomenon, its periodicity flattened out until it was no longer an interruption but a permanent condition.[46] For the socialist politician and philosopher Pierre-Joseph Proudhon, there was only one revolution, "selfsame or perpetual."[47] But this seems to mean that having replaced the past, revolution had also acquired many of its characteristics, overthrowing the consistency of the known only to establish the consistency of the unknown.

In any case, revolutions are never partial phenomena, but even in their oldest version involve total change. The idea of permanent revolution simply extends this logic to time, so that revolutionary change is no longer punctual but occupies the entire course of history. At this, its fullest extent, revolutionary novelty seems to have achieved a state something like that of Parmenidean being turned inside out. Binding all of space and time into a single totality, revolution comes to constitute an absolute with all the characteristics of Parmenides' block universe, but with change substituted for changelessness. Arendt argues, in fact, that the revolutionary movements of the eighteenth century consciously cast their innovations in absolute terms so as more effectively to fill the gap left by the dispersal of absolute monarchy.[48] Nevertheless, revolution lost its old periodic and repetitive character to become both arbitrary and necessary at once, rather more like an a priori truth than a fact of nature.

Common use of the term *revolution* for every incidental change may not be much of a misuse, then, if everything that happens is an episode in a revolutionary process both total and perpetual. Journalistic abuse of the term is certainly an effect of the common assumption that unrest is a constant in modern times. The model of novelty that comes from and helps to support this assumption is the peculiar and yet familiar one in which nothing changes the fundamental fact that everything changes. The new no longer needs to return, because it never really goes away. Like Parmenides' great sphere, it does not revolve, nor does it move: there is no space, free of itself, to move into.

THE SCIENTIFIC REVOLUTION

Some early abuses of the term *revolution* were so influential that they persist despite criticism and disbelief. In various scholarly accounts, the Industrial Revolution, for example, has been multiplied, stretched out, demoted to lower-case, and dissipated, but it still survives in common parlance and in academia.[49] Something even more drastic has happened to the Scientific Revolution, a term that may have been coined as late as 1939 and which has already fallen into disrepute. Considerable scholarly mistrust has collected around the vivid picture suggested by the term *revolution*, which seems to bring into the same insurrectionary brigade a diverse collection of actors, principles, and practices, spread out over a considerable amount of time.[50] And some historians have argued that science not only did not but cannot foment revolution, because it advances incrementally and cumulatively, preserving as much received wisdom as possible. The historian of science I. B. Cohen finds this a prevalent belief among scientists themselves.[51] Yet, if the Scientific Revolution has been erased from history, some object of historical study still occupies the same intellectual space, an inconsistency that the historian and sociologist of science Steven Shapin mocks when he begins his recent survey: "There was no such thing as the Scientific Revolution, and this is a book about it."[52]

Some of this difficulty is certainly caused by the odd history of the term *revolution*, which has almost reversed its meaning in the course of time. It is hardly a coincidence that the first scientist known to have described his own discoveries as revolutionary, in the modern sense of that term, is Anton Lavoisier, who worked between the American and French revolutions.[53] Cohen has discovered a few instances earlier in the eighteenth century in which intellectual advances were described as revolutionary: Fontenelle on calculus in 1720; Clairaut on Newton in 1747; and d'Alembert on Descartes in 1751.[54] In other words, the term *revolution* came first to be applied to scientific advance just as it was shifting its meaning from cycles and repetitions to sudden upheavals. The unsettled nature of the concept of revolution is evident in Fontenelle, who represents calculus as one of "the rises and falls of empires, morals, of customs, and of beliefs which succeed one another ceaselessly," though he clearly believes that it represents an irreversible advance over the mathematics of the past.[55] A term that had been used to describe a periodic return to the past was being stretched to announce something like the very opposite.

Even in the eighteenth century, the concept of revolution was elastic enough to cover both possibilities: complete, irreversible upheaval and repetitive return to the past. An influential example of this potent combination had been offered in the Renaissance by Francis Bacon, who deployed the ungainly term *instauration* so as to advocate return and renovation at once. Bacon rather pridefully takes biblical scripture as his model, comparing instauration to the work of reform, and he defends scientific investigation as a mimetic recapitulation of the Creation itself.[56] Science, by this account, uncovers the original novelty packed into nature by its first creator, much as the church was supposed to do within its sphere of influence. Bacon's idea that humankind could recover its original Edenic knowledge of and mastery over nature was apparently widespread in the seventeenth and eighteenth centuries, and it gave the Scientific Revolution a religious justification and a traditionally circular shape.[57] Return to origins did involve a new beginning, for science as for religion before it, insofar as it enabled the recapture of the original novelty of the first things.

Once it was imagined as a revolution, then, scientific advance recapitulated the pattern established by renaissance and reform, models that were consciously applied to science as authoritative examples.[58] By reinventing the wheel, as it were, the Scientific Revolution also reinvented an ambiguous kind of novelty. To be new and original, from Bacon onward, meant to disclaim ancient authority and start over on one's own.[59] If there was a scientific revolution, the authority figure it hoped to depose was certainly Aristotle, or at least the systematic understanding of the natural world that had grown up around the authority of Aristotle's name. Instead of consulting old books, which merely repeated what had been said since Aristotle's time, the modern scientist was supposed to use observation and experimentation.[60] Having an original relation to nature meant having insights into it that were new and original.

Whether actual scientific practice between the time of Galileo and that of Darwin actually respected this principle is one of the basic controversies in the history of science. Since Kant, revolutionary leaps in science have often been defined as dramatic shifts in some basic worldview that precedes and interprets experience.[61] Shifts of this kind are drastic and total because they involve complete conceptual systems, not just aggregated bodies of practical experience. Passed by the philosopher Alexander Koyré down to the physicist, historian, and philosopher of science Thomas Kuhn, this version of the scientific revolution finally identifies it with religious conversion, as requiring a conceptual reorientation so total and so drastic that Kuhn compares it to "neural reprogramming."[62] Though observation and experimentation are obviously involved in science, changes in the meaning of empirical evidence cannot be derived from the evidence itself and must be imposed from outside. New facts do not lead to new conceptual paradigms, but require the support of new paradigms before they can be accepted as fact at all.[63]

Kuhn's theory has been understood as undermining the pretensions of Enlightenment science to have replaced traditional authority with an original relation to nature. In its own rhetoric, though, the Scientific Revolution followed fairly closely the pattern established by revolution and renaissance before it, mixing up the appeal to nature with appeals to ancient authority and the claim of novelty with that of precedent. Aristotle was felt to interpose himself between the modern scientist and nature, not because nature stood all around for any contemporary to see, but rather because nature had existed in its purest state at the very beginning of human history, where it had been observed by authorities far more primary than the Greeks. Thus it was common to claim that obeisance to Aristotle and Galen prevented the development of a truly Christian scientific philosophy, one based on the scriptures.[64] Galileo himself appealed to the authority of Solomon and Moses, who "knew the constitution of the universe perfectly."[65]

Some of this ostensible respect for authority must have been strategic, such as the defense of heliocentrism that traced it back to the pre-Socratics.[66] The attack on Aristotle was sometimes softened by ascribing all errors to later commentators and sophisticators of the original Peripatetic wisdom, as Aristotle himself was sometimes blamed for perverting the course of earlier Greek philosophy.[67] But some of these appeals to earlier and purer scientific authorities were based on the genuine belief that ancient authority was closer to nature and therefore more thoroughly acquainted with it. Since, as Bacon contended, the sciences "flourish most in the hands of the first author," the purpose of later investigators was to remove centuries of accreted error and recapture the real novelty of the earliest authorities.[68] Even René Descartes, otherwise keen to display his own originality, traced his geometric methods back to Alexandrian mathematicians, and sometimes claimed not to be offering new ideas but rather to be reviving "the most ancient of all."[69]

If revolution is understood in its earlier sense, as implying a return to an original novelty, then the notion of a scientific revolution is somewhat easier to defend. Revolution in the older sense does not so much defy as re-create authority. Its project of renovation is unending, not because the new is always different and keeps advancing in time, but rather because original truths progressively disappear under layers of obscurity and ignorance. Until recently, science must have conformed to such a model almost by definition, since it claimed nothing more for its discoveries than that they lifted the veil on some part of nature that had always existed despite human ignorance of it. Even if nature is infinite, in size and divisibility, and there is always more of it to discover, it is hard to say whether science ever discovers the new, assuming that what is disclosed was always there to be noticed. But this is not the only model of novelty active in early modern science, which imagined ways of being new that operate even now, when science seems able to invent as well as discover.

THE NEW SCIENCE AND ANCIENT ATOMISM

If such important proponents of modern science as Bacon and Descartes were concerned to describe themselves as reviving an original novelty, lost in the past, then it might seem that the common label "the Age of the New" would have to be retired along with "the Scientific Revolution." This would call into question the boasts of a whole bibliography of famous works, including William Gilbert's *New Physiology* (1600), Kepler's *New*

Astronomy (1609), Bacon's *New Organon* (1620), Galileo's *Two New Sciences* (1638), Robert Boyle's *New Experiments* (1660, 1665, 1682), and the unblushingly ambitious *New Philosophy of the Universe* by Francesco Patrizzi (1591).[70] What, then, to make of such unambiguous pronouncements as Bacon's "The true and lawful goal of the sciences is none other than this: that human life be endowed with new discoveries and powers"?[71] Of course, it is not too hard to reinvest such chestnuts with the reservations they originally carried. Bacon, for instance, also decried an "extreme . . . appetite for novelty."[72] But it would be hard to utterly dissipate the atmosphere that gathered as new celestial bodies appeared, new continents were first visited, and new inventions were introduced.

Another term often used to cover these developments, "the new science," is not just preferable to "the Scientific Revolution" in being a little more modest; it also depends on a different model of novelty. While revolution implies punctual, total, and even violent change, the new science is a repetitive, gradual method of advance. From Kant to Kuhn, the metaphor of revolution has been used to downplay the empirical side of science, while "the new science" has been understood as the first coherent formulation of empirical methods and standards. In this sense, revolution, for all its apparent violence, involves a change of ideas and ideals, while the new science advances by means of practical discoveries and inventions. One thing the two models do have in common, though, is that they are both very old. The scientific revolution is one in a series of revolutions going back to the cycles of Empedocles and Plato, while the new science was, among other things, an explicit revival of the mechanical atomism of the Epicureans. One of the most important findings of the scientific revolution, as it roamed back beyond the works of Aristotle, was a model of novelty entirely different from that of revolution.

Though the new science was one of the main features by which Enlightenment philosophers distinguished the modern era from the darkness of the past, it was itself traced back to influential precursors, the earliest of the classics. The philosopher and mathematician Nicolas de Condorcet, for example, identified the beginnings of modern science, lost for centuries, in Pythagorean mathematics and the mechanical philosophy of the Greek atomists.[73] Thus the two most important structural innovations of the new science were fitted out with distant ancestors.

With the establishment of a general theory of equations, mathematics in the seventeenth century became the model for and the precursor of a whole new technology; it was, in the sociologist Randall Collins's words, "a machine for making discoveries."[74] Aimed toward the future though it was, the mathematical model still often found its justification in Pythagoras or Plato, whose philosophies were used to substantiate the belief that mathematics is actually the native language of the cosmos.[75]

If so, and if, as Collins says, mathematics is a machine, then it follows that the universe itself is mechanical in nature. This, of course, was the explicit claim of new scientists from Galileo to Leibniz, who were intent on displacing Aristotelian teleology and outfitting nature with a set of mathematical laws.[76] Though their claims were supported by results—often rather dramatically so, in a series of famous experiments from Galileo's inclined plane to Boyle's vacuum pump—they were also authorized by appeal to the ancients, who were said to have invented the mechanical philosophy themselves. Lucretius's *De rerum natura* was rediscovered in 1417, and by the eighteenth century, at least according to Whitehead, "every educated man read Lucretius, and entertained ideas about atoms."[77] Regardless of whether this is an exaggeration, Greek atomism, as adapted by Epicurus and presented in Lucretius's poem, did provide a philosophical basis and much of the intellectual background for the mechanical model of science developed between the Renaissance and the Enlightenment, bringing with it a very different way of conceptualizing the new.

Boyle liked to deny that he was an Epicurean and often claimed that he had never read *De rerum natura* all the way through. If so, he gleaned enough from his fragmentary readings to make up over a hundred references to Epicurus or Lucretius in his published works, and to develop a "corpuscular" philosophy remarkably like Lucretius's atomism.[78] Galileo also had to fight off accusations of Epicureanism, suspect because it supposedly taught a godless hedonism, which were brought on by his descriptions of the *particelle minimi* of nature, apparently rather like those of atomism.[79] Descartes was another who disclaimed the influence of Democritus and Epicurus, perhaps because it made his vortices seem less than original.[80] Even Pierre Gassendi, usually accounted the foremost Enlightenment champion of Epicurean atomism, carefully adjusted its precepts so that they could support the Christian voluntarism of his time.[81] In other words, the influence of Epicurean atomism was so pervasive it made the new science nervous about its own originality. In fact, it was a widely acknowledged paradox in the seventeenth century that the "new philosophy," insofar as it was synonymous with the "corpuscular philosophy," was not particularly new.[82]

European scientific debate between the Renaissance and the Enlightenment arrived at Epicurean atomism very largely by retracing the steps along which it had been developed in the first place. Christian belief in God's ability to create the universe from nothing did not make it any easier to imagine any other such episodes, or even to make creation of new things from unformed matter seem plausible.[83] Descartes even assured his readers that mechanical causality was only "a variant on the simply and universally accepted axiom 'nothing comes from nothing.' "[84] In logic, this meant that there could be "nothing in the effect which was not previously in the cause," so that the Enlightenment was as fully armored against the very possibility of novelty as if there had never been any such thing as the "new science."[85] The same logical principle, adapted to physics, dictated that the amount of motion in the universe must be constant, so that movement at one spot had to be absorbed by its contrary elsewhere.[86] The result is a block universe just as tightly packed as that of Parmenides, whose very terms are echoed by Isaac Newton when he bases the cosmos on a God who "endures forever, and is everywhere present; and, by existing always and everywhere . . . constitutes duration and space."[87]

Of the various ways to mediate between the logic of continuity and the apparent facts of change, workers in the new science preferred atomism, partly because it had been criticized by Aristotle, whose Scholastic descendants they hoped to displace from authority, and partly because it was so obviously ancestral to their mechanistic philosophy. As it was explained by Bacon, atomism preserved continuity and consistency, which were the only real characteristics of the most basic particles, while also allowing for variety and change, their epiphenomenal expression and only perceptible effect.[88] Locke later made much the same distinction, between the corpuscular substructure of matter, its real essence, and the phenomenal properties that can be observed and that constitute its nominal essence.[89]

In between these two, some version of a corpuscular or atomistic philosophy was developed by Boyle, Descartes, Galileo, Gassendi, and Newton, to cite just the most prominent examples. Boyle's particles were very, very small, but finite, while Galileo's were apparently infinitely small.[90] Descartes also believed that matter is infinitely divisible, though Gassendi disagreed.[91] Newton, who preferred not to speculate about invisible entities, decided somewhat vaguely that "God in the beginning form'd Matter in solid, massy, hard, impenetrable, moveable Particles, of such Sizes and Figures, and with such other Properties, and in such Proportion to Space, as most conduced to the End for which he form'd them."[92] This neatly evaded all the most controversial points, especially the existence of empty space, disbelief in which set Descartes off from most of his contemporaries.

These were not trivial disagreements, of course, and some corpuscles, especially those of Descartes, differed profoundly from the others and from their common prototypes among the Greeks. As mechanisms of change, however, all corpuscles and atoms shared the essential property of making new things through recombination. Atoms themselves were never created or destroyed, and the laws that governed their means and forms of combination were also fixed; but within these limits the system generated all that appeared and disappeared in the phenomenal world. As Boyle put it:

> Not that there is really any thing of substantial produced, but that those parts of matter that did indeed before pre-exist, but were either scattered and shared among other bodies, or at least otherwise disposed of, are now brought together and disposed of after the manner requisite to entitle the body that results from them to a new denomination, and make it appertain to such a determinate species of natural bodies, so that no new substance is in generation produced, but only that which was pre-existent obtains a new modification or manner of existence.[93]

For Boyle, as for Bacon, perceptible things acquired their particular character and maintained their difference from other things by virtue of their "texture," which is to say the pattern assumed by the atoms in their constitution.[94]

Atomism, in its revived as in its original form, has the advantage of explaining how there can be things at all, given the tendency of an eternal, consistent reality to coalesce into an infinite, spherical blob. In fact, it accounted for the divergence of things so well that it also explained how there can be so many of them, how the stock of new things can seem well-nigh inexhaustible. Boyle follows Lucretius in arguing that the sheer multiplicity of the world can be explained only by its inherently relational character, that such a multitude of qualities, invested in such a plenitude of bodies, could come about only through the infinite multiplication of new relations.[95] Since even a small number of particles can propagate an exponentially huge stock of relations, a vast, swimming sea of minute particles the size of the world should be able to spawn enough new things to keep creation going for a good long time.

As a model of reality, atomism has a number of other consequences, beyond making novelty easier to rationalize. On the positive side, at least as far as the new scientists were concerned, it did away with all the old Aristotelian categories, all the different causes, and most especially final cause, and the cumbersome machinery of form and matter, most especially prime matter.[96] Not that corpuscularianism was necessarily at odds with Aristotle, who did teach that matter was divisible into four basic forms and thus made possible a combinatorial view of reality.[97] But atomism cleared away a great many intermediate steps and apparently metaphysical entities, leaving a purely material fund of basic particles, directed by purely mechanical laws of relation. Even if the particles themselves could not be observed, and thus constituted something of a scandal for an ostensibly empirical system, their relations were apparent and could be described mathematically. In fact, the nature of the atom was such that it could be approached only in quantitative terms, as a sum of relations, though even this was an advantage to a science founded on new developments in advanced mathematics.

The most serious difficulty presented to the new science by old-fashioned Epicurean atomism was the random nature of the relations and associations of the basic particles. Infinite variety actually seemed much easier to rationalize on an Epicurean basis than the existence of a single useful structure such as the human eye, the precise adjustment of which to the conditions of life on earth can hardly be explained by pure chance. Critics of Epicureanism from Aristotle to the philosopher and utilitarian William Paley made much of this weakness, turning what was on one level the great strength of the atomic theory, its ability to account for change and to allow for novelty, into its greatest weakness.[98] On the other hand, Gassendi, who had been drawn to Epicurean atomism because it included the *clinamen*, or swerve, felt that the purely random nature of these tiny variations actually ruled out the exercise of free will, thus becoming a kind of determinism after all.[99] Approached from either vantage point, atomism seemed most vulnerable in its most characteristic aspect: the combinations or relations from which all new things were supposed to arise.

Certain obvious solutions lay close to hand. The prodigious gap between a random rain of particles and the ordered and generally efficient structures of nature could be filled, for example, by divine agency. For Boyle, as for most other scientists of his time, the fact that matter chooses the useful, viable configurations out of all those randomly available to it was strong evidence of the existence of God.[100] But it was also possible to apply the same principle of reduction that had derived the particles themselves to the relations between them, which might in turn be expected to fall into a small number of categories. Lucretius himself had tried to address the suspicion that randomly associated atoms could never collect in anything like the structures of nature by postulating various consistent configurations, like nets or webs or crystals. He also spoke of fixed laws restricting the atoms to certain viable shapes.[101] In this, he merely argued from observation, noting that animals tend to reproduce their kind, without really trying to supply any underlying reason for the regularity.

For some of the new scientists, however, it seemed reasonable to suppose that if matter consisted of only a few basic units, their movements might also occur in fixed patterns. According to Descartes, for example, the arrangement and motion of the particles were just as stereotypical as their shape and size.[102] As science began to establish rules of motion for macroscopic objects, it started to seem reasonable to believe that these were in operation all the way down, so that the motions of the smallest particles were not in fact random at all but followed immutable laws of nature. Of course, these were so general they could hardly explain the existence of particular organisms, much less structures like the eye—but it was a significant comfort just to think that there were laws, especially since their existence seemed to imply a divine lawgiver.[103] The accidental universe of Lucretius was thus remodeled in the style of divine reason. The habit of mind that imagined matter coming in uniform packets also found it congenial to conceive of time and motion in the same way.

Partly to justify and partly to illustrate the notion that the recombination of atoms could be reasonable and not just random, proponents of the new science deployed an old metaphor contained in their ancient sources. Christian Europe had long thought of nature as a book, and from Paracelsus onward scientists had been advised to read it instead of the pages of authority. But Galileo had something different in mind when he spoke of "this grand book, the universe." Whereas the traditional Book of Nature was composed of a multitude of signs, the meaning of which was apparent in visible similarities, Galileo's book was "written in the language of mathematics, and its characters are triangles, circles, and other geometric figures."[104] At its base nothing more than a claim that everything in nature can be measured, which is to say represented by numbers, Galileo's statement also claims that mathematics is not representational at all—the basic geometric figures, such as Plato's triangles, are the basic building blocks of the universe. To be "written in the language of mathematics," in this sense, is to be created in geometric shapes according to mathematical principles.

In Galileo's case, then, the alphabetic metaphor is just a conceit, and the "reading" involved in science is not really reading at all, since it is not the decoding of a representational scheme but the progressive distinction of an essential structure from the accidents of appearance. Much the same is true, though, in many other statements of the same scientific principle that seem more explicitly alphabetical. When Bacon speaks of the "ABCs of nature," he is speaking not of signs in the astrological sense familiar to the Middle Ages but of "simple natures,"[105] basic building blocks, which resemble the letters of the alphabet only in that they are not apparently decomposable into more basic units. But it was conventional to think of letters as an appropriate example of basic building blocks, because they had been treated that way in European philosophy from at least the time of Plato. The new science found the Lucretian version of this metaphor particularly congenial for the same reason Lucretius had first turned to it, because it helped to explain away the most serious difficulty of Epicurean atomism.

Boyle, for example, explicitly uses the analogy of the alphabet to demonstrate that a few simples, combined according to fixed principles, can generate a result as large and complex as "all the books of a great library [in] all the languages of the world."[106] The metaphor appeals, not just because it seems to promise infinite variety and endless novelty, but also because it suggests that each and every instance, no matter how various or new, will also be legible. The older medieval Book of Nature enticed investigators because its meaning was partly withheld; it had to be read. The newer form of the alphabetic metaphor reassured scientists that nature was intelligible; it could be read. That it was intelligible also meant that nature could not have come about by accident—no more, according to Gottfried Leibniz, than "a library forms itself one day by a fortuitous concourse of atoms."[107] Though Leibniz used this analogy in argument against a purely random version of Epicureanism, he was himself the proponent of the grandest combinatorial scheme of all: an "alphabet of human thoughts," from which all knowledge, that already encompassed and that yet to be known, could be generated.[108] His ambition illustrates another advantage of the alphabetic metaphor: by teaching that reality could be read, it suggested that it might also be written.

Language, conceived as a combinatorial system, thus seemed to offer an authoritative prototype for a model of the new that otherwise threatened to run off into gibberish. The familiar fact that language can be so various and yet still manage to make some kind of sense brought not just order but also meaning to a system that lacked an obvious purpose, since it was basically mechanical. Perhaps the linguistic analogy also helped turn to advantage other features of atomism that might otherwise have seemed distinct weaknesses. Though it was certainly challenging and exciting for Bacon, Boyle, or Descartes to propose their scientific programs, then entirely new, once accepted they were each supposed to run on like clockwork, so that any future novelty of thought or discovery would have to be merely incremental and additive. Setting science up on sound foundations meant that future revolutions would not be necessary or possible, no matter how much the term might be used. All science would be what Kuhn calls—trying to keep the condescension from becoming too obvious—"normal science," which putters along adding this to that, happy within its paradigm. Language, bound to the demands of communication as it is, always changes very slowly and within familiar parameters, but this is necessary if it is to keep its chief advantage, sociality. The gradual, mechanical, incremental change promised by the combinatorial model is a far more sociable process than revolution, and it rightly finds its authoritative prototype in language, which is collectively created, communally maintained, and altered only by the accumulation of a multitude of tiny changes.

But the linguistic analogy did not help with what is probably the most formidable problem, that of finding the novelty. If the new arrives in the form of unprecedented combinations of preexisting elements, where exactly is it to be located? Relation is a notoriously difficult philosophical problem, so that a kind of novelty that inheres only in relations is one that will always be a little hard to identify with any precision.[109] Versions of this problem arise in practice all the time, in distinguishing the exact step, out of a complex and socially dispersed process of change, that made the real difference—in naming the one person, in a dense social network of overlapping investigations, who made the actual discovery. Discovery and invention, two of the major ways in which novelty appears to the modern world, are thoroughly social processes now, and their identification with particular moments and particular individuals is a well-maintained fiction.[110] That it is a necessary fiction suggests the residual strength of the models of renaissance and reform, which are punctual, ideal, and total, where the combinatorial model is gradual and empirical. Though Kuhn strictly distinguishes between normal science and scientific revolutions, he also maintains that normal science will produce revolutions from its familiar routines. The idea that nature does something very much like this, producing revolution from routine by deriving fundamental novelties from incremental repetition, became the basis for a model of novelty with more influence, right now, than any other.

3

DARWIN'S RENOVATION OF THE NEW

THE PROBLEM OF EVOLUTIONARY NOVELTY
In his attempt to explain how Saladin Chamcha has been
turned into a demon—to explain, that is, how this bit of extravagant newness has come into the world of *The Satanic
Verses*—Mohamed Sufyan turns to Darwin, the "great
Charles," who apparently has an advantage over classical experts on change such as Ovid or Lucretius in having
science on his side.[1] Or, to be more precise, Sufyan cites
Darwin's measured acceptance of Jean-Baptiste Lamarck,
whose theory of environmentally induced change comes
much closer to accounting for the "mutation in extremis"[2]
that has seized his friend. Sufyan's pedantry makes his
daughter roll her eyes, and Rushdie's narrator seems to
share her skepticism—not an unreasonable reaction
when science is called on to explain the fantastic. But the
narrator has long since anticipated Mohamed Sufyan on
the arcane subject of Lamarck, who is cited at the very beginning of *The Satanic Verses* when the question of newness is introduced;[3] and Sufyan's interest in unconventional theories of evolution leaks out into other parts of
the novel, where several comments are made about the
controversy over punctuated equilibrium. More than once
in the course of his story, Rushdie invokes the theory of
evolution as if it were the modern world's best attempt
at accounting for the new, but then amends it so that it
becomes "a thing of dramatic, cumulative transformations . . . more revolution than evolution."[4]

Rushdie's ambivalence about the power of evolution as a theory of the new is not a bit less intense than that of the science itself. Considered from the first to have been a major intellectual revolution, Darwin's theory is supposed to have brought newness of a very fundamental kind into a world that had previously felt quite comfortable with stasis as a norm. The essence of evolution, according to the evolutionary biologist Julian Huxley, is the realization of ever new possibilities.[5] Making change the basic constant of biological existence, giving novelty the kind of physical authority previously enjoyed by forces such as gravity, Darwin apparently shifted the momentum of nature itself. Innovation became one of the innate tendencies of things, since, as the feminist theoretician Elizabeth Grosz puts it, "life is always challenged to overcome itself, to invent new methods, regions, tactics, and goals, to differ from itself, to continually invent solutions to the problems of survival its universe poses to it."[6]

And yet, despite this fundamental commitment to the new, the definition and explanation of evolutionary novelty have always been among the most contentious issues in the science. As the evolutionary biologist Armin Moczek states in the abstract of a recent survey, "The origin of novel traits is what draws many to evolutionary biology, yet our understanding of the mechanisms that underlie the genesis of novelty remains limited."[7] In fact, the very definition of evolutionary novelty is uncertain, despite many years of research and discussion; and the increasing appearance of articles, symposia, and dissertations on the topic suggests that it is less settled than ever.[8] A whole history of scientific controversy about the shape and nature of evolutionary novelty is currently being revived and reenacted, so that even the ideas of Lamarck, as thoroughly repudiated as any theory of the past, can be respectfully addressed, not just in fanciful novels but also in advanced research.[9] If evolution is, now more than ever, not a theory but a bundle of theories, with a contentious variety that appears even in Rushdie's brisk account, it is very largely because of tensions introduced by the concept of novelty.

For all its fanciful and satirical humor, then, *The Satanic Verses* fairly represents a considerable conundrum where newness is concerned. For the contemporary world in general, and not just for Mohamed Sufyan, evolution offers one of the most influential methods of explaining the new. As an all-purpose figure of speech, *evolution* has long since transcended biology and appears in book titles ranging from *The Evolution of Natural Resource Law and Policy* to *The Evolution of Broadcast News*. As a model of change, it is mapped onto almost any process that can be imagined as occurring in successive stages.[10] As a literal explanation, it is proposed in etiologies of everything human, from society to consciousness to the arts.[11] Still, the role of novelty in the evolutionary scheme remains a puzzle, even for specialists in the field. While evolutionary theory provides a wholly modern, scientific perspective on the problem of change, it still seems subject to the most ancient philosophical conundrums: "What is meant by 'new'? Is it more than reshuffling and rearranging?"[12] How, it still makes sense to ask, even for the most serious students of evolution, does newness come into the world?

One way to address this question of the new, if not to answer it, would be to trace the history of its appearance and reappearance in the development of evolutionary biology and theory. Though one crucial part of Darwin's theory, the idea of common descent, gained fairly quick and wide acceptance among scientists, its main mechanism of change, natural selection, was originally thought to be incapable of accounting for radical novelties. Thus the early twentieth century was a veritable zoo of competing alternatives, each attempting to repair this apparent deficiency in the Darwinian system. These were winnowed down by the neo-Darwinian synthesis of the mid-twentieth century, but that very process then came under attack, partly on the grounds that its streamlining had also subordinated evolutionary novelty to variation and adaptation. Explaining radical novelty has therefore been the stock-in-trade of heterodox evolutionists virtually since the publication of Darwin's *The Origin of Species* in 1859. The refusal of this controversy to disappear means that despite common assumption, the science of evolution does not offer a single model of novelty, available for easy application, but a series of models, still competing to answer the essential question Darwin posed for the modern world.

THE EVOLUTION OF EVOLUTION

Nothing seems more obvious than the great store of incidental novelty that nature produces and refreshes every day: new individuals, new parts, new behaviors, new results of all kinds. In fact, given all this creativity, it is remarkable how little of the full spectrum of possibility is actually occupied and how much of what there is in nature might seem, from a cosmic perspective, redundant. In a sense, then, the real miracle of life is not just its creativity but its consistency. This, at any rate, is the way it appeared for many centuries, when the purpose of generation was understood to be mainly that of maintenance. According to Aristotle, "Nothing is more natural than for a living thing to make another like itself, an animal producing an animal, a plant a plant, in order that, as far as its nature is able, it may partake of the eternal and divine."[13] Thus the anecdotal fact that like produces like becomes the normative principle of continuity, whereby nature fulfills its intrinsic purpose by maintaining itself unchanged. Centuries later, Immanuel Kant rehearsed much the same argument: "As far as experience goes, all generation known to us is *generatio homonyma*."[14] This apparent empirical fact also represents, however, a logical necessity, since *generatio heteronyma* would involve a basic violation of the inner purpose that keeps organisms together in the first place. If an organism is a unified whole, then there is nothing in it from which difference might emerge; and if it has a single definitive purpose, then departing from that purpose piecemeal is impossible or fatal.

The capacity to reproduce is still one of the most important parts of any definition of life, and insofar as reproduction is understood as "self-replication," it will tend to emphasize continuity.[15] It is fairly easy to see, then, why organic generation and reproduction would have been the source of some of the earliest models of novelty, those based on the principle of cyclical recurrence. According to these models in their simplest form, novelty is reproduced like everything else and is basically the same every time it comes around. It is also easy to see why the fundamental biological problem to be addressed, for most of scientific history, was not evolution, or even variation, but continuity. What has to be explained is the uncanny ability of living things to maintain their essential forms generation after generation. Scientists hoped to discover the single principle or mechanism by which all the various reproductive strategies of nature managed to deliver the same result, faithful replication, time after time.[16] Even when Darwin deflected this research program by placing more emphasis on the variation generated by reproductive systems than on the similarity, the general context and many of the assumptions remained the same. Thus the terms within which evolutionary theories of novelty would work were first laid down by theories with a very different intent.

The most influential account of generation for many centuries was that of Aristotle, who taught that the form that makes one organism different from another is a reflection of the practical process by which each carries out particular functions.[17] In the abstract, this means that organisms are divided into kinds, or species, by virtue of the functions they fulfill in the world. Species are not ideal types but rather immanent forms maintained by a teleological process in which organisms live partly to perform a certain function and partly to replace themselves with others that will do the same.[18] Confirmation of these ideas was apparent to Aristotle in the development of animal embryos, which begin, according to his observations, as an undifferentiated mass, from which the adult form emerges, part by part. This process, which became known as epigenesis, was formalized for European science by the physician and anatomist William Harvey, who believed that each embryo is a creation *de novo*, which emerges from a primary mass, organ by organ, each part the material cause of the next.[19] This model of development, in which the adult pulls itself into existence, hand over hand, conforms rather closely to the model of novelty now commonly referred to as evolution, a process of advance in which each stage starts in the old and ends in the new. But it was in fact a completely different account of generation and development, one to which Aristotle was utterly opposed, that first acquired that name.[20]

Aristotle's model of generation, like much of his philosophy, was developed in opposition to the ideas of the pre-Socratic atomists Democritus and Leucippus, and to Empedocles, who first taught that matter is divided at base into distinct substances.[21] The most influential version of this idea for later European philosophy and biology was contained in Lucretius's *De rerum natura*. In accordance with the atomistic physics of his poem, Lucretius offers an account of generation in which organisms "keep concealed in their bodies many elements, mingled in many ways, that are derived from the ancestral stock and transmitted from father to father."[22] This account differs from Aristotle's in that the elements distinguishing one organism from another exist unchanged from the beginning of time. The particular forms that living entities assume are determined by random combination of these elements, though all the combination seems to have happened very early in the life of the universe, when the conditions of existence eliminated the unviable results, leaving only those seen in the present. Lucretius, in other words, did not believe that the primordial elements could be rearranged into new kinds of organisms.[23]

Aristotle and Lucretius thus establish competing accounts of the consistency of natural kinds, which reflect their fundamental disagreements about the elementary physics of organic generation. Though both sides agree that generation is essentially duplication and that like always begets like, their dispute about how such consistency is accomplished established a distinction that remained fundamental for later biology. As the biologist E. S. Russell put it in the first pages of his classic account, the atomists saw generation as dependent on inherent formal predispositions in matter, which, since it was heterogeneous at base, came already distinguished into types. Aristotle, on the other hand, believed that an essentially homogeneous matter is pressed into the different kinds we see by the necessary functions that different organisms perform.[24] Of these two models, one emphasizing form and the other function, it was the former that originally came to be known as evolution.

Biological science in the seventeenth and eighteenth centuries, influenced by the general atomism of the time, developed a theory of generation that depended on the combination of preexisting parts, abstracted from the parents' bodies and transmitted to their offspring.[25] For some early scientists, these parts were in fact miniature replicas of the final organs to be realized. This had been the original notion of Empedocles, who rather scandalized Aristotle by imagining tiny limbs dancing together at random to make whole animals.[26] Scientists as late as the philosopher Nicolas Malebranche apparently believed something like this as well: "apple-trees, apples and apple-seed for infinite or almost infinite centuries to come, in the proportion of one perfect apple-tree to an apple-tree in the seed."[27] The problem of fitting a near infinity of apple trees inside itself was not squarely faced or, for that matter, definitively dismissed, until the naturalist and biologist Karl Ernst von Baer's embryological research in the early nineteenth century.[28] By that time, however, most scientists had come to think of the preformed replicas as representations of some kind. After Empedocles, the Greek atomists had imagined generational particles as containing a pattern that carried form from parents to offspring; and even Jan Swammerdam, often ridiculed as a mechanical preformationist, apparently believed that seeds carry a kind of "rational similitude" and not a fully formed miniature.[29]

In any case, it was Swammerdam's preformationism that was first referred to as evolution.[30] Since the term literally means to unfold something previously compacted or rolled up to its full size and extent, this application is appropriate for a theory that the biologist François Jacob illustrates by reference to paper flowers that expand when put in water.[31] By some such process, the indescribably small, preformed replicas were supposed to be compacted, collected, transmitted, and then reconstituted into a living being. The evolutionary biologist and historian of science Stephen Jay Gould has also suggested that such accounts are more appropriately called evolutionary insofar as they are "internalist," reliant on distinctions and forms inherent in each organism rather than forces and demands external to them.[32] What the term *evolution* implies in such cases is that the new organism simply unfolds until it assumes a predetermined size and shape. Of course, such usage also implies that in its first and most appropriate application, evolution means something like the exact opposite of what it is supposed to mean today, that it is the antithesis rather than the epitome of novelty.[33]

Explaining the new was not originally a problem for science, since it did not believe that novelty was possible as anything other than a random mistake. Something fundamentally different and yet well organized enough to be considered a new species was particularly repugnant to good sense. As the philosopher and historian of science William Whewell phrased the common wisdom in 1840, "Nothing has been pointed out in the existing order of things which has any analogy or resemblance of any valid kind to that creative energy which must be exerted in the production of new species."[34] But it can be felt in Whewell's tone that the common wisdom was already struggling with some opposition, and that the problem of novelty was beginning to impose itself on a science dedicated to explaining continuity. The meaning of the term *evolution* had begun to change as embryologists refuted preformationism and replaced it with a model of gradual development much closer to Aristotle's epigenesis.[35] And the possibility of expanding that term to designate a larger process of change, involving whole species rather than individuals, was at least presented by the popular analogy established between embryonic development and species development. The anatomist Johan Meckel's influential discovery of what looked like gill slits in the early-stage embryos of mammals suggested that individual organisms passed through a series of evolutionary stages before arriving at their final form, though it was not necessarily taken to suggest that whole species had traversed these stages in the distant past.[36]

This possibility was first presented in an inverted form when it became clear from fossil remains that species had once existed that were now extinct. In extremely slow stages, the truth of the matter forced itself on a reluctant science: by the late seventeenth century, it was clear that fossils were indeed biological remnants and not mineral deposits of some kind; by the early nineteenth century, the naturalist Georges Cuvier had established that at least some species identifiable in the rocks did not match any known in the present; in the 1830s, Charles Lyell's *Principles of Geology* disposed of the notion that one or more catastrophic floods could have accounted for the extinctions.[37] None of this mandated belief in evolution. Cuvier, in fact, took extinction as a sound argument against the possibility of biological adaptation, and Lyell vexed Darwin for years by resisting the implications of his work.[38] But the fact that species had disappeared from the face of the earth did raise the general possibility of change and, for some at least, presented the particular problem of replacement. If creation is always a perfect whole, wasting nothing and wanting for naught, then it seems that the demise of old species requires the introduction of new ones.

The notion that such new species might arise in some fashion from the remains of the old seemed somewhat more feasible in an age that had experienced political revolution. The ancient atomists had not believed that one species could turn into another, but they did believe that a species could die out and that the eternal elements of the living world would then be rearranged in the form of a successor. The metaphor Lucretius used for this process, that of a relay race, is apparently mandated by a tradition at least as old as Plato, and it implied linear rather than circular change, replacement rather than evolution.[39] When Cuvier came to describe the same process of extinction and replacement, he used the term *revolution*. What he had in mind was a series of successive catastrophic changes, major upheavals that would nonetheless leave the earth in something very much like its earlier state, though with some new actors in the old roles.[40] In other words, he had a more cosmological than a political idea in mind, a more repetitive than progressive time line, as did Kant, who used the same terminology late in his life.[41] But the idea that there were "revolutions in nature" was attractive to the revolutionary in politics, especially to Cuvier's opponents in France, who were pleased to find in nature the same kind of change they hoped to see in the state.[42] Evolution thus became a model of novelty at all, and not the metaphor for mere realization that its etymology implies, in part by association with a similar shift in the meaning of revolution.

DARWIN'S SOLUTION

By the time Darwin published *The Origin of Species*, even a cautious scientist like Richard Owen could admit, "The origin of species is the question of questions in zoology; the supreme problem which the most untiring of our original labourers, the clearest zoological thinkers, and the most successful generalizers have never lost sight of."[43] Though Owen uses Darwin's title, the issue to be addressed is even clearer in Alfred Russell Wallace's contemporaneous paper, which he called "On the Law Which Has Regulated the Introduction of New Species." Before Darwin and Wallace, the likeliest supplier of biological novelty was the only source of novelty at all, the deity. Though Cuvier and Lyell disagreed about the way in which extinctions come about, they employed the same expedient to replace extinct species: special creation.[44] Cuvier and Lyell also agreed in despising the most prominent alternative, the transmutationism of Lamarck, who held that species changed as individual organisms adapted to the environment. Though Lamarckism was both supported and opposed because it seemed implicitly revolutionary, it had a steadiness of its own, since Lamarck believed that species always evolve in one ever-ascending direction, in a continuous process of promotion that current commentators like to compare to an escalator with all the steps always full.[45]

Having concentrated for so many centuries on the problem of stability, biological science was poorly equipped to explain its opposite. In fact, the generally miraculous nature of early explanations for the supply of new species shows how little modern science had added, by this point, to the very limited sources of novelty traditionally provided by philosophy. The brilliance of Darwin's contribution lies in the way it avoided this whole difficulty by deriving novelty from the same source that had previously ensured continuity. According to the historian of science Janet Browne, Darwin's taxonomic work on barnacles convinced him that individual variation within a species "was a natural consequence of reproduction," that it did not require any special conditions because differences between members of a species would be passed on in the course of ordinary reproduction just as surely as the similarities.[46] Even if reproduction were perfect, it would still tend to reproduce variation along with everything else and thus sustain a constant supply of difference. But, of course, reproduction is not perfect. For organisms with sexual reproduction, at least, variations are not just passed on but added to, combined and recombined, thus producing and maintaining a source of new variations.

On this principle, Darwin constructed his theory, which he tended to call "descent with modification through natural selection," relying on an analogy between artificial selection and the work of nature. At least once, though, he alters his terminology to speak of "slow and gradual modification, through descent and natural selection," giving descent an equal role in the gradual modification of species.[47] As Jacob puts it, "The theory of evolution had turned reproduction into the mechanism responsible for both maintaining and varying structures."[48] Against what he called "the common view of the immutability of species,"[49] Darwin pointed out their obvious variability; against the notion that changes in species over time could only be explained by catastrophic events or divine intervention, he suggested that constant replication of and selection from minute individual differences would provide enough variation to account for the grosser differences between species. Thus he proposed a model of biological change in which the process that had long been counted on to maintain species could be seen as a crucial part of their evolutionary transformation.

Many modern accounts of Darwin's theory point out that it depends on and then helps to promote an entirely new attitude toward variation. Observers had always noticed the obvious fact that individual members of a species differ from one another in many ways, but such variation had been considered inessential and temporary, since any truly major differences would presumably make the individual unviable or at least sterile.[50] Since variation was by definition accidental, it could hardly accumulate in any particular direction. Again, Darwin preserved much of the conventional wisdom by agreeing that variation is accidental, at least with respect to the future needs of any individual organism; but instead of assuming that this random quality doomed variation or made it trivial, he saw it, amplified by natural selection, as building up instead of canceling out incidental differences until they become radical novelties.

Depending as it does on the random combination of preexisting traits, Darwin's theory seemed to many of his contemporaries a modernized revival of an outmoded atomism. Sending a copy of Aristotle's *Parts of Animals* to Darwin late in his life, his friend William Ogle remarked, "I can fancy the old teleologist looking sideways and with no little suspicion at his successor, and much astounded to find Democritus, whom he thought to have been effectually and everlastingly squashed, had come to life again in the man he saw before him."[51] Though Ogle was a supporter, the association with atomism was frequently exploited by Darwin's challengers, including the Rev. Dr. J. M'Cann, as quoted by Darwin himself in *The Descent of Man*: "The teaching that atoms leave their impressions as legacies to other atoms falling into the places they have vacated is contradictory of the utterance of consciousness, and is therefore false."[52] As M'Cann's language suggests, Darwinism was often received as a late variant of Lucretius's Epicureanism, a doctrine whose influence over European science had always been qualified by misgivings about the role in it of happenstance. The classic argument of design theorists, as the philosopher of science Elliott Sober shows, has always treated Darwinism as if it had nothing more to offer by way of explanation than the swerve of falling atoms.[53]

What it had to offer instead, of course, was natural selection, which plays the role in Darwin's system that had always been played in Enlightenment science by fundamental laws of nature, supplying the need most felt in classical atomism by bringing the random combination of basic parts into form and order. In this way, Darwin manages to reconcile the classic alternatives of chance and necessity, since the variations arise randomly but are then subjected to the force of necessity, as administered by the conditions of existence. Although the relationship between these principles is presented in almost all accounts of Darwinism, by scientists as different as Jacques Monod, Ernst Mayr, and Stephen Jay Gould as a balance or reconciliation,[54] it might be just as accurate to say that Darwin transforms chance into necessity. Alfred Russell Wallace expresses something fundamental about Darwin's system as well his own when he describes variation as "a constant and necessary property of all organisms," rather as if it were a physical property like mass.[55] Obviously, when randomness becomes "constant and necessary" the accidental is demoted, as it were, one step, to become a merely local effect of an overarching necessity. This occurs in Darwin's system because natural selection, by determining which variations will be passed on, also determines which traits can appear in the future.[56]

Evolution happens as it does, sustaining consistent kinds and starting new ones, because of the press of environmental necessity, which constantly feeds its results back into the available pool of variation. Because he emphasizes environmental adaptation in this way, Darwin is often considered a functionalist like Aristotle, who also believed that organic forms reflect functional demands. But the early opponents who thought they saw in Darwin a reincarnation of Greek atomism also had a point. Like Lucretius, Darwin saw nature as a collection of differentiated units, so that organic forms are largely constrained to the combinations possible for those units. For this reason, Darwin can also be considered a formalist, since the shape and structure of organisms are not solely determined by the press of function but also constrained to particular forms.[57]

Another way of putting this would be to say that Darwin arranges a grand reconciliation of two different ways of explaining natural change, drawing them into a circle, so that functional necessity determines formal constitution, which then presents itself to a new set of functional demands. This circle does not become a vicious one, because function never completely delimits the form it hands on to later generations; some traits are always neutral in terms of survival. Darwin also opened this circle so that it could include a number of other factors for change, among them sexual selection and direct environmental influence.[58] But the essential beauty of his system lies in the way it turns an old pair of ideological antagonists into an interdependent couple, so that form is but inherited function, which can itself be defined as fitness for particular environments. What turns a prior opposition into a cycle is the additional factor of time, which allows functional distinctions to build up as form, and form to change as it meets different functional necessities. Though the theory of evolution made it easier to accept the notion that species might change, it was itself dependent on Darwin's willingness to think of nature in historical terms.[59]

Resolving the old opposition of Aristotle and Lucretius as he does, Darwin also reconciles what had been two quite different models of novelty, having first made significant alterations in each one. Like other models of novelty based on nature, evolution involves cycles of recurrence: the whole process depends on the necessity that species recreate themselves, generation by generation. For Darwin, though, the cycle of generation escapes the circular by incorporating an element of recombination, wherein particular traits and features are selected from a constant and constantly changing pool of variation.[60] In this he recalls the old atomists with their random rearrangements, but his model differs from theirs in being repetitive and recursive. According to the doctrine passed from Empedocles down to Lucretius, the atoms dance only once and then the forms of nature are fixed, except in certain extraordinary circumstances. Darwin arranges evolution as a cyclical pattern of recombinations, thus making a new model of novelty in what is apparently the only way possible, by merging two old ones.

The specific shape of Darwin's model of novelty is very largely determined by its heritage, and by the changes Darwin effects in the old models as he brings them together. Because he saw nature as particulate, always already divided up into discrete structures, traits, or features, he tended to see change as happening piecemeal. Traditional functionalists from Aristotle to Cuvier had seen each one of nature's structures as exquisitely adjusted to every other one; as late as 1916, E. S. Russell found it hard to forgive Darwin for dismantling nature into independent bits.[61] For classical Darwinists, though, this is the only way that evolution can happen at all, since functional interdependence makes it hard to change one part without changing all the others. If nature were not a "mosaic," as Gould puts it, with parts that are at least semi-independent, then it could not be rearranged.[62] The smaller the pieces, as the atomists realized, the greater the possibility of rearrangement—but this condition also means that change will be gradual and generally undramatic.

Darwin gladly embraced this necessity, and he was quite happy to say, with "the experienced naturalist," that "nature is prodigal in variety, but niggard in innovation."[63] However friendly he might have been toward variation and change, Darwin was not fond of novelty as such, and he shied away from the word itself, which he tended to use as a synonym for *fashion*, as denoting the love of change for its own sake.[64] This practice was partly based on predilection, since he was personally a conventional man, and partly on conviction, since he tended to assume, with Lyell, that natural change would be continuous and slow since it had to be produced by regular laws working consistently.[65] This conviction, passed on to later generations of Darwinists, helped to make the entire science suspicious of dramatic novelty, as if it could be achieved only by supernatural means.[66]

Thus the tempo of evolution, by Darwin's metronome, is decidedly on the slow side, which is one reason why it usually cannot be witnessed on the fly. Like a glacier, evolution is a river that refutes Heraclitus's rule and flows without seeming to go anywhere at all. Again, Darwin was perfectly content with a model of change that tended to approach stability, and it did not seem to him a dismal fact that "the production of new species must always be slow."[67] If it was slow, the evolutionary change that he imagined was also steady, because it was cumulative. It is in this way that the cyclical and recurrent aspect of Darwin's model of novelty repairs the deficiencies of pure recombination, which would have the tendency to dissipate if it were not recursive. Darwin offers an example of how this process might work as a model of cultural change in *The Descent of Man*. Imagine, he suggests, that "one man in a tribe, more sagacious than others, invented a new snare or weapon"; if it were more effective, his fellows would imitate it from sheer self-interest, and the tribe would grow in numbers, thus offering chance a greater opportunity to produce further inventors.[68] The general stock of novelty increases insofar as new developments help to guarantee their own survival.

Of course, to be entirely true to his own system, Darwin probably should not have started this illustration with an innovation as major as a new weapon. Working incrementally as it does, evolution is far more likely to have started with a minor modification, introduced accidentally, to some aspect of an existing weapon. For the model of cumulative change implies that all novelty, at every scale, is the result of novelties arising at the very lowest scale. Darwin maintains that "as natural selection acts solely by accumulating slight, successive, favourable variations, it can produce no great or sudden modification; it can act only by very short and slow steps."[69] In fact, natural selection does produce great modifications, but only by adding up slight ones. Once again, the cyclical aspect of Darwin's model helps it to overcome one of the most obvious deficiencies of simple recombination, which had never been imagined, not even by Lucretius, as an explanation of continuous, developmental change. By Darwin's reasoning, a small step can count as a big one when it contains within itself the results of a great many preceding small steps.

By similar small steps of its own, Darwin's theory arrives at a model of novelty as such. A mere quantitative increase, of course, has never counted as novelty. As Aristotle might have put it, coming-to-be more or less is drastically different from coming-to-be as such. One of the classic deficiencies of the atomist model is that it merely recombined qualities fixed in nature from the beginning of time and thus seemed to reduce difference to a matter of quantity. There were different recipes for different dishes, but they all used the same ingredients, just in different proportions. In Darwin's version, however, in which recombination is made recursive, there is a dialectical transformation, as Jacob puts it, and "quality is produced from quantity."[70] Though it is difficult—perhaps even impossible, as Mayr admits—to tell just where in a sequence of quantitative changes a qualitative difference appears,[71] it is also hard to gainsay the fact that somewhere between, say, the *Urschleim* (protoplasm) and the blue whale, such a change has occurred.

In terms of biological classification, this means that species and genera are but variation writ large. For Darwin, even the splendidly inexplicable novelties that had always seemed to distinguish human beings, developments such as language, were the cumulative results of beginnings visible far distant on the family tree. *The Descent of Man* slowly and steadily derives all the most spiritual qualities of humankind from their prototypes among the other animals, so that the difference between the faithfulness of the family dog and the faith of his master is a difference of degree that has insensibly become a difference in kind. Darwin does draw one or two sharp lines across this pattern of development, one for the appearance of the mind and one for life itself, both of which he sets aside as "problems for the distant future, if they are ever to be solved by man."[72] Otherwise, everything above the bare rock can be explained as the recursive accumulation of infinitesimal variations. All novelty, according to this model, is the hybrid offspring of recurrence and recombination, like the theory of evolution itself, which, by crossing these classic alternatives, achieves an explanatory vigor denied to either one alone.

AFTER DARWIN

For William James, writing in 1880, the "triumphant originality of Darwin" lay in the clear separation he enforced between the two phases of evolutionary change: the random causes of biological variation, on one hand, and the necessary processes by which it is selected and preserved, on the other.[73] James's account of Darwin's theory allows him to celebrate the first part of it while dismissing the second, which he found less congenial. Natural selection, rebranded as "survival of the fittest," had become the watchword of social Darwinism and was being used to assert an absolute environmental determinism. For James, though, Darwinism was a theory of accidental variation, the source and exact nature of which were beyond the reach of science. By showing that biological reality always begins in sheer contingency, "that we all have five fingers not because four or six would not do just as well, but merely because the first vertebrate above the fishes happened to have that number," Darwin, according to James, puts the environment firmly in its place.[74] James sees evolution so exclusively as a matter of "spontaneous variation" that he comes to view it not as including natural selection but almost as refuting it.

James thus offers a particularly clear view of the peculiar fate of Darwin's theory in the first decades of its success. Understood as a theory of spontaneous variation, evolution helped to inspire a burst of new thinking about novelty, which became a distinct philosophical issue only at the end of the nineteenth century. C. S. Peirce as well as James in the United

States,[75] F. C. S. Schiller and other pragmatists in Britain, and Henri Bergson in France derived from Darwin an account of novelty that was free of the old fear of chance. As James sees it, evolution as a physical explanation of human activity is not reductive but expansive:

> The new conceptions, emotions, and active tendencies which evolve are originally produced in the shape of random images, fancies, accidental out-births of spontaneous variation in the functional activity of the excessively instable human brain, which the outer environment simply confirms or refutes, adopts or rejects, preserves or destroys,— selects, in short, just as it selects morphological and social variations due to molecular accidents of an analogous sort.[76]

Putting accident at the heart of nature in this way, according to James, is what makes novelty possible, since "predetermined and necessary outgrowths of the being already there" can never be new.[77]

From this point of view, of course, natural selection was little more than an embarrassment. But James was hardly alone in his attempt to prune Darwinism of this unpleasant excrescence. At the end of the nineteenth century, natural selection was generally regarded as a major logical flaw in Darwin's system, a purely negative factor that could never allow, much less account for, evolutionary novelty.[78] Even in the early twentieth century, Russell regarded Darwinism as better at explaining the persistence of vestigial organs than at accounting for the appearance of new ones.[79] Though there were also considerable doubts about the power of gradual change of the kind Darwin postulated ever to amount to anything dramatic, it was very largely because of natural selection that "creativity" became a major scientific and ideological problem for early Darwinists.[80] In short, Darwin established novelty as an issue for science and philosophy to face, but without converting very many to his particular explanation of it.

From James's point of view, one of the beauties of Darwin's theory was that it could not account for either the origin or the transmission of variants, since it did not include a specific, verifiable mechanism of inheritance, and thus seemed to leave the whole matter open to chance. Darwin's own theory, in which particles called gemmules accumulated in the bloodstream and were passed on from generation to generation, was almost entirely conjectural. As the evolutionary biologist August Weis-mann, the botanist and geneticist Hugo de Vries, and the biologist and geneticist William Bateson, aided by the rediscovery of the researches of Gregor Mendel, began to establish a more solid account of biological continuity, they also developed a theory of evolutionary novelty that was almost as free of cause and determination as James could want. Weis-mann's demonstration that general physiological changes could not be recorded and transmitted through the germ line has often been seen as the deathblow to survival of the fittest as coined by the philosopher Herbert Spencer, since it seemed to show that acquired characteristics could not be passed on to later generations. But if change could not come in from the environment, then this meant it had to arise somehow within the materials of inheritance themselves, in the factors that were just be-ginning to be known as genes. Mere rearrangement, it was widely be-lieved, could not lead to anything so dramatic as a new species, since extreme variations would inevitably be washed out in the general tide of genetic sameness.[81] Novelty, therefore, would have to come from changes in the genetic material itself, by way of what de Vries called mutation.

For several decades around the beginning of the twentieth century, mutation was solidly ensconced as the only possible source of evolution-ary novelty.[82] As Bateson put it in a symposium celebrating the centenary of Darwin's birth, "Selection determines along which branch Evolution shall proceed, but it does not decide what novelties that branch shall bring forth."[83] According to the account of mutation first offered by de Vries, new species arise as the result of random, spontaneous changes in the genetic material itself, experienced by whole species in bursts of change that are concentrated enough for the new characteristic to be passed on and thus established.[84] Sudden, discontinuous, spontaneous, and apparently random, the model of novelty established by the muta-tion theory differed in several fundamental respects from that originally offered by Darwin. As de Vries put it, new species are formed "by certain leaps,"[85] by what biologists then and now are apt to call "saltations" out of a kind of inverted respect for Darwin, who believed so firmly in the old scientific maxim: *Natura non facit saltum* (Nature makes no leap).[86] Dar-win's evolutionary notion of evolution was replaced by one that hardly seemed entitled to the name, since it did not see change as gradually unfolding from implicit origins but rather as exploding quite suddenly more or less from nowhere.

It is easy to see why this saltatory model of novelty appealed to James, and why Bergson would have found de Vries's work "striking."[87] For the mutation theory seemed to free the principle of novelty from centuries of inhibition. Stripped of natural selection as Darwin had proposed it, and therefore of any vestige of Aristotelian functionalism, evolution appeared as a modern form of atomism in which the old *clinamen*, or swerve, was no longer a weak and somewhat embarrassing makeshift but rather a major engine of change.[88] Mutations had always been known to biology as sports or monsters, and it was still often assumed by biologists of this time that most mutations would be nonadaptive and perhaps fatal. But this did not necessarily weaken the case so long as it could be assumed, as de Vries did, that "mutations are the rule."[89] Though mutations are random, spontaneous, and nondirectional, they are also regular enough in their appearance to account for the appearance of new organs, new species, and even new taxa. The mutation theory thus achieved a quantitative advantage over Epicurean atomism, dramatically increasing the possibilities of change by making randomness regular without subjecting it to any particular rule.

The mutation theory also surpassed traditional atomism in a qualitative sense, since the biological novelty it imagined did not arise from mere recombination of existing characteristics. Mutation, as de Vries understood it, meant a substantial change in the genetic material itself — a change, moreover, that is discontinuous with any prior state. Though he suggests that it "is perhaps appropriate to compare such a change with a chemical substitution," he actually had no idea how to account for it.[90] This notion of discontinuous change violates not only the scientific maxim *Natura non facit saltum* but also the broader truism behind it: *Ex nihilo nihil fit* (Nothing comes from nothing). Science did not believe that nature could advance in leaps because a leap implies a gap, a break in the chain of cause and effect. A leap defies the absence of an immediate, antecedent cause and achieves an effect, as it were, out of nothing. In supposing that nature can change by leaps and not by steps so tiny they approach a continuum, the mutation theory proposes a kind of qualitative novelty impossible under any model previously imagined by European science.[91]

As it happened, however, the mutation theory was both incorrect and unnecessary—incorrect because de Vries's original experiments were performed on a plant that turned out to be genetically anomalous,[92] and unnecessary when later geneticists showed how even minute genetic changes could ultimately give rise to major evolutionary novelties. Still, the tension within evolutionary biology between continuous and discontinuous theories of change has not disappeared but remains a major variable in the evolutionary model of novelty.[93] And the notion that major qualitative novelties such as mind or language might somehow be explained by the purely quantitative relations among genetic factors remains what it has been since the beginning of the twentieth century: one of the fondest hopes of revisionary Darwinists.

EMERGENCE

When Julian Huxley came to characterize the early twentieth century as the nadir of Darwinism, he gathered the apostates into two camps, that of Bateson and that of Bergson.[94] Like many later biologists, Huxley himself was much more strongly influenced by the latter, to whom he paid elaborate tribute in the first pages of his first book.[95] This influence seems more than a little odd, since Bergson was not a biologist and thus hardly deserves a position side-by-side with the scientist who gave genetics its name. But Bergson achieved his considerable reputation, in philosophy as well as biology, in much the same way that Bateson did, by offering to restore to the theory of evolution its power to explain creativity.

Like most biologists of his time, Bergson complained that natural selection, as a merely negative force, an editor that can only cross out errors, could not account for the progressive creation of new forms of life.[96] Conversant with the research of Weismann and de Vries, he agreed with the latter that the store of ordinary variations was insufficient to explain the major novelties on which evolution must depend.[97] Though he was much taken with "the sudden 'mutations' which we now hear of," he felt that exclusive reliance on these merely accentuated the absurdity of explaining living change as the mechanical recombination of parts.[98] And yet Bergson did not believe in creation *ex nihilo* any more than the Greek philosophers he was so apt to criticize. "That new things can join things already existing is absurd," he agrees, not only ontologically but also experientially, because this would imply that the mind can present to itself something that it has not already imagined.[99] If it is impossible to imagine any way of adding to the available store of reality, then the only way to explain novelty is to change the arithmetic and make evolution a matter of division and multiplication instead.

Going back to embryology, to the original source of the metaphor of evolution, Bergson insists, "Life does not proceed by the association and addition of elements, but by dissociation and division."[100] What he seems to have in mind is a primordial biological entity, a single complex cell, all of it absolutely new in the context of unliving, mineral reality, which then divides itself into two equally new halves, and so on. In this way, "nature's simple act has divided itself automatically into an infinity of elements," working outward from the center "by concentric waves which go on enlarging."[101] Though nothing is ever added to the sum of life, the total amount of novelty always increases as life divides itself into ever more complex forms, multiplying as it divides. In this way, life manages to draw from itself more than it contains[102] and produces qualitative novelty without first having to accomplish a quantitative increase. Biological development of this kind is continuous, without breaks or flying leaps, but it also makes distinct progress and eventuates in forms and structures that could not possibly have been predicted in the bud.

Bergson supported his ideas with only the most general sort of references to actual biology, which offered little more than a jumping-off point for his philosophy; and he found it impossible to believe that a purely material force could sustain this process of self-division and multiplication indefinitely, in face of the inevitable tendency of material things to decline and fall apart. Thus he assumed, from mere observation of the ability of life to thrive and increase, that some vital influence must be counteracting the heavy weight of sheer materiality. Though vitalism of this kind had been a common feature of earlier biological theories, it was regarded with some suspicion by the early twentieth century, so that scientists taken with Bergson's ideas had to work around it. Perhaps the most significant and influential such adaptation, especially for the history of novelty, was the emergent evolution of the ethologist and psychologist C. Lloyd Morgan.

Morgan was in the direct Darwinian line, as it were, having served as literary executor to George Romanes, who had been Darwin's closest disciple.[103] Nonetheless, he did not believe that conventional Darwinism had accounted for major evolutionary novelties such as mind or language; nor did he think that the mutation theory offered much advance over other models of quantitative recombination. He agreed with Bergson that some account of qualitative novelty was necessary in order to explain the full course of evolution, but he specifically disclaimed Bergson's vitalism.[104] Instead, Morgan went back to a concept first presented in the mid-nineteenth century by the philosopher John Stuart Mill, who had pointed out that many unexpected qualities emerge quite naturally from the association of known quantities, as wetness emerges from the combination of hydrogen and oxygen.[105] In a sense, this kind of novelty is nothing but the same recombination that had been serving science since the Greek atomists, but Morgan insisted that new relations did more than simply add the old elements together: the relation between them constituted a substantial, qualitative novelty in itself.[106] Thus the qualitative advances that seemed most difficult to explain by natural selection, developments such as the human mind, could be seen as emergences, sums arrived at by multiplication rather than simple addition.

Emergent evolution, as a more scientific alternative to Bergson's creative evolution, had a certain influence in the first few decades of the twentieth century. As late as 1927, H. S. Jennings, a prominent American biologist and president of the Zoological Section of the American Association for the Advancement of Science, offered emergent evolution as the best available explanation for major evolutionary novelties.[107] Morgan's religiosity, his interest, even if rather glancing, in eugenics, and suspicions of residual vitalism in his theory, not to mention the success of R. A. Fisher and Sewall Wright in showing how genetic variation and natural selection could work together to produce new species, doomed his work to inconsequence. But emergence became a familiar term again in the 1970s as computers helped scientists model self-organizing systems that seemed to produce the sort of novelty Morgan had described. Though Jennings had offered emergence as the sort of natural phenomenon that is particular to the life sciences, evidence of emergent properties in physics has helped to free the concept from some of the suspicion of mysticism that had previously hampered its influence.[108]

The most popular of all emergent effects, then and now, is almost certainly language. Even Alfred Russell Wallace found it difficult to believe that natural selection could bring forth a result as complex as human communication, which he explained by means of supernatural causes. More recently, the anthropologist Terrence Deacon has insisted that language cannot have evolved "in the standard sense of that term. Language is an 'emergent' phenomenon in ways unlike almost any other biological product."[109] Whatever the scientific merits of this position may be, it expresses something fundamental about the troubled role of novelty in evolutionary theory. Evolution has always implicitly taken language as a privileged model, simply because of the etymology of the term. Though the Latin *evolvere* simply means to unfold or disclose, in its substantive form *evolutio* refers precisely to the way a scroll is unrolled to full length.[110] But this association with the scroll is not merely topological. In fact, *evolutio* refers to the unrolling and reading of a scroll, and the standard quotation from Cicero strongly emphasizes the latter: "'Quid poetarum evolutio voluptatis affert?' (What pleasure does the reading of the poets provide?)"[111] The notion of evolution as the simple manifestation of something already latent has always been accompanied by another idea, in which the new emerges from the old by some process like the one that produces meaning from inert graphical marks.

Thus the ancient tradition, stemming from the *Theaetetus*, of relying on the homely example of the alphabet to explain how novelty can arise from the reassociation of old and known elements continues in the development of evolutionary theory. As Bergson says, in a virtual paraphrase of Cicero, "Consider the letters of the alphabet that enter into the composition of everything that has ever been written: we do not conceive that new letters spring up and come to join themselves to the others in order to make a new poem. But that the poet creates the poem and that human thought is thereby made richer."[112] Thus poetry is enlisted to show how the new can emerge from what seems a mere reshuffling of the old. More recently, Stephen Jay Gould concludes his massive revisionary study of evolutionary theory with some pertinent words from Friedrich

Nietzsche, who says "that anything in existence, having somehow come about, is continually interpreted anew, requisitioned anew, transformed and directed to a new purpose." Evolution thus assumes its historically secondary and more modern meaning as "a continuous chain of signs, continually revealing new interpretations and adaptations."[113] This chain of signs, each one modifying the significance of the one before, is the revisionary biologist's version of the evolutionary scroll, the unrolling of which is just a topological metaphor for the constant rereading of nature.

One way of explaining how evolution might have given rise to language, in other words, is to claim that evolution actually *is* a language. Darwin himself was fond of a simpler version of this argument, in which the family trees produced by early philologists serve as prototypes for the branching trees of evolutionary descent.[114] Since his time, evolutionary theory has resorted to literary analogies to support its explanations of novelty, following the ancient argument that language shows how unexpected qualities can arise from the recombination of known quantities. The most recent of these analogies was offered by information theory, which was deployed in the 1950s to illustrate and substantiate the explanation of biological novelty established by modern genetics. Influential and controversial, the definition of genetic inheritance as the transmission of information began as an analogy and then developed into a forceful new version of the ancient model of atomistic recombination. By this time, however, the social and physical sciences had fundamentally reconfigured the very notion of randomness on which that model had always relied for infusions of the new.

4

CALCULATING CHANCE

The great accomplishment of evolutionary biology, according to the philosopher and mathematician C. S. Peirce, was to establish the existence of "an element of indeterminacy, spontaneity, or absolute chance in nature."[1] Against the prevailing determinism of the late nineteenth century, much of it inspired by a very different reading of Darwin, Peirce argued for an "arbitrary heterogeneity"[2] in things that could account for real ontological novelty. But Peirce's version of the arbitrary is not quite as open and freewheeling as it sounds, for he saw in nature "a spontaneity which is to some degree regular."[3] "Pure spontaneity," as he explained it, is not exactly unrestricted, since it is always "restrained within narrow bounds by law, producing infinitesimal departures from law continually, and great ones with infinite infrequency." Such a principle, he claimed, is the only way to "account for all the variety and diversity of the universe, in the only sense in which the really *sui generis* and new can be said to be accounted for."[4] Making spontaneity as regular as the rules it supposedly violates, Peirce intends to verify its presence and its forcefulness in the world, but he is also aware of having produced a bit of a paradox. In his zeal to stand up to determinism, with its doctrine of mechanical necessity, Peirce makes spontaneity and chance almost as reliable as necessity itself. If the new and unexpected can be "traced out with mathematical precision into considerable detail," then perhaps it could even be predicted and thus come to be expected after all.[5]

As counterintuitive as it may sound, calculating chance is a common-place activity, the particular province of probability theory, on which Peirce wrote a good deal in the course of his life. At one time, he treated probability as a matter of logical inference, as a way of measuring the relative reliability of particular arguments.[6] This is Peirce's adaptation of the older and more traditional form of probability theory, which tries to balance arguments and to measure degrees of believability. The sciences of the nineteenth century had, however, given Peirce strong precedents for the study of a different kind of probability, inherent in the objective facts of physical existence. Evolutionary biology was one such science, since it tried to estimate the influence of variations within a population that were random, at least in relation to the demands of natural selec-tion. For Peirce, an even more precise model was provided by physics. It was, he says, "the peculiar function of the molecular hypothesis in physics to open an entry for the calculus of probabilities."[7] Here Peirce rephrases as an opportunity the necessity that faced the physicists James Clerk Maxwell and Ludwig Boltzmann when they proposed to treat bulk properties such as the temperature of a gas as effects of their constituent molecules, which became possible only when it was assumed that the essentially innumerable molecules could be treated statistically, in terms of relative frequencies.

That the swirl of elementary particles could be modeled in this way seemed to make Maxwell and Boltzmann the heirs of Epicurus and Lucretius, but with a much sounder account of the *clinamen*, or swerve.[8] No longer a quasi-mythological episode, the random swerve of particles could now be calculated and relied on. Though Maxwell was no more capable of actually observing an atom than Lucretius had been, he did have sophisticated methods of representing the aggregate effects of gas molecules—methods that, because they were probabilistic in nature, gave the random a new and apparently scientific basis. Probabilistic rea-soning of this kind thus had the paradoxical effect of substantiating the improbable. Once he had adapted the formulae of statistical mechanics to population biology, R. A. Fisher claimed that "the effects of chance are the most accurately calculable, and therefore the least doubtful, of all the factors in an evolutionary situation."[9] In biology as in physics, probability gave the random a sound mathematical basis, establishing it as a constant in the real world. Though the fundamental constituents of reality might remain the same, new combinations and rearrangements might come into being in ways both indeterminate and ultimately cal-culable. Probabilistic approaches in the sciences thus gave thinkers like Peirce a chance to make the new as sure and certain as any other scientific phenomenon.

Even for its most sophisticated students, though, probability is "a difficult and complex notion."[10] Is the probable a matter of logical inference and therefore a subjective factor, a kind of limit that human knowledge constantly approaches? Could we always turn the probable into the certain with enough time and intelligence? Or is it, as Peirce liked to suppose, an actual fact of existence, an inevitable indeterminacy in the basic physical relations that make up the world? If so, what are we to make of an indeterminacy that is inevitable, a spontaneity that, as Peirce put it, could always be counted and counted on? *Can* we count on a principle like probability, which is reliable in the abstract, in the long run, all other things being equal, but not necessarily in any particular situation on any given day? If the success of probabilistic reasoning in the sciences of the nineteenth century substantiated for Peirce the status of real ontological novelty, it delivered that boon in a form that was never very easy to grasp.

In fact, the effect of probabilistic reasoning on the sciences has itself been unpredictable. Early probability theorems made eighteenth-century sociology far more certain of human behavior than it had been, but probabilistic theories made nineteenth-century physics comfortable with a kind of uncertainty that would have filled earlier scientists with horror. By way of information theory, probability has informed vast stretches of the contemporary world and seems to have destabilized and insubstantialized physical reality itself by turning everything into electronic bits that can be sent, stored, and manipulated. Some of the most influential contemporary models of novelty thus base themselves on the assumptions of information theory. But the greatest early success of information theory in the sciences, which came when it transformed the basic terminology of molecular genetics, is now often regarded as having returned biology to a rigid determinism not seen since the days of social

Darwinism. Probability theory has always been concerned with the basic question of novelty: must the future be like the past? It is partly because the theory has returned so many different answers to that question that modern ideas about novelty are as richly ambiguous as they are.

PROBABILITY

Though probability may have become a difficult and complex notion, in its earliest form it was simplicity itself. Classically, the probable was that which most serious witnesses would find believable. If reality is more or less consistent and unchanging and if a common notion of good sense can be assumed, then the probable is relatively easy to determine. Even such a diligent skeptic as the philosopher David Hume came to depend on this sort of reasoning in his argument against the idea of miracles. "A wise man," he says, "proportions his beliefs to the evidence." Where the evidence is incontrovertible, he is confident. Where it is less reliable, he depends on "what we properly call *probability*," by which Hume means "the usual conformity of the facts to the reports of witnesses."[11] The more common and consistent these reports, the more probable is the testimony they contain. It is, of course, the whole purpose of such an argument to impeach the improbable and to rule the unprecedented out of court altogether. Hume allows for uncertainty, especially in such innocuous and routine cases as the English weather, and he does not believe that the apparent consistency of nature is guaranteed by anything other than our habitual experience of it. But utter violations of that experience are not to be credited, so that past experience puts a limit on future experience and protects us from the illusion of radical change.

It occurred rather early to canny businessmen that the relative certainty of canny businessmen in general could be calculated so that things such as contracts and annuities could be valued fairly and efficiently.[12] Mathematics thus began to inform the estimation of probabilities, and the reason behind reasonable expectations came to be less a matter of habitual custom and more a matter of abstract calculation. So long as it can be assumed that reality is fairly consistent, then such calculations are rather trivial. It is really not much more than common sense to say, as Jacob Bernoulli did in the eighteenth century with the aid of a good deal of sophisticated math, that choosing from an urn full of black and white balls will sooner or later produce a highly reliable notion of their proportions.[13] What we really want to know is to what extent reality may be said to resemble an urn full of black and white balls. In other words, what early probability theorists such as Bernoulli hoped to be able to determine was the chance, in a system less restricted than the urn of black and white balls, that any given observed frequency was stable and would continue in the future. The application of sophisticated mathematical formulas to such questions gave scientists such as Pierre-Simon Laplace great confidence in their ability to determine future patterns; and yet the very entry of abstract standards into an arena traditionally dominated by custom and habit showed that past experience was no longer a reliable guide. Bernoulli and Laplace both believed that chance is a figment created by ignorance, so that a full and complete account of the present will give a very reliable estimation of the future.[14] But the very fact that they had to calculate what had previously been left to common sense showed that in some respects at least, the past alone was no longer a reliable guide to the present. Though eighteenth-century probability theory denied the possibility of radical novelty, its very existence testified to the kind of unexpected and improbable change that challenged traditional experience.

Statistical representations of large numbers of human beings in the abstract, which became common in the early nineteenth century, suggest all by themselves an inescapable ignorance and obscurity, as the face-to-face acquaintance possible in small groups gives way to numerical approximation. The kind of certainty provided by tradition and custom is replaced in such situations by a mathematical certainty offered as a kind of ironic compensation. The mathematician Siméon Denis Poisson's "law of large numbers" claims that ignorance of the individual case is overcome by sheer multiplication, and that the consistency lost as tradition declines is replaced by a different kind of consistency discernible only in the vastest mass. What this law dictates is that irregularities, so long as they are independent of one another and of particular determining causes, will cancel out and produce stable mean values.[15] What it meant in practice is that social statistics of various kinds were observed to settle at fairly steady values, with such reliability that the variations were thought to be mere errors of measurement.

Thus the practice ultimately used by the biological and physical sciences to bring a manageable version of chance into their disciplines was first introduced by the human sciences to rule it out. According to Poisson, the law of large numbers is "a fact of experience that never goes wrong."[16] The average incidence of various social occurrences, such as suicide, once found to be approximately stable, came to seem constant and then to be *a* constant, as if governed by a physical principle such as gravity. For social scientists such as the astronomer and mathematician Adolphe Quetelet or the historian Henry Thomas Buckle, constants came to function as norms, so that variations, dismissed as errors, ceased to be real evidence at all.[17] Finally, descriptive regularities, which were at bottom nothing more than arithmetical means, were turned into prescriptive laws so that they could function as causal explanations of themselves.[18]

The statistical law was a popular and influential feature of the social sciences in the nineteenth century, though it is a fairly peculiar kind of law. As the philosopher Ian Hacking points out in what is still the most widely cited study of nineteenth-century probability theories, the first step, taken by Quetelet, is to treat mere averages as if they are real quantities, facts of physical existence so concrete that it would not be absurd to look for an actual "average man."[19] The regular appearance of a physical phenomenon seems to imply some consistent causal force, some necessity like the law of gravity to which everything must submit. But statistical laws are exceptional in this sense in that they imply causality without specifying even a distant cause.[20] Once statistical regularity came loose from its basis in mere counting and became something more than a numerical artifact, it seemed to constitute causality in and of itself.

As a mathematical discipline hitched to the social sciences, probabilistic reasoning eliminated the new and different even more completely than it had when it meant little more than the common wisdom. Mathematical necessity thus confirmed the idea of mechanical necessity, the orthodoxy Peirce was complaining against in 1892, which decreed "that the state of things existing at any time, together with certain immutable laws, completely determines the state of things at every other time."[21] Still, a law based on statistical probability contains certain loopholes that leave room for the irregular, for chance, and even for novelty. Because there was no real physical cause behind the statistical laws deduced by Quetelet or Buckle, because these tended to mystify the whole notion of causality, the necessity they proposed remained abstract and distant. To say that in the long run some particular thing is overwhelmingly likely to happen is not at all the same as saying that every apple must inevitably fall to earth. The philosopher Quentin Meillassoux has recently radicalized what he calls "Hume's problem" by proposing that if "in the long run" means something like "in a nearly infinite amount of time," then there is room within the probable for all sorts of unprecedented events. Meillassoux turns Hume's chapter on miracles upside down by arguing that the nonappearance of the unprecedented might be due to the relatively tiny part of time and space covered by our experience. In fact, he turns probabilistic reasoning upside down by explaining the apparent regularity of our universe, "the immense numerical gap between those possibilities that are conceivable and those that are actually experienced," by suggesting that human experience as a whole is contained within a run of dumb luck, in which the continued tendency of the dice of time and space to come up lucky seven does not mean that they won't, at some point in an infinite number of future throws, come up snake eyes.[22]

Even in the strictest and most deterministic versions of probabilistic reasoning, however, the probable exists in a tense relationship with the improbable. Because probability is a matter of ratios, the common and predominant is always defined by its relationship to the uncommon and rare. Does this mean that the common and the uncommon are opposites, as Hume certainly seemed to believe when he cited common wisdom as a way of disproving the existence of miracles? If so, why is the distinction between the two, in any statistical system, gradual instead of being sharp and bright? Is the probable ever anything more than predominantly probable, or more probable than something else, which is itself probably more probable than something else again? What would seem particularly sharp and bright would be the distinction between the improbable and the impossible, separated as they are by a statistical gap that is both infinitesimal and uncrossable. But probability actually has very little to do with the impossible. Though it may handle the rare with some confidence, probabilistic reasoning is rather helpless when it comes to the unprecedented, where there is no prior frequency from which to calculate a probability in the future.[23]

Given the difficulty of actually driving the probability of anything down to zero, some serious statisticians have argued—in unwitting parallel to Meillassoux—that given a large-enough sample, "any outrageous thing is likely to happen." Using "the law of truly large numbers," even the likelihood of a miracle might be calculated. If we take the common notion of one in a million as the going rate of the impossible, then about 250 US citizens would experience something impossible on any given day.[24] Thus modern probabilistic reasoning seems to establish a steady ratio for the miracles against which Hume had directed the authority of a much simpler version of the probable. In giving mathematical support to the old notion of common wisdom, nineteenth-century probability theory had not just made it more objective and easier to verify—it had also given later philosophers and scientists the tools they would need to establish the real existence of the radically new and different.

STATISTICAL MECHANICS

Boltzmann once proposed to name the nineteenth century for Charles Darwin, so profound was his respect for the transformation that Darwin's ideas had effected by bringing probabilistic reasoning to bear on the mechanical view of nature.[25] Though Darwin was certainly aware of Quetelet, whose work on sex ratios he mentions in *The Descent of Man*, it is not at all certain that the statistical approach had much direct influence on his work.[26] What he shared with Quetelet and with statistical methods in general was the concentration on large numbers of relatively similar individuals. Where nineteenth-century sociologists analyzed modern urban populations, Darwin analyzed the perpetuation and transformation of whole species. It was not until the 1920s, with the advance of genetic research and the study of statistical probability, that R. A. Fisher was able to show that there is in fact enough regular variation in any gene pool to power evolution. As Fisher modeled it, evolution was a probabilistic process that preserved a strong element of freedom and even chance, though the mathematical formulae in place were absolutely certain.[27] As he put it toward the end of his life, evolution is always "new; not merely new in time like a new penny, but new in its nature and potentialities."[28] If this is not exactly the radical heterogeneity that Peirce imagined, random at its very base, it still sees the unpredictable and new as the effect of actual physical causes and not just the result of limited human knowledge.

For inspiration and authority, Fisher had relied on the example of statistical mechanics, basing his analysis of genetic variation on the model of the ideal gas studied in the nineteenth century by Maxwell and Boltzmann.[29] Where classical thermodynamics had dealt with physical substances considered in the mass and had treated properties such as heat as if they were real physical volumes themselves, flowing from place to place like water, Maxwell and Boltzmann assumed that substances were collections of atoms, the aggregate actions of which constituted bulk properties such as heat.[30] Since it was hardly possible to account for the movements or positions of single atoms, even if they could have been directly observed, Maxwell and Boltzmann worked with averages instead. The molecules of any given volume of gas were understood as being distributed across a number of different states, which were schematized so that they were limited in number and distinct from one another, like the boxes on a sheet of graph paper. The different ways in which the gas molecules could be distributed among these states were mapped out mathematically, following the precedent of and using some of the same formulae as the social sciences of the eighteenth century. Understood by analogy with the human population of a modern society, the apparently chaotic movements of a mass of gas particles could be grasped in terms of relative frequencies. The law of averages, Maxwell and Boltzmann both asserted, is just as applicable to molecules as it is to "marriages at a given age, crimes, and suicides."[31] Thus the overall state of a volume of gas at any one time could be expressed in terms of the probable ratios of the many, many possible distributions of individual gas molecules into their microstates.

Classical thermodynamics had long provided some of the most profound arguments against the possibility of real novelty. Since the first and most basic law of physics dictates that energy cannot be created or destroyed, it does not seem possible for the ontologically new to arise, unless that could somehow be accomplished without access to additional energy.[32] But the second law of thermodynamics is even more daunting, especially if it is expressed in probabilistic terms. One way of expressing that law, one that spread much discontent in the late nineteenth century, is that any isolated system will tend to seek equilibrium. The dissipation of heat will tend to continue, in other words, until a constant temperature is reached and no useful energy remains.[33] This is the celebrated "heat death" of the universe, belief in which gave the decadence some of its pseudoscientific basis. As Boltzmann reformulated this law for statistical mechanics, it stated that molecules in any system will tend to spread out among the states possible for them. Since this is the most probable distribution, the second law now amounts to the prediction that isolated systems will always approach their maximum probability. Or, to put it another way, the improbable is steadily less likely to happen the longer any system remains in isolation, which is a very difficult situation for the creation of ontological novelty, especially if the universe itself is understood to exist in isolation.

Given these basic laws, it is rather difficult to see why Peirce would have looked to Maxwell and Boltzmann as authorities on the existence of real novelty, or how Fisher might have used their work to underpin an account of creative evolution. The second law in particular seems to have promoted the social regularity observed by Quetelet until it has become one of the basic physical necessities of the universe. As implacable as it may seem, however, statistical mechanics actually helped to push all sorts of questions about probabilistic reasoning to their limit, so that some of the deepest paradoxes of the probable could appear. One of the most important of these was a problem that Boltzmann found particularly puzzling: if equilibrium is overwhelmingly probable, why do we find ourselves in a world that is generally so far from it?[34] Why, in fact, is there a world at all, and especially *this* world, which seems to have built up a rather immense deficit of probability by creating ever more complex organisms from what seem to be simpler and less organized precursors? Boltzmann explored a number of ways past this difficulty, all of them depending on what might seem to be one of the main weaknesses of probabilistic mechanics: the state of a system at any given time need not approach very closely to its most probable state. Boltzmann therefore anticipated Meillassoux by suggesting that all sorts of improbabilities might be possible if our world is considered to be just a sliver of infinite time and space.[35]

Smaller and subtler questions also opened up fissures in the apparently deterministic world of the basic laws. Statistical mechanics depends on a number of schematic idealizations in order to arrive at its conclusions, and the exact status of these is subject to much skeptical discussion. Might it be possible to regard probability itself as one of these idealizations? Are molecular distributions fully determined by fixed laws such that a perfect accounting could dispense with probabilistic approximations, or is elementary motion at the molecular level actually random, so that a probabilistic approximation is the best that science could ever hope for?[36] As Maxwell put it, "The limitation of our faculties forces us to abandon the attempt to express the exact history of each atom, and to be content with estimating the average condition of a group of atoms large enough to be visible."[37] Thus the problem remained for him the incidental limitation of human faculties and the current low capability of research techniques, so that statistical methods, reliable as they were, remained a makeshift that might, in theory, give way to a full accounting of exact trajectories.[38] From Maxwell's own experiments, however, Peirce drew another conclusion, that what he called "tychism," or absolute chance, existed in the basic physical constituents of the universe.[39] Even what Maxwell once called "absolutely perfect data and . . . the omniscience of contingency" would not suffice to make prediction possible in all cases.[40]

This disagreement raises a basic question about probability itself, a question that has arisen in various ways throughout the history of probabilistic reasoning—whether it is an approximation of an underlying state that might, in principle, be expressed more exactly, or whether it is itself the sharpest possible representation of a state of things that is ineliminably random.[41] Even limiting the definition of probability to the second case leaves significant questions. Probability has often been understood as the relative frequency of some set of random events, extrapolated in some way from an actual observed frequency to a virtual frequency to be approached as the number of trials approaches infinity. What is the relationship in such cases between the actual frequency of any particular result and the most probable frequency, assuming that frequency is attainable only with an infinite number of trials, which could not be reached in any practical sense? Though it would seem that the actual frequency of an infinite set of trials, if such were possible, should match the most probable frequency, probability theorists disagree as to whether this is necessary even in principle.[42] For some, in other words, probability is not an uncertainty about relative numbers that could be cleared up if we could but perform an infinite number of trials but a propensity inherent in the individual instance, an indeterminism that is an objective and actual quality of things.[43]

In these various ways, then, probability theory has made an increasingly certain place for the improbable, which has been promoted from its old status as avoidable error to its current position as an inevitable aspect of physical reality.[44] In fact, probability theory in general seems to have produced a paradoxical situation in which explanations for physical reactions combine deterministic processes to produce a merely probable outcome.[45] If all the individual molecules in any given sample obey the basic laws of conventional mechanics, then nothing about their particular microstates should be indeterminate, only the possibility of their being in any given microstate at any given time. But how does this relative uncertainty arise from the more basic and more determinate situation of the individual molecules? One way around this difficulty is to treat probability as Maxwell did, as if it were the effect of insufficient information. Then the problem is to understand how such a purely subjective phenomenon as human ignorance could play the quite actual role in physical systems assigned to it by statistical mechanics.[46]

The scientific practice that began in an attempt to bring certainty to the apparently chaotic arena of the human sciences thus ended by importing uncertainty deep into the heart of the physical sciences. Even Maxwell came to believe in an essential indeterminism, an opening in the laws of physics for free will, which he based on the notion of "singularities," turning points in a process where a tiny influence might have an exorbitant effect—where, moreover, similar influences might at different times have different effects.[47] The venerable physical axiom "That from like antecedents follow like consequents" is now overturned, in what Maxwell both grandly and sadly calls "a world like this, in which the same antecedents never again concur, and nothing ever happens twice."[48]

INFORMATION THEORY

To assure his readers that endless novelty might in fact be derived from a limited number of fixed elements, Lucretius used what was already at that time a venerable analogy by comparing nature to the alphabet. In later times, the same analogy was used against the Epicurean system. In *Gulliver's Travels*, Jonathan Swift mocks the powers of chance with his satirical account of the Grand Academy of Lagado, which pretends to produce knowledge by the random manipulation of individual words. At the same time, similar arguments were deployed to defend belief in divine creation, on the grounds that it is just as impossible to imagine that human bodies could have come together randomly as to think that a book might be written by the chance arrangement of letters.[49] Later, the alphabet analogy was used on behalf of a "life force" by scientists such as Claude Bernard, who maintained that "physico-chemical means of expression are common to all natural phenomena and remain mingled, pell-mell, like the letters of an alphabet in a box, till a force goes to fetch them, to express the most varied thoughts and mechanisms."[50] Despite the commonsense view expressed in Freud's warning that "letters of the alphabet . . . do not occur in nature," the linguistic analogy has been a fairly constant presence whenever probability reasoning applies itself to nature.[51]

One way of understanding information theory is to see it as the most recent and the most fully developed of such analogies. At its base, information theory is another extension of probabilistic reasoning, one that modeled itself on statistical mechanics, just as statistical mechanics had modeled itself on the sociology of Quetelet.[52] From its relatively simple beginnings in signal processing, information theory came to have a profound influence on evolutionary biology and then, via cybernetics, on systems theory, in addition to the central role it has had in computer science. Its influence is now such that it is commonly claimed that everything can be expressed in terms of information, or even that everything just *is* information. This habit represents the furthest extension of Norbert Wiener's original claim that information represents a new category of existence, neither matter nor energy—a claim that seems to grant the world a general pardon from the laws of thermodynamics.[53] Information figures so largely in contemporary explanations of the creation of life partly because it seems capable of increasing in extent and complexity in ways that simple matter cannot. For this reason, it is the most powerful contemporary model of novelty, a modern successor to the Epicurean system, translated through several centuries of probabilistic science. Linking numbers to letters as it seems to do, information theory also helps to transform measurement into meaning and thus to give the sheer randomness of the probabilistic system a significance it would not otherwise enjoy.

In the beginning, the problem addressed by information theory was nothing more exotic or far-reaching than finding the best possible method to encode a telegraph signal so as to maximize speed of transmission and overcome the noise inevitable in any electronic circuit. Early experimenters, including Thomas Edison, had made a number of practical improvements, but the effort was first put on a sound scientific basis by the electrical and communications engineer Harry Nyquist, who introduced what turned out to be the basic mathematical expressions in 1924.[54] Nyquist himself used fairly homely terminology, such as *signal*, for the object of his study; but when his work was elaborated in 1928 by the electronics researcher R. V. L. Hartley, the quantity to be maximized was called "information." To signify the novel and provisional nature of the term, Hartley bracketed it with scare quotes in the abstract of his article, and he noted that since "information is a very elastic term," it would be necessary to define it at the outset.[55] But he did not actually offer such a definition himself.

When the mathematician and electronic engineer Claude Shannon published his influential reformulation of the work of Nyquist and Hartley in 1948, he called his paper "The Mathematical Theory of Communication," but he generally followed Hartley's lead in referring to the quantity to be measured as "information." Years later, Shannon confessed to some regret that the term had taken on such grandiose connotations, when all he had been concerned with was "getting bits from here to here."[56] The quantity that Shannon's theory actually attempted to measure, so that it could be maximized, was something like "letters per unit time,"[57] which was considered in the abstract. Consequently, as far as the theory was concerned, the "letters" to be transmitted did not need to add up to anything intelligible at all. Very early on, the cybernetician Heinz von

Foerster complained about the term "'information' in situations where there was no information at all, where they were just passing on signals," and he suggested that the field be renamed "signal theory, because information was not yet there. There were '*beep beeps*' but that was all."[58]

As early as 1952, the philosopher Rudolf Carnap and the philosopher and mathematician Yehoshua Bar-Hillel tried to address the fact that Shannon's theory measured only the frequency of certain symbols and not what those symbols might be taken to stand for. They attempted to formalize the actual semantic content of particular statements using Carnap's theory of inductive probability rather than the statistical probability that Shannon had adapted from statistical mechanics.[59] In a sense, then, this disagreement about the use and application of the term *information* rests on a deeper disagreement about the nature of probability. For Carnap, probability has to do with degrees of belief,[60] and his system is basically a formalization of inductive reasoning, a way of putting logic where Hume had put common sense. In Shannon's system, probability has nothing to do with belief or logical inference but only with numbers, the frequency distributions of certain symbols. One of the reasons the term *information* was able to slide so easily back and forth between semantic significance and signal efficiency is that the underlying probability theory had always concerned itself alternately with human subjectivity and with mathematical regularities. The tension between these had often amounted to a useful confusion, as human subjectivity seemed to acquire an objective, calculable quality, while mathematical regularities seemed to gain meaning and significance they did not actually have. The extraordinary career of information theory, despite the fact that the original meaning of the term *information* was so restricted, is a spectacular example of this useful confusion.

As an application of probabilistic reasoning to human communication—one dedicated, as the scientist and mathematician Warren Weaver puts it, "not so much to what you *do* say as to what you *could* say"[61]—information theory was a significant extension of the statistical methods by which novelty had previously been modeled. As Shannon explained it, *information* was essentially a synonym for "choice and uncertainty."[62] A source, understood as producing signals symbol by symbol, is capable of generating more information the more different symbols it has available, and the more varied the frequencies and arrangements of those symbols. The more redundant or predictable the source, the less information it can generate. Information, then, is equivalent to novelty by definition. As the philosopher of science Bernd-Olaf Küppers puts it, "The information value of a message is coupled to its expectation value: the lower the expectation value of a message, the higher its novelty and thus its information content."[63] In one of his few nonmathematical examples, Shannon offers Basic English as the extreme of redundancy and *Finnegans Wake* as its opposite, the furthest extension of the avant-garde in information capacity as well as literary style.[64]

In fact, it would have been clearer and more straightforward if Shannon had used a term like *novelty* rather than *choice* or *uncertainty*, which are descriptions of a psychological state, not a physical system. Already, in these basic descriptions, the subjective condition of a human receiver is very closely associated with the objective capacity of a signal generator. The probability values of a signaling system are simple frequency ratios, but the expectations of a human receiver are like the degrees of belief associated with the very different kind of probability to which both Hume and Carnap appeal. Thus baked into Shannon's terminology is some ambiguity concerning whether information is to be understood as a subjective or an objective category.

This can and did lead to confusion. One very basic problem presented by Shannon's definition is the counterintuitive equivalence it sets up between *information* and *uncertainty*. In common parlance, information is more usually said to remove uncertainty, to inform. From Shannon's point of view, this is really an irrelevant confusion, since uncertainty is for him an objective feature of a signaling system, which might more carefully be described as combinatorial complexity.[65] In this sense, the measure of information as uncertainty is a measure of a system's capacity to convey a wider, more various, and less redundant series of signals. This capacity is sometimes more or less helpfully restated as potential uncertainty.[66] Or, the definition is twisted just a bit so that the transmission of information can be identified with the removal of uncertainty or the resolution of it.[67] To some extent, this difficulty has to do with the difference between a system, in which information exists only potentially, and a signal sent through that system, which conveys information in actuality.

But the apparent mirroring of information and uncertainty remains as an ineliminable confusion in every explanation of information theory, and the equivocation between signal generator and human receiver persists as an almost constitutive ambiguity in the concept of information. The objective probability of a simple frequency distribution comes to be associated, through terms such as *uncertainty*, with probability defined subjectively as degrees of belief.

The uncertainty measured by information theory is often compared to a measurable characteristic of the physical systems studied by statistical mechanics that is known as entropy. In crude terms, *entropy* is often defined as the degree of disorder in a system.[68] More precisely, higher entropy means that molecules are more evenly distributed across the possible energy levels in a system—that the system, in other words, is closer to equilibrium and thus less capable of generating useful energy.[69] One consequence of this sort of distribution is that as the probability distribution of the molecules flattens out, it is more difficult to specify the energy level of any particular molecule. A rather cumbersome way of restating this situation in terms of information was first suggested by the physicist Leo Szilard in the 1920s. The lack of specificity that occurs as the probability distribution of the molecules flattens out, as all levels become equally probable, that is, can be considered as a lack of information, insofar as it becomes more difficult to know much about the molecules in the system. Entropy in this sense is more or less the opposite of information, or it might be equated with the loss of information.[70]

Shannon was apparently the first to notice a similarity in the mathematical formulas used to calculate entropy in statistical mechanics and those used to calculate information in information theory, a similarity arising from the fact that these are both probabilistic situations. In statistical mechanics, entropy is "the logarithm of the number of ways in which the physical system can be configured," while Hartley's formula for measuring information was essentially "the logarithm of the alphabet size."[71] The relationship between the two situations is basically that of a "mathematical analogy," as the engineer John R. Pierce puts it.[72] In fact, by one account at least, the term *entropy* was originally suggested quite flippantly when the mathematician and physicist John von Neumann said to Shannon, "You should call it entropy for two reasons: first, the function is already in use in thermodynamics under the same name; second, and more importantly, most people don't know what entropy really is, and if you use the word *entropy* in an argument you will win every time."[73] Scholars have argued ever since about the merits of using one word for these two different situations. Some, including John R. Pierce and Jeffrey S. Wicken, insist that the two entropies are not equivalent in any but a very basic mathematical sense, and that nothing but confusion has arisen from von Neumann's puckish advice.[74]

One reason for some scholars' distress in this respect is the fact that entropy is usually used as a measure of information sent, though what it actually represents is something like the informational capacity or carrying power of a signal system. *Entropy* is also usually used as a synonym for *uncertainty*, since it is a function of the number of possible choices available in a system. This means, then, that discussions of entropy end up recreating some of the basic confusions surrounding information and uncertainty, so that some scientists, including Norbert Wiener himself, define *entropy* as "the negative of the amount of information contained in the message,"[75] though Shannon originally defined it as a positive measure. The apparent difference between the two comes from the fact that their verbal descriptions approach the same situation from different vantage points—Shannon with the *potential* information identified with the entropy of a system, and Wiener with the information actually *produced* by a particular signal.[76] Nonetheless, the fact that two pioneers of information theory might be supposed to relate the term *information* to entropy not just in different but in diametrically opposite ways illustrates a very tentative quality in the terminology of the discipline.

On the other hand, it might be argued that the very ambiguity of the concept of entropy has made it so useful that it cannot be excluded from discussions of information theory. The list of possible synonyms for *entropy—uncertainty, ignorance, randomness, complexity*—illustrates the split personality of information itself, since some of these are subjective terms appropriate to a human receiver or observer, while others are objective conditions of a probabilistic system. Since entropy aims to measure all of these, it makes them all seem equally objective—though it is rather difficult to see how our ignorance of the positions of particular molecules could be an objective quality of the gas they compose. Entropy thus brings into information theory one of the basic tensions in probabilistic reasoning, the tension between subjective degrees of belief and objective frequencies, but in this new situation the tension turns out to confer a real advantage. For quasi-psychological terms such as *uncertainty* and *ignorance* make it seem as if the merely mathematical frequencies measured by information theory have some semantic significance, at least potentially. Fitted out with synonyms such as *uncertainty*, the quantities measured by Shannon's equation seem to transcend mere combinatorial complexity and thus to acquire real meaning. On the other hand, linking a subjective state like uncertainty to a numerical quantity, whether this is defined as randomness or complexity or something else, makes it seem as if such states are actually measurable. If uncertainty is quantifiable, then knowledge must be quantifiable, and thus the actual content of messages could be measured and not just the relative complexity of the symbol systems that convey them.

Warren Weaver insisted at the outset, in the commentary that accompanied Shannon's original paper, that "*information* must not be confused with meaning."[77] Shannon himself had warned in the second paragraph of his paper that the "semantic aspects of communication are irrelevant to the engineering problem."[78] Actually, even these warnings are a bit too narrow, since information theory is intrinsically indifferent to content in general, meaningful or not, and also to the pragmatic aspects of messages, such as context and effect.[79] Weaver carefully separates the act of communication into three layers, which he calls technical, semantic, and effectiveness, apparently so as to concentrate on the first, the only one really relevant to information theory. In the space of two pages, however, he laminates his layers back together, insisting quite explicitly that information theory concerns all three.[80] By the end of his essay, the indifference of information theory to considerations other than signal efficiency, which had originally been presented as a limitation, has been turned into an advantage, as if the purely abstract nature of the theory gave it a scope "so general that one does not have to say what kinds of symbols are being considered—whether written letters or words, or musical notes, or spoken words, or symphonic music, or pictures."[81] For the close of his essay, Weaver delivers the grand pronouncement that "entropy not only speaks the language of arithmetic; it also speaks the language of language."[82]

Translating numbers into letters in this way, matching one to the other as if they were simply two different codes, makes the simple frequencies studied by information theory seem to be combinations of a very different kind, the kind that makes up words out of letters and sentences out of words, one that is not amenable to probabilistic analysis at all. Of course, letters do occur in specific frequencies in particular languages, and individual words occur in specific frequencies in existing pieces of text. Thus it would be possible to calculate the likelihood of a particular letter or string of letters occurring in a given sample of some natural language.[83] But it is not possible to use these frequencies to reverse engineer a new piece of text, because the logical and linguistic relationships that make language intelligible involve much more than mere frequency. In Weaver's essay and in later pronouncements on the power and scope of information theory, the fact that existing examples of actual language can be coded and sent is inflated until it is confused with the ability to generate linguistic statements. When he claims that information theory can actually speak, Weaver implies that a signaling system can vastly exceed its actual powers to record and transmit.

Thus, as Terrence Deacon puts it, "For more than half a century we have known how to measure the information-conveying capacity of any given communication medium, and yet we cannot give an account of how this relates to the content that this signal may or may not represent."[84] In a sense, then, information theory can measure what it cannot define, and this situation obtains at the general level as well as the specific, in the case of the term *information* itself. The formula for measuring the informational capacity of a particular system, or the informational content of a particular signal, is often taken as if it amounted to a definition of information. But this is a little like assuming that being able to measure out a pint will also tell us something about the flavor of ice cream. As Deacon says, "Although we use the concept of information almost daily without confusion, and we build machinery (computers) and network systems to move, analyze, and store it, I believe that we still do not really know what *it* is."[85] Information theory's basic constitutional indifference to issues of meaning returns as its inability to define the basic quantity itself.

On the other hand, the fact that information has no real character of its own, that its ontological status is rather like that of other units of measure such as inches or meters, is part of its tremendous usefulness and one source of its ubiquity as a concept. Since anything combinatorial can be measured in terms of information—since virtually anything can be expressed in terms of information—it naturally seems as if anything can be converted into information. Information thus comes to seem the basic stuff of the universe. For many writers at the present time, this is not a metaphor but a literal description,[86] and the appeal of information as an account of existence comes in part from its apparent power to generate novelty in ways not generally thought possible for purely physical systems.

One way of understanding this capacity is to recall Wiener's claim that information is a new category of existence, different from both matter and energy. One consequence of this privileged situation is that information is not bound by the ordinary laws of conservation that limit physical reality and can therefore spontaneously increase itself. Another and far older context might be provided by the argument in the *Theaetetus* to the effect that nature creates new forms by combination, in the same way that language creates new meanings out of a few standard symbols. It is often argued by contemporary information theorists that information arises as a kind of unearned increment, a surplus like the mysterious surplus that emerges when three letters are combined to evoke the idea of a cat. Though it is most certainly not the case that any random combination of letters creates a new word that has an unearned bonus of novel meaning, the fact that information was associated from the outset with novelty made it easy to assume that every message generates some novelty, unless it fails as a message. If everything is ultimately expressible as information, and if information always increases the store of novelty by definition, then it is not hard to imagine the "history of the universe in terms of information-processing revolutions, each arising naturally from the previous one."[87] Some of these latter-day cosmogonies have been frankly religious, with information serving as a shiny new version of the *logos*; but others have been quite rigorous scientific proposals, such as that of the theoretical evolutionary biologists John Maynard Smith and Eörs Szathmáry, who have mapped out the history of life on earth as a series of "major changes that have taken place in the way in which information is encoded, and transmitted between generations."[88]

The value of these proposed accounts of the history of the universe depends a great deal on context, and on the particular twist given in each case to the meaning of *information* as a term. However, insofar as they depend on the notion that information can spontaneously increase itself, they do run into difficulty, since it is not physically possible for information to increase in the course of transmission.[89] Indeed, because of the inherent presence of noise in any transmission channel, information inevitably degrades in the process of transmission, so that it would seem more likely, in the abstract, for any cosmic message to degenerate as it is passed from generation to generation. If information is to be understood in a more-than-physical sense, as involving meaning of some kind, then the difficulties become even greater. Bernd-Olaf Küppers insists that "there are no 'informational perpetual-motion machines' that can generate meaningful information out of nothing." Meaningful information always depends on other meaningful information to acquire, maintain, and transmit its content, so that any real process of communication inevitably requires extra information in order to work, using up informational resources instead of creating more.[90]

Küppers thus denies the basic assumptions behind informational cosmogonies and reduces the whole project to what he sees as its actual basis: "Or are the processes by which [information] arises in nature or society nothing more than processes of transformation: that is, translation and re-evaluation of information, admittedly in an information space of gigantic dimensions, so that the result always seems to be new and unique?"[91] In other words, information theory is another combinatorial scheme, not that much different from the Epicureanism of Lucretius, that relies on a rather exaggerated analogy with language in order to claim that something radically new can arise from the shuffling and reshuffling of the same old deck of cards.

THE GENETIC CODE

Perhaps the most influential use of information as a model for novelty has occurred in the years since Francis Crick and James Watson revolutionized the field of genetics. Very early in their work on DNA, one of the central mysteries to be explained was the exact way in which the four nucleotides of the DNA strand could be matched to the twenty amino acids that make up all proteins. What Crick disarmingly called "the problem of how, in protein synthesis, a sequence of four things (nucleotides) determines a sequence of many more things (amino acids)" came to be known as the coding problem, partly because of the convention of representing the nucleotides by the initial letters of their names, but mainly because the prototypical rules for generating sequences of twenty things from an array of only four were established by coding theory.[92] Strictly speaking, a system that generates twenty letters from an array of four is a cipher and not a code—an apparently minor but actually rather significant difference, since ciphers work on single letters while codes work on larger units.[93] Thinking in terms of code rather than cipher made it easier to elevate Crick's rather practical problem of efficient matching to a different level, a level at which the phrase "genetic code" seems to imply that something meaningful is being transmitted as the sequences of four things are shuffled to make the sequences of twenty.

Once the relationship between nucleotides and amino acids was conceptualized as a code, it was quite natural to further conceptualize the "something meaningful" passed on by the code as information. In the beginning, information as used in this way designated nothing more than the specification for a particular amino acid sequence.[94] By 1958, however, Crick had begun to speak of information as something different from nucleotides and amino acids, but passed from one to the other. Initially, he put the term in scare quotes, as if to set it off as a hypothetical entity; but, as in the earlier history of information theory itself, the scare quotes soon dropped off and the hypothetical became actual.[95] In the same year, François Jacob and Jacques Monod began to use the term in the same way, to designate what Jacob later called "the univocal transformation of one system of symbols into another."[96] In fact, what Jacob had in mind here was not symbols at all but actual physical entities: the sequences of four nucleotides that give rise to combinations of twenty amino acids. But the fact that these sequences could be represented by letters of the alphabet made them, in Monod's words, "the logical equivalents of an alphabet," and their logical equivalence soon gave way to a literal identity, so that Monod refers to them simply as "an alphabet."[97]

The information metaphor seemed so natural at the time because information theory was at the peak of its influence, as the old and rather mundane coding problems originally worked on by Shannon were attached to the new science of cybernetics, which offered itself as a general clearinghouse for all the issues raised by communications, computers, and automation.[98] By the early 1960s, *information* was common in discussions of genetics, where it was readily adopted even by scientists as distant from the original research as Ernst Mayr, who defined genes in 1962 as "the carriers of 'bits of information,' to use the happy term of information theory."[99] As Mayr's locution suggests, the "happy term" was at this time still little more than a figure of speech. In the early days of information-based microbiology, some proponents suggested that it be used in such a way, as a "semi-quantitative" term, as the research biologist Henry Quastler put it.[100] Some fifty years later, John Maynard Smith suggested that *information* and all the associated terms that have accumulated around it—*transcription, translation, editing, proofreading*—are generally used in just this way, as analogies founded on an apparent isomorphism between genetics and language.[101]

Other scientists have defended *information* as a scientifically exact term for the genetic characteristics that are altered, preserved, and passed on in the process of inheritance. The historian of science Lily Kay describes a fascinating TV roundtable, "Genetic Information and the Function of Language," including the linguist and literary theorist Roman Jakobson, François Jacob, and the anthropologist and ethnologist Claude Levi-Strauss, at which Jacob insisted that genetic information is "genuinely inscribed in the chromosomes . . . exactly like a phrase in a text."[102] More recently and more notoriously, the ethologist and evolutionary biologist Richard Dawkins has insisted that when seeds fall from trees it is literally and actually raining instructions: "It couldn't be any plainer if it were raining floppy discs."[103] Jacob and Dawkins claim that *information* is not merely an analogy, because genes are quite literally symbolic—a somewhat convoluted situation that Dawkins makes more complicated by use of a purposely outrageous metaphor.

As Jacob later explained it, the "nucleic-acid message" is based on a combinatorial system like the alphabet, in which a distinct and limited number of units can be manipulated in any number of ways to yield an infinite set of outcomes.[104] The freedom of this system to lead in any direction is based on two crucial characteristics: the individual units of DNA are only arbitrarily attached to any particular protein sequence, and the units can be combined and recombined in any way. In other words, as Maynard Smith puts it, the DNA code is arbitrary and therefore symbolic, and it is this necessary gap between the vehicle and the tenor, the sign and the referent, that gives a limited genetic code the ability to make an infinite variety of living forms.[105] Unlike language, the genetic code is not literally literal; that is to say, it is not really made up of letters but actually of nucleotides, but the unitary and combinatorial qualities of the nucleic acid system make it seem alphabetic, and the loose and changeable relationship of the nucleic acids to the amino acids gives it the figurative freedom of linguistic expression.

The linguistic model, in other words, helped modern biological science, as it had helped Darwin, to understand the elementary puzzle of evolution, the problem of novelty. According to Jacob, the two most crucial properties of living things, "stability and variability, are based on the very nature of the genetic text," which is stable because it is always composed of the same few elements but variable because those elements can be combined to create any result.[106] Genetic lineages, like languages, change over time, and genetic sequences that have existed since the beginning of life itself promote new life-forms, just as old words acquire new meanings. Thus the biological variation so important to Darwinism comes to be associated with linguistic variability, change, and ambiguity, so that Maynard Smith can praise the arbitrary and symbolic nature of "genetic signals" because it makes possible new and various life-forms.[107] By the same token, though, the limited size of the alphabetic set offers an analogy to scientists for the continuity of evolution, so that the biologist and philosopher Francisco Ayala can compare the common ancestry of the world's life-forms to the way the various books in a library share the same few letters.[108] *Information*, in such instances, is just a scientistic term for language itself, which appeals because it seems to offer a model that derives real change, real novelty, from a mere recombination of preexisting elements.[109]

Still, if the process of genetic reproduction and transmission is to be understood as a sign system, it is a rather extraordinary one, since it causally links one bit of physical reality to another by means of a chemical reaction—not the sort of thing that linguistic symbols can usually accomplish.[110] And the past history of information theory, which had long since transcended its original indifference to semantic meaning, allowed geneticists to further promote the genetic code so that the probabilistic shuffling and reshuffling of gene frequencies over time acquired a virtually spiritual significance. Jacob, for example, begins *The Logic of Life: A History of Heredity* with a truly sibylline pronouncement: "The organism thus becomes the realization of a programme prescribed in its heredity. The intention of a psyche has been replaced by the translation of a message."[111] Replacing, in this case, also seems to mean acquiring the characteristics of, since the genetic message is invoked here as if it were the intention of a psyche. As extravagant as they are, these pronouncements are not particularly exceptional for the time. In 1967, the biologist Robert Sinsheimer insisted that "every human being is born knowing how to read this book in every cell of his body," consciously and perhaps polemically making the individual cell more literate than the mind itself.[112] Inevitably, DNA came to be celebrated as a biological Rosetta Stone, a living Linear B, "a language much older than hieroglyphics, a language as old as life itself."[113]

Since the original identification of information with language was itself little more than a metaphor, such claims amount to building one analogy on top of another. In recent times, many writers and scientists have objected to this two-step process by which genes are turned into bits of language. If the genetic code is a linguistic system, it is one without punctuation, consisting entirely of four-letter words created randomly and combined without any syntax; one in which messages are sent in one direction only and never answered.[114] Furthermore, it is a language that works with physical entities and chemical reactions, not with symbols and concepts.[115] If, however, the analogy has tended to spiritualize what is after all a material process, it has also tended, according to critics, to make that process much too rigid and deterministic. When Crick postulated as the Central Dogma of molecular biology that information can flow only from DNA to amino acids and never back again, he established the basis for a conception of genetic transmission as a simple act of decoding a preexisting set of instructions.[116] As Monod and Jacob elaborated the analogy with information transfer, they insisted that the informational content of DNA originated within it and was not modified by its transactions with other parts of the cell.[117] The Central Dogma thus came to be seen as a newer and more rigorous version of the old preformationism.[118] Ironically, the linguistic analogy, which had traditionally been used in order to support the notion that real novelty could arise from a purely combinatorial process, now had the effect of restricting the scope of novelty in biological inheritance.

As the theoretical biologist Gerd B. Müller puts the old question, "Given the existing basic architecture, how could unprecedented elements be added if variation were the only mechanistic possibility?"[119] According to Müller, accounts of evolution dominated by molecular biology have simply sidestepped this question and ignored the whole problem of evolutionary novelty.[120] Developmental biologists interested in explaining novelty have therefore shifted the informational metaphor from "information-transmission" to "information-expression."[121] Just as linguistic signals need the support of other signals in order to yield their meaning, the genetic code needs supporting information from other parts of the cell and from the environment in order to reproduce itself effectively.[122] In other words, the code needs to be interpreted in a given context instead of simply being decoded.[123] It is this process of interpretation and the influence of a variable set of contexts that allow for evolutionary novelty.

Though most developmental biologists insist that factors beyond gene transmission have an important influence on the nature of and changes in living forms, the theoretical biologist Mary Jane West-Eberhard moves the main causal force out of the cell altogether. When she argues that "DNA is condition sensitive and dependent upon materials from the environment," she is not just suggesting that the environment interprets the information that DNA contains.[124] She means to assert something unconventional enough to require italics: "*the most important initiator of evolutionary novelties is environmental induction.*"[125] Changes in environmental conditions favor developmental variations of one kind or another, as, for example, birds with one beak type feed more easily than others of their species when certain kinds of seeds are available; and this difference, fixed first by environmental factors, gradually comes to be represented in the genome.

West-Eberhard also believes that novelty can be introduced into the evolutionary process by means of learned behavior.[126] In fact, she insists that novel traits arrived at by learning are even more influential over the course of evolution than genetic changes, since "a learned novel pheno- type influenced by evolved motivation and reward criteria is not random with respect to fitness in the same way a mutant genetic mutant novelty is [sic]. A learned novelty is a product of the assessment of alternatives, which are screened by a system of differential rewards."[127] In her version of the evolutionary scheme, the unique "innovation of a single individual could spread in a population and even become propagated through gen- erations as a learned tradition."[128] Organisms, as West-Eberhard sees them, are restless experimenters, even the most basic and apparently simple of them, and their constant trial-and-error work with the envi- ronment keeps alive within any species all sorts of useful variants, from which natural selection can take its pick. In her view, "an organism has the unmachinelike ability to respond to a new situation or to a new gene with the production of a new trait, and then to multiply, through repro- duction, the ability to produce this trait."[129] Real novelty, in this theory of evolution, is neither random nor determined but invented by particular organisms as they cope creatively with a changing environment.

Evolution thus becomes a series of creative improvisations, the results of which are continuously deposited in the genetic record, which is then recombined by inheritance so that it can yield further new opportunities for innovative responses. Novelty in this case is not an effect of probabi- listic reasoning, or the qualitative result of quantitative recombination, but the purposeful contribution of a life-form challenged by its environ- ment. Though this may seem to have replaced the random swerve of the Epicurean system with something almost vitalistic in its sheer willful- ness, West-Eberhard's version of evolution actually brings probabilis- tic reasoning closer to its first formulations. As the philosopher Hans Blumenberg explains the ideas of Epicurus, the swerve, the original ran- dom event in the creation of all things, reoccurs in human beings as acts of free will, in the ability of active beings "to introduce absolute begin- nings into reality."[130] What makes the world possible at all, the first in- fringement on absolute necessity, also makes living beings what they are, free from complete determination. Life, in this sense, is just a process whereby the first random swerve of the atoms is fed back into the cosmos to create more new things. For the Epicureans, this was little more than a hopeful myth, an assertion of their own against the far more apparent powers of fate and determination. For at least some contemporary biologists, however, it is the most sophisticated and flexible version of the only model of novelty that continues to make sense.

NOVELTY IN THE TWENTIETH CENTURY

PART II

5
THE STRUCTURE OF SCIENTIFIC DISCOVERY : KUHN AND WIENER

NEWNESS ACCORDING TO KUHN

Just past the midpoint of the twentieth century, just before the outburst of novelty that came to be known as
the Sixties, two scientists—apparently unknown to each
other—finished preparing new accounts of the nature of
scientific discovery. Thomas Kuhn's *The Structure of Scientific Revolutions*, which appeared in 1962, almost instantly
became the most visible and influential example of a new
philosophy of science, and is often said to be one of the
most widely read books ever published. Norbert Wiener's
Invention, on the other hand, was only "finished" in 1959
in that it was abandoned then, as Wiener turned to other
projects. It was not read by anyone until 1993, thirty years
after Wiener's death. Kuhn's book is the definitive statement of a serious philosopher and historian of science,
while Wiener's is little more than a potboiler, one of a
number of projects conceived in his later years to exploit
his vast celebrity as the Father of Automation. For Kuhn,
The Structure of Scientific Revolutions was a beginning,
and he spent the rest of his life elaborating, explaining,
and altering it. *Invention* was one of Wiener's last works, a
kind of addendum to a lifetime of achievement in mathematics, physics, information theory, and cybernetics. In
a sense, *Invention* is an account of a particular scientific
revolution, the one Wiener had himself fomented, which
at least in its outward form did not very much resemble
the model offered in Kuhn's book. Nonetheless, Wiener's

self-conscious attempt to account for this particular scientific revolution and Kuhn's much more ambitious account of scientific revolutions in general have much in common, and the similarities between them can tell a good deal about the ways in which twentieth-century science came to understand the role of novelty in its inventions and discoveries.

Kuhn wrote his book in the hope of changing the way the history of science was conceptualized, so that it would no longer be possible to think of it as proceeding additively, on a single basis of understanding, closer and closer to nature itself. The gist of the argument is thus contained in his question-begging title, which asserts what the book will try to prove: episodes heretofore understood as additions to knowledge were actually revolutions that altered the basic nature of scientific inquiry.[1] This new theory of scientific invention and discovery, insofar as it seemed to make scientific advances more abrupt and unexpected, also seemed to emphasize their novelty; and for this reason *The Structure of Scientific Revolutions* is perhaps the most influential and significant model of novelty to be offered in the twentieth century. Because of the central role of the new in definitions of modernity, it might also be said that Kuhn's book is one of the most significant interpretations of the twentieth century itself. It is certainly the case, as Kuhn suggested at the time, that the argument of the text would turn out to be widely influential outside the history and philosophy of science.[2] Because of its direct and indirect influence over certain art critics in particular, *The Structure of Scientific Revolutions* had a very powerful role in shaping midcentury theories of modernism in the arts.

Kuhn's focus of attention is on scientists, on the way they study the physical world, and he does not make objective claims about the nature of the world they investigate. Still, it is hard to imagine his project without some reference to important modern developments in physics, the discipline that Kuhn had once hoped to pursue himself and to which he always remained oriented. These developments, including non-Euclidean geometry, Einstein's theories of relativity, and Werner Heisenberg's uncertainty principle, have in common the way they make relative to a particular observer the features of the physical world, such as space and time, which had seemed to constitute the very structure of objectivity.[3] Not oddly, then, Kuhn's logic begins with and his model depends on the situation of observational particularity, to which he gave the name *paradigm*.

Though almost every aspect of Kuhn's theory has come in for concerted critical discussion, the paradigm is probably the single most controversial element in his book, and his definition of the term changed considerably over the years.[4] In the beginning, though, a paradigm was for him a sort of perceptual framework. He often uses the metaphor of eyesight in describing a particular scientific perspective, which makes it seem as if the limitations of it are actually physical; but he also rather often uses psychological analogies and examples, as if the paradigm were a kind of unconscious, individual mindset.[5] Thus the paradigm sometimes seems to be a matter of individual predilection, but even in the book's first edition it also has a collective aspect as a mode "of community life," as Kuhn puts it.[6] Appealing directly to the philosopher Ludwig Wittgenstein at one point, he describes a paradigm as a "competent body of rules" that does not just govern but actually constitutes traditional practice.[7] By the end of his life, he had come to see the paradigm in linguistic terms, as a lexicon, an accepted system of symbols with which scientists had to work in order to be understood.[8]

Whether it is defined in perceptual, psychological, sociological, or linguistic terms, a paradigm is a worldview, a way of looking at the world that comes to be a world in its own right. Though he does seem to believe in the ontological independence of physical fact, Kuhn finds a number of different ways to say that for us, "when paradigms change, the world itself changes with them."[9] Frequently, a crucial "as if" or "in some sense"[10] intervenes to moderate this claim, and at least once in *The Structure of Scientific Revolutions* he cautions his readers that even after a revolution, scientists are "still looking at the same world."[11] But Kuhn's book would not have had anything like the effect it did if it had not been seen to claim that worldviews have all the qualities of the world itself, in that they are complete and all-encompassing. This is why paradigms are incommensurable, as Kuhn famously claimed, because there is no independent standpoint outside any worldview from which one worldview might be objectively measured and compared to other worldviews.

Though worldviews are plural, even at particular moments in history, they have for Kuhn all the same characteristics that the world had for Parmenides and the pre-Socratics who followed him: unity, completeness, and thus eternity. Since a worldview is complete and self-contained, whatever develops within it must already have been present there, at least by implication. For a worldview to change in any fundamental way, therefore, it must in effect become a different worldview. The most pressing question about a worldview, then, is the question that Parmenides posed in relation to the world itself: how can it allow for anything new? Kuhn is so fundamental to modern thought because he restates Parmenides' foundational question about existence as a question about human knowledge. If there is no such thing as a "pure-observation language," if the most basic "operations and measurements are paradigm-determined,"[12] then how can science ever produce knowledge not already implied by its paradigms?

Of course, this is also an ancient philosophical question, at least as old as Plato, if not quite as old as Parmenides—but it had a particularly painful resonance in the twentieth century.[13] Scientific discoveries have such notoriety and prestige in the modern world in part because they seem to exemplify modern independence of thought and freedom of inquiry, but philosophers since Pierre Duhem had been steadily sharpening Hume's skeptical sense that theory is always underdetermined by fact, that even scientific theory can be impervious to contrary evidence.[14] When Kuhn, working in this tradition, suggests that a set of assumptions can literally blind scientists and deafen them to competing arguments, he seems to diminish the prestige of science by making it seem as subjective as any other modern practice. The most daunting thing about a worldview, though, is that it is no less total for being subjective, so that a scientist's most fundamental assumptions can never be questioned even though they are ungrounded and implicitly questionable. Science seems stuck, in other words, with the worst of both worlds, with limited, subjective points of view that have all the authority of objective fact. Modern scientific thought is just as closed and self-contained as tradition—not in spite of its subjective nature, but precisely because its partiality is too perfect to be affected by another point of view.

In other words, Kuhn raises in relation to knowledge the fundamental question, which is not where do new ideas come from? but how can new ideas come at all? Though it seems fairly obvious that new ideas have occurred, since modern notions differ in so many respects from those of past times, it is not at all clear how a worldview, defined as Kuhn variously defines it, can permit itself to be altered. Thus it is no accident that his book must work its way through most of the traditional ideas about novelty or that it turns out to be a virtual anthology of the classical models of the new. At one time or another, he sees scientific change as religious conversion, revolution, atomistic recombination, and evolution. The last of these is the most appealing of all, since it helps Kuhn to imagine how the others might be arranged in a cycle, which is itself the time-honored way, since the pre-Socratics, of allowing for the appearance of change while still respecting the unity and stability of all things.

Kuhn begins his exposition of this cycle with an account of science locked within its paradigm, a situation he regards as "normal" since it is the state in which scientists must spend the vast majority of their time. Normal science devotes itself to the paradigm more or less the way that worker bees devote themselves to the hive, feeding and sustaining it, tidying it up, constructing the very cells within which hive life exists. Science in this mode is, within its given limits, cumulative and accretive.[15] It does not aim at, and in fact actively avoids, any but the most incidental novelty. In fact, Kuhn goes so far as to say that normal science actually suppresses novelties, since they may have the effect of subverting the paradigm that gives scientific inquiry its shape and structure.[16] Not just conservative but actively intolerant, normal science works hard to find what it expects to find and regards disconfirmation as failure.[17]

As unattractive as this may sound, it does correspond fairly closely to one common view of the way modern science works, once the Scientific Revolution sets it in motion. With that one push for momentum, science hums along with machinelike regularity according to basic principles, respecting agreed-upon constants and conventions, rearranging and recombining the building blocks of nature so that the fundamentally rational structure of everything becomes clearer and clearer. One result of this view of science is a redefinition of scientific discovery so that it is no longer thought of only in terms of dramatic personal breakthroughs. The notion of mechanical invention and scientific discovery as dispersed, impersonal social events, ones that work more by rearranging the old than by repudiating it, is now especially influential. "Intellectual creativity," according to the sociologist Randall Collins, "comes from combining elements from previous products of the field."[18]

This is in fact one of the basic beliefs with which Kuhn begins *The Structure of Scientific Revolutions*, one that seems just as relevant to what he will call revolutions as it is to "normal science." To ask, "Who first conceived of energy conservation?" he says at the beginning of the book, is to ask the wrong question.[19] He continually quarrels with the Romantic view of scientific discovery as the work of particular individuals driven by quasi-divine inspiration. In a sense, then, the term *normal science* is redundant, or even misleading, if it is taken to imply that some other sort of science is possible. Normal science, science conducted within a paradigm with the intention of reinforcing and advancing its presuppositions, is the only kind of science there is. To imagine some other kind of science is to imagine inquiry that works outside a paradigm, which Kuhn flatly insists is impossible: "There is no such thing as research in the absence of any paradigm."[20]

Revolutionary science, then, is not a different kind of science but an episode in the course of normal science. As Kuhn tells it, anomalies build up in the practices or findings of scientists until they force a crisis of faith in the entire paradigm, which finally comes down like a ton of bricks.[21] Kuhn himself is rather vague about the nature and origin of anomalies, and this seems to be one of the few aspects of his theory that has not inspired an extensive tradition of criticism and exegesis.[22] According to Ian Hacking, an anomaly is "a novelty that runs counter to what is expected."[23] But it is hard to see how the unexpected can arise when, as Kuhn adamantly insists, it is impossible to check the cherished assumptions of a paradigm against an unmediated account of nature. Even the search for a "pure-observation language," he maintains, is constricted by "a host of expectations about nature" that cannot be eluded.[24] But Kuhn does believe in "fundamental novelties," and he does say that they come about when "nature has somehow violated the paradigm-induced expectations that govern normal science."[25] One way of understanding this apparent inconsistency might be to suppose that paradigms are not really worldviews in the most comprehensive sense but simply *scientific* worldviews, around which there is a fairly large penumbra of natural phenomena that are not considered within the paradigm simply because they have not achieved the status of scientific fact. Kuhn does not maintain that such phenomena are not seen at all but rather that they are seen as mistakes, or even as frauds, and not as facts, until they reach some specific pressure and break their way through the boundaries raised around the paradigm.

Once this happens, the change that comes over the scientific mind is total. Kuhn calls these changes revolutions because he sees them as following the pattern of political revolution. As Hacking paraphrases this in the book's introduction: "Everything is overthrown. A new world order begins."[26] A revolution, as Kuhn defines it, is occasioned by a failure of the political system so comprehensive that it can be resolved only by the introduction of a completely new system.[27] Though Kuhn goes to some lengths to explain and justify this parallel, he also relies rather heavily on a different model, the gestalt switch: "What were ducks in the scientist's world before the revolution are rabbits afterwards."[28] As criticism built up around this concept, mainly because it seemed to confuse an individual psychological event with a much more general social change, Kuhn backtracked quite a bit; but in the beginning the gestalt switch must have appealed, because it seemed an authoritative description of an instantaneous and total replacement of one worldview with another.[29] Sometimes, Kuhn's descriptions of the gestalt switch shade off into another metaphor that he often uses to illustrate this sort of crisis: religious conversion. "Scientists then often speak of the 'scales falling from the eyes.'"[30] Since there is no reasonable way for the new paradigm to be judged by the standards of the old, since the terms each applies are incompatible with the other, the shift from one to the other cannot be a rational process. "A decision of that kind," as Kuhn put it in one of his most controversial statements, "can only be made on faith."[31]

Kuhn's accounts of the revolutionary process are, in short, quite various, and a good deal of debate has ensued in the years since 1962 over some basic questions, including the role of individuals in what seems necessarily to be a collective change. Whether it is to be seen as individual and psychological or collective and political, though, a Kuhnian revolution always conforms to the classic model of novelty derived from Christian conversion and then applied to the political dislocations of the eighteenth century. In fact, Kuhn sometimes seems determined to trace out the full history of this model, to use all the metaphors it offers for change that is total and instantaneous. But his revolutions respect the tradition of the term in an even more basic sense, in that they are also implicitly circular. In a long career that involved a good deal of self-criticism and revision, Kuhn never compromised on what turned out to be one of his most controversial claims, that science does not progress toward an objectively true account of nature. Though one paradigm may be superior in some sense to another, scientific revolutions in general do not accumulate but simply vary. On a more abstract level, though, the pattern he describes is not just various but actually circular, since revolutionary science always leads back to that which is its source: normal science.

It is in this circular relationship between normal and revolutionary science that Kuhn's theory most resembles yet another common model of change and novelty: evolution. *The Structure of Scientific Revolutions* often makes casual use of evolution as a half-dead metaphor for incremental advance,[32] but it also sometimes appeals directly to Darwin's actual theories for support, particularly in arguing against the idea of teleology.[33] At one point, Kuhn refers to "the evolutionary view of science developed here"[34] as if he were consciously following Darwin's example.[35] Regardless of whether this is true, *The Structure of Scientific Revolutions* does resemble *The Origin of Species* in one essential respect, in arranging an interdependent relationship between recombinant and revolutionary novelty. Normal science combines and recombines its basic elements until sufficient anomalies arise to cause a revolution, which then feeds these anomalies back into a new version of normal science. Thus normal science replicates itself in subtly different forms, generation after generation.

Kuhn's model thus shares with evolution a particularly elegant solution to the basic problem of novelty, for it turns out that normal science produces anomalies, or deviations from its paradigm, in the course of the same process that ordinarily produces confirmations of it. As he says, "Normal science, a pursuit not directed to novelties and tending at first to suppress them," is nevertheless "effective in causing them to arise."[36] But this is not quite strong enough, for the methods of normal science are not just effective but absolutely necessary to the production of novelty. It is because the normal scientist is so devoted to the tried and true, so meticulous in his subjection to the paradigm, so determined to perfect it in every way, that he inevitably finds those few instances in which it does not suffice. Thus Kuhn maintains in *The Essential Tension* that "work within a well-defined and deeply-ingrained tradition seems more productive of tradition-shattering novelties than work in which no similarly convergent standards are involved."[37] One rather weak way of putting this is to say that "tradition-shattering" is a concept that is meaningless outside a tradition, that the very concept of anomaly is dependent on the existence of accepted laws. But Kuhn's notions in this respect are not so abstract, and he argues quite extensively that it is the practical doggedness and not just the abstract dogmatism of normal science that makes it inevitably revolutionary.[38]

By the same token, the goal of revolutionary science is the reestablishment of a paradigm and thus the reinstitution of normal science. Under fire for much of his life as a wild-eyed relativist, Kuhn came to insist rather more than he might have that "the basic scientist must also be a firm traditionalist."[39] Thus it is now more common to emphasize the conservative tendencies of his theory and even to insist that in the instantaneous transition from paradigm to paradigm there is no room for freedom of thought.[40] What first presented itself as a theory of scientific revolution now looks more like the description of a closed system in which revolutions are really little more than temporary embarrassments. At the same time, though, it is Kuhn's insistence that revolutions do not advance the cause of science in a linear and progressive fashion, that they merely lead it back into a more or less steady state, that remains one of the more controversial aspects of his theory; and it is hard to see how he might have preserved the relativism at this level of the theory without relativizing in some way the effects of revolution.[41]

Normal science and revolutionary science are thus like two sides of a Möbius strip, leading to each other so ineluctably that they seem in fact to be the same. Or, to take a metaphor from Kuhn himself, they are like one of those famous figures that illustrate a gestalt switch—the rabbit and duck that Wittgenstein favored or the two faces that turn out to frame a vase. The difference between normal science and revolutionary science is not just motivated by a gestalt switch, as Kuhn explicitly claims in his book, but perhaps actually constituted by one. Revolutions do not always seem to be revolutionary at the time, as he says, and it is often only in retrospect that what seemed to be a stable tradition with a few flaws turns out to be an accumulation of exceptions so dire as to lead to revolution. Even though the difference between tradition and revolution is as stark as black and white, their relationship as figure to ground can reverse itself in the blink of an eye.

Viewed from this perspective, Kuhn's theory seems a restatement in relation to scientific knowledge of the claim that biologists such as François Jacob have made in relation to evolution, that continuity and change are in a sense the same, insofar as they are both guaranteed by the same physical mechanisms.[42] Kuhn actually struggled with his relationship to Darwinism, particularly when it came to finding a precise analogy for biological novelty.[43] What he was looking for was some intellectual version of a genetic mutation, or better yet, of the ordinary variation that is produced and transmitted in the course of reproduction. Later in his life he came to think of scientific revolutions on the model of speciation[44] Though the immediate influence of Darwin was apparently strong, the evolutionary model itself is constructed on the basis of the ancient compromise whereby novelty is allowed into an unchanging world either as a reproduction of the old or as a rearrangement of its elements. With Darwin's example before him, Kuhn links these two together in a dynamic system that derives novelty from a closed intellectual world without violating its unity or consistency.

Perhaps this is why Kuhn's work has been controversial for so many different reasons, why it has looked radically anti-intellectual to some and authoritarian to others, because it preaches dramatic change and fundamental consistency in more or less the same words. But the long-running debate about Kuhn's book, in the course of which virtually every syllable of it has been subjected to withering criticism, has also signified the continuing irresolution of the problems that his work promised to resolve. For what Kuhn came to see as an "essential tension" between tradition and innovation—essential because the two terms not only depend on each other but by his account actually come to produce each other—is far more commonly experienced as one of the abiding torments of modernity. A life of numbing routine, broken by spasmodic episodes of revolutionary violence, which then merely reestablish the same routine with a slightly different name—this is probably the most negative image that can be offered of the modern condition. Even on a purely intellectual level, Kuhn's theory seems to sentence us to a particularly modern kind of orthodoxy, one that can never really be challenged because it depends on nothing outside itself. What might look to others like contradictions—when innovation reinforces consistency, or when what seems the perception of difference reestablishes the systematic ignorance of difference—actually occur in Kuhn's system as moments in a self-sustaining cycle and thus lose even the slim potential for change inherent in contradiction.

WIENER AND CYBERNETIC NOVELTY

Kuhn lived through what was almost certainly the most significant scientific revolution of the twentieth century, and yet he had nothing to say about it, perhaps because it did not come about in a manner very much like the pattern described in his book. The advent of the computer, the introduction of information as an all-purpose measure of everything under the sun, the arrival of the Internet and of networks in general as the ultimate media of communication, exchange, and storage—all this certainly constitutes a revolution by Kuhn's or any other definition. If a paradigm shift is to be understood as a dramatic change in perspective, with a whole new terminology to replace the old, then the common contemporary notion that anything can be expressed as and potentially even converted into information is one of the most dramatic and influential paradigm shifts in modern history. Information is quite literally a new language, and the change it has fostered in common views of the physical world is at least as pervasive as the ones brought about by Isaac Newton and Albert Einstein.

Though it was common to speak of these developments in revolutionary terms, as a new Scientific Revolution or a second Industrial Revolution, they do not seem to support Kuhn's theory at all well. There was no buildup of anomalies, no sense of unease about the reigning paradigm, no shift of allegiances from an old orthodoxy to a new one. In fact, if a revolution requires the overthrow of something old before the establishment of something new, then perhaps the coming of the information age was not a revolution at all but rather the arrival of something simply unprecedented. The whole grand transformation began with some fairly mundane engineering problems, the solutions to which turned out to have application far beyond their original context. In one fairly trivial sense, however, the development of these solutions did correspond to Kuhn's ideas about scientific discovery, in that they were arrived at independently by several practitioners: information theory by Claude Shannon and Norbert Wiener; basic computer design by Wiener, John von Neumann, and the mathematician Alan Turing. Though Wiener tends to get less credit than the others for these seminal ideas, he became a far more famous public spokesman for them, and for a time he was the popular face of the information age.

For Wiener, developments in information processing mattered most because they might help to reorganize the whole process of scientific discovery, and the practice he hoped would emerge from this change did resemble in some respects the one that Kuhn discerned as an ideal pattern in the past. Wiener also imagined a cyclical scientific process in which a highly organized effort would give rise to innovations, which would then loop back to make a new version of the old organization. Expressed in such general and abstract terms, of course, this looks like a model of change that might have been offered by almost anyone at almost any time, but Kuhn and Wiener share enough philosophical and scientific influences to suggest that they were in fact working on a common problem. And they have shared a rather similar fate, once-notorious symbols of change that have come to be seen as oppressive and reactionary.[45] Perhaps this odd reversal in public estimation has less to do with Kuhn and Wiener than it does with the intractable conflict they were both trying to solve.

Wiener's encounter with philosophical aspects of the problem of novelty began at Harvard in the first years of the twentieth century. A child prodigy more or less force-fed by his father, a Harvard professor, Wiener knew the most famous philosophers in the nation as neighbors and family friends.[46] Heavily influenced by William James, whose lectures he had attended as a very young man, Wiener entered Harvard as a graduate student in 1911, at the age of sixteen. James had just died, but his final published work, *Some Problems of Philosophy*, identified novelty as one of the issues most pressing on the discipline. The problem, as James puts it, is the conflict between perception and conception, since perception "yields a perfect effervescence of novelty all the time," while conception so reduces everything to identity that "no novelty can really come." Since the intellect inevitably understands what is in terms of what was, "there can be nothing genuinely new under the sun."[47]

James had been inspired by Darwin to hope that evolutionary biology might suggest a solution to this problem, and he was also influenced by Henri Bergson, whose work he had found both congenial and challenging.[48] As if in negative response to these hopes, Josiah Royce, the Harvard philosopher with whom Wiener was to start his dissertation, published an essay, "The Reality of the Temporal," in which he deprecates the influence of Bergson and pooh-poohs the "new theories of time."[49] As Royce sees it, the notion of unmediated perception is a delusion. Though he agrees with Bergson that our ordinary conceptions of temporal experience are mere conventions with no necessary connection to the actual, he does not believe it is possible even to think about, much less experience, anything outside their confines. Novelty itself, he argues, is a concept and "not an immediate datum of sense."[50] Thus even the uniqueness of each individual moment comes to us indirectly, in the context of a preexisting category, that of "the new." Bergson may very well be right, then, and each moment may be a unique expression of the essential novelty of time; but there is no way to bring this raw fact to consciousness, and thus no way for us, in the course of everyday experience, to say that any particular moment differs from other such moments in the past.[51]

Between them, James and Royce identify two related problems that were to occupy Wiener throughout his life. The first is the variation of phenomena over time, and especially the possibility of variations that are truly undetermined by the past. As a student of advanced math and physics, Wiener was to learn that there are such situations, and ways to account for them, at least approximately. But he was also to spend a good deal of time worrying about the second issue debated by James and Royce, that of conceptual novelty. What effect could real ontological novelty have if human logic inevitably subsumes the new to the old? If Royce is right, then the inescapable conformity of intellectual categories makes the whole issue of ontological novelty moot. How is scientific discovery possible, if the very conditions of inquiry prevent an awareness of the new?

The effect of these debates is clear in the work that Wiener began to do at Harvard. He studied scientific method and symbolic logic with Royce, and he wrote a dissertation comparing two different attempts to produce a comprehensive algebraic system of logical relations, one of which was that of the philosophers Bertrand Russell and Alfred North Whitehead in *Principia Mathematica*. This he presented rather proudly to Russell himself at the beginning of a postdoctoral fellowship at Cambridge.[52] Wiener's work with Russell overlapped with that of Wittgenstein and T. S. Eliot, the latter of whom he came to know well. These three very different students shared with their teacher a concern with symbolic logic, a sense that the symbolism of mathematics, the grammar of language in the abstract, and the categories of logical thought must be related. But Russell was developing a theory of logical atomism, which holds that there are things which can be understood apart from their relations to other things, whereas Wiener, like Royce before him, and like Eliot, who was studying the similar idealism of the philosopher F. H. Bradley, believed that everything is ultimately understood in relation.[53]

Eliot was particularly interested in an essay with the straightforward title "Relativism," which Wiener published in the *Journal of Philosophy, Psychology, and Scientific Methods*.[54] In using this term, Wiener does mean to say that "all reality that we know is relative and partial."[55] But he also uses the term in another, slightly different sense, to designate the idea that things are known only in relation, as parts of a system. Sounding a bit like the later Wittgenstein, Wiener maintains that things come to be intelligible according to a set of rules, a grammar. Thus "any new knowledge we acquire must be internally relevant to our previous knowledge: that only in proportion as it is thus relevant is it knowledge at all."[56] Unavoidable as it is, though, any particular grammar is still only particular and idiosyncratic. As Wiener puts it, all languages are actually idiolects, binding particular speakers to particular situations. There is no grammar of grammars, no "*total* context" within which different ways of seeing and saying might be evaluated.[57] Thus he comes at the end of his essay to a notion of science in which its truths are only approximate, since "we never judge whether any scientific hypothesis is better or worse than another by any criterion which is itself known to be more than approximately true."[58]

This essay is probably the best single expression of the philosophical convictions that Wiener took from his years of study with James, Royce, Russell, and others with whom he had more incidental contact, such as G. E. Moore and Edmund Husserl. Very early on, he connected the logical relativism of this essay to the theory of relativity on one hand and to an ethical relativism on the other. In both cases, he says in an essay titled "The Highest Good," there is a system of relations to which observations must be referred, within which they can make sense.[59] In the essay, the term he uses for this context is *Bezugsystem*, which might cover any of a number of reference systems, including one based on geometric coordinates. But even such apparently simple geometric concepts as points and lines, he asserts in another essay of this time, are intellectual constructs, not empirical facts.[60] What he really means by *Bezugsystem*, then, is something very close to what Kuhn means by *paradigm*, and the problem he thus approaches as a philosopher and a budding scientist is the one that Kuhn set out to explore: how scientific discovery might be possible at all if everything to come is inevitably understood within a context determined by the past.

As Wiener tells it himself, the version of this problem most prevalent in the physics of his time was the conflict between Newtonian mechanics and the research into thermodynamics that eventually resulted in quantum mechanics.[61] Kuhn devoted his longest and most complicated book to the same conflict, which began as scientists such as Max Planck were attempting to reconcile the principles of mechanics with the second law of thermodynamics. It was difficult for such scientists to accept the idea that a mechanical system, in which every action has its reaction and energy can never simply disappear, could lead, as the second law says it must, to an irreversible increase in entropy. Surely, Planck assumed, this apparently unidirectional change could be somehow reduced to "conservative," that is to say, classically reversible, mechanics.[62] At the same time, the probability calculations that James Clerk Maxwell and Ludwig Boltzmann had relied on would be shown to be theoretical conveniences, and all reactions would turn out to be explicable in purely mechanical terms.[63]

Kuhn's book is about the "break with tradition" that occurred when scientists finally had to qualify their belief in Newtonian mechanics instead.[64] Giving up the idea that molecules had necessarily to act in the same way as planets not only opened up a new understanding of the atom, it also helped to justify belief in real indeterminacy and an asymmetry in time. As Wiener says, "This transition from a Newtonian, reversible time . . . has had its philosophical echoes."[65] If the indeterminism lurking within the probability calculations of Maxwell and Boltzmann turns out to be actual and not artifactual, if physical systems are not all driven by symmetrical forces that could in principle be reversed, then the old Newtonian time, "in which nothing new happens," has given way to a different kind of time, "in which there is always something new."[66] The paradigm shift from Newtonian to quantum mechanics, in other words, opens up to physical science the fundamental novelty that James and Bergson had always said was perceptible beyond the boundaries of conventional concepts.[67]

Wiener's earliest scientific ambition was to develop a mathematical model capable of predicting the course of a stochastic system, one with an ineliminable element of the random in it. A real-world version of such a system is to be seen in any glass of water containing a little dust or pollen, as the grains jostle and push one another around in a pattern that turns out to be truly random. This effect, known as Brownian motion, served as a crucial prototype in analyzing and modeling atomic behavior, and to Wiener it presented a fascinating instance of a system "in which what happens in the future will have very little to do with what has happened in the past."[68] In such cases, probability calculations that had previously been used to estimate the possible distributions of molecules of gas in a container were now used to predict the relative likelihood of one or more of the possible future states into which the system might evolve.[69] In other words, Wiener was helping to develop mathematical models for novel developments in Bergsonian time.

Wiener would not have been as famous and influential as he was if he had not also found a set of technological problems that could be attacked with the same tools of analysis. Electronic signals, such as those transmitted by telephone or telegraph, also contain, in addition to the necessary fluctuations of the signal, other fluctuations that have a random quality much like Brownian motion.[70] These unwanted fluctuations, commonly and technically known as noise, can be filtered out only insofar as they can be effectively modeled, a task calling for the same probability calculations originally developed in ideal gas theory and then applied to other situations such as Brownian motion.[71] But the signal itself must also be characterized in some way, so as to identify in particular terms what it is that is being freed of noise. This is where Wiener's work converged on the information theory developed at the same time by Claude Shannon.

During World War II, under wartime rules of classification, Wiener prepared and privately circulated a paper that was ultimately published under the title "Extrapolation, Interpolation, and Smoothing of Secondary Time Series with Engineering Applications." Part of this paper covered much the same ground that Shannon was simultaneously exploring, though in relation to continuous signals such as those carried by the telephone rather than discrete ones such as those sent by telegraph. The problem in both cases was the same: how to code a signal so as to make the best use of the carrying capacity of the line given the necessary corruption of the signal by noise. Wiener was particularly concerned with filtering and thus with the inevitable tradeoff between signal and noise. The problem, as the mathematician P. R. Masani puts it, is this: "To reduce the effects of noise we will have to make the instrument insensitive, thereby diminishing its accuracy and utility. To make it accurate, we will have to increase its sensitivity, but then it will begin to register noise along with the message, and again lose its usefulness."[72] Given the essentially random nature of the phenomena in question, probability calculations are used to make the best of a bad job, to find the optimal tradeoff—given the nature of the information to be transmitted and the capacity of the medium of transmission—between signal and noise.

In a more general sense, then, Wiener was involved in finding ways to describe, as faithfully as possible, a Bergsonian flux in actual time and space, a continuous novelty, in which the future is only partly determined by the past. As Masani puts it, "The transmission of messages via a medium (or channel) is an intrinsically statistical phenomenon in Bergsonian time."[73] But Wiener's mathematical models of this novelty were useful only insofar as they made it possible to extract order from constant flux. As he says in the introduction to *Cybernetics*, "The telegraph and the telephone can perform their function only if the messages they transmit are continually varied in a manner not completely determined by their past, and can only be designed effectively if the variation of these messages conforms to some sort of statistical regularity."[74] A signal is, in this sense, a constantly modulated novelty, a piece of news that counts as news only insofar as it fits within the recognized channels of communication. In other words, Wiener's mathematical and technological researches, for all their advanced accommodation of the novelty actually present in phenomena, had recreated the original situation that bothered James, in which the immediacy of percept is always traded off in relation to the usefulness of concept—and the new ends up being subsumed in the old after all.

Wiener came to regard information theory as the basis of the more general scientific effort he called "cybernetics," which he liked to think of as "a second industrial revolution,"[75] a revolution *within* the previous revolution and not against it. In technological terms, the most important difference effected by this revolution would be the reconceptualization of machines as communications devices, processing messages before they process anything else. This is the aspect of cybernetics that brought notoriety to Wiener as the Father of Automation. But Wiener was just as interested in cybernetics as an innovation in scientific methodology, an innovation necessitated, in Masani's words, "by the existence of processes for which time is Bergsonian."[76] In order to study and learn from such processes, science would have to be modeled on them with the same sort of creativity, driven by an essential randomness but controlled and channeled by a process of continuous modulation. Thus, beginning with his study of stochastic processes in nature and working through information theory, Wiener came, in cybernetics, to a concept of scientific discovery that corresponds very closely to Kuhn's and suffers from some of the same difficulties.

At first, it might seem hard to associate cybernetics, which was always very proudly innovative, with the part of Kuhn's cycle that he called "normal science." For one thing, cybernetics was by definition interdisciplinary, while Kuhn's version of science, in its "normal" phase, was very strictly confined within conventional disciplinary boundaries. Reading Wiener, though, it often seems that what excites him about cybernetics is not its interdisciplinarity as such but the way it overcomes disciplinary boundaries. Wiener was elated early on to find "that people working in all these fields were beginning to talk the same language, with a vocabulary containing expressions from the communications engineer, the servo-mechanism man, the computing-machine man, and the neurophysiologist."[77] This is, after all, the goal of communications and the purpose of reconceiving the factory and the laboratory as networks, so that distance can be overcome and everyone involved can speak the same language.

Just as every channel has its noise, however, a cybernetics group, even one in which everyone succeeds in speaking the same language, will inevitably encounter some impediments to perfect communication. In fact, communication increases noise in the very process of sending a signal, so that it might be said that the cybernetic situation produces scientific cooperation and confusion at the same time. But the point of a cybernetic organization is that the confusions, the failures of communication, are treated not as errors to be eliminated but rather as signals in their own right, novelties to which the system should respond. This is made possible by the process known as feedback, in which "an error of performance is returned to the system as a partial basis of its future performance."[78] Noise in the cybernetic system thus plays much the same role that the anomaly does in Kuhn's theory, except that cybernetics is set up from the beginning to reassimilate the anomaly and not to resist it, so that the cycle is thus made much more compact. In this sense, cybernetics might be said to represent the perfect fusion of normal and revolutionary science, their simultaneous instantiation as versions of each other, without the unfortunate moments of stasis and upheaval that plague Kuhn's system.

Like Kuhn, Wiener was also conscious of a general intellectual debt to Darwinian evolution, which seemed to him "a mechanism by which a more or less fortuitous variability is combined into a rather definite pattern."[79] As a kind of signal system, cybernetics creates its own sort of "variability" by the recombination of standardized elements, like an alphabet, in which an element of the fortuitous is always present. It also depends on a recurrence, which is recursive, when the fortuitous element is fed back so as to become part of the system. Linking recurrence and recombination together in this way, Wiener recapitulated the synthesis that Darwin had accomplished for the theory of evolution and developed a new model of novelty by combining aspects of the old. Wiener also felt that evolution offered science in general a viable model of teleology, at least insofar as biological processes of change often seem purposeful. But he did not believe in the idea of general progress any more than Darwin before him or Kuhn after. In his case, then, this means that any local directionality that nature may show is included within a more general stasis, as variability is always reintroduced into a newly stable system. Over the years, even Wiener began to suspect that this circularity might tend to cancel novelty in the very act of preserving it.

THE FATE OF NOVELTY IN THE CYBERNETIC AGE

For a few years in the mid-twentieth century, cybernetics was both popular and influential, and Wiener played on a public stage the same role that Kuhn played in philosophy—as the representative of a revolutionary new way of looking at science. As cybernetics increased in prominence, however, Wiener found himself becoming a cyberneticist of a different kind. Having derived the term originally from the Greek for "governor," he ultimately found himself trying to hold back the engine he had invented, for fear it would blow its top. Again and again, he warned in his later works against the illicit application of scientific ideas beyond their original field of relevance, the commercial and military cooptation of scientific advances, and popular enthusiasm for technology in general as it turned into idolatry. Despite his efforts, he became famous as the Father of Automation, perhaps the very worst of all possible synonyms for the self-reflexive systems he had envisioned.

Wiener's misgivings about his own project seem to have two different sources: one historical and political, the other rather more fundamental. As Wiener saw it, a cybernetic system aims to achieve the ideal state of homeostasis, which he modeled after the self-correcting balance achieved by many biological systems. But a balanced homeostatic state is always, in his view, a hard-won and temporary stay against the basic laws of thermodynamics, which decree that any organization of matter will always degrade into a junk pile of its constituent parts. More particularly, though, Wiener came to see contemporary capitalist democracies as not just prone to lose homeostatic equilibrium but as actively antihomeostatic. Where information could not flow freely, because "control of the means of communication" was in the hands of the few, inhibited by "privacy and anonymity" and "by the laws of libel," feedback could not work properly.[80] It is simply not in the interests of "Fascists, Strong Men in Business, and Government" to let information take its natural course.[81]

Instead of the ideal self-control to which Wiener had dedicated cybernetics, he viewed modern society as governed by external control, but the result is not a static tyranny. Instead, the antihomeostasis of contemporary society expresses itself in "business cycles of boom and failure, in the successions of dictatorship and revolution, in the wars which everyone loses, which are so real a feature of modern times."[82] In other words, without useful feedback about its situation, or with too much feedback for the system to process, the machine of society veers wildly out of control and in its flailings destroys those it is supposed to protect. It is in this way that contemporary societies bear the brunt of both extremes, suffering through the dislocation and uncertainty of a wildly unstable system while also feeling that it is impervious to change.

Wiener felt so strongly about the dangers of this situation that he dared and ultimately suffered the fate of becoming a crank, denouncing the commercial and military sponsorship of science at MIT, an institution that had turned such funding into a science of its own. But he also harbored deeper and more significant doubts about cybernetics itself, doubts that seem to go all the way back to his studies with Royce. What if the recursive process on which cybernetics is based does not preserve the anomalous by using it but simply reduces it to order, just as traditional concepts did? What if perception without concepts is in fact blind, so that it is humanly impossible to reorganize scientific research to be responsive to the actual novelty to be found in nature? These are doubts about cybernetics in general, and as such they echo much contemporary criticism of information theory and the cybernetic project. Yet they are also doubts about the very possibility of conceptual novelty in the sciences, and as such they shed some harsh light on Kuhn's project as well as Wiener's own.

Wiener's most candid and unguarded ideas about novelty are included in two of his least-read books, one of which was not published until almost thirty years after his death. Asked in 1954 by the editor-publisher Jason Epstein at Doubleday to write a short, nontechnical book about his "philosophy of invention," Wiener produced a draft that did not finally appear until 1993.[83] Wiener had withdrawn the draft, because he had become so much more engrossed in one of the anecdotes in it—the story of the electrical engineer and physicist Oliver Heaviside, whose work had been of instrumental importance to long-distance telephone communication.[84] Instead of polishing his book on invention, Wiener wrote a novelized version of the Heaviside story, which was published as *The Tempter* in 1959. Thus the two books together constitute a single effort to define innovation and to show how its best effects are often thwarted.

According to the account given in *Invention*, Wiener sees new ideas as emerging in four stages, arranged in such a way that each stage is a necessary though not a sufficient cause of the next. Though he presents the stages as typical, they actually seem to constitute historical stages as well, from the most primitive type of invention to the most advanced and complex. The first stage, or moment, as Wiener puts it, is intellectual: "Some person or persons must have introduced [the new idea] in their own minds."[85] Though Wiener leaves open the possibility of plurality here, "the effectiveness of the individual is enormous."[86] The second stage is technical, which, in its first appearance in the book, Wiener defines rather modestly: it is merely the necessity of "proper materials or techniques."[87] The third stage is social, insofar as any successful invention depends on collaboration and communication, especially between intellectual and technical workers. Thus the mere existence of proper materials or techniques is not enough unless there is some significant relationship between people with ideas and people with practical knowhow.[88] The last stage, finally, is economic, since there must be "some way to promote" the invention once it has been made feasible.[89]

Though this scheme looks like the genesis of any particular invention at any time, the stages actually contain within them a cryptic history of the development of invention as a process and thus of innovation as a general concept, a story that has a number of twists and discontinuities in it as well as a tragic ending. The first level, the intellectual, represents perhaps the very oldest notion of novelty: divine inspiration.[90] A truly original idea, Wiener says in a candid moment, is virtually "an Act of Grace."[91] Lucky accidents of this kind occur only to individuals, particularly to Promethean individuals who are marked off from their fellows in some way. Wiener was always drawn to scientists who fit this model, such as the physicist Willard Gibbs, who was little understood in his own time, or Heaviside, who had been, according to Wiener, both scorned and cheated.[92] Thus Gibbs appears in *Invention* in Wiener's list of scientists who made the great Promethean gamble and dared the gods.[93] At this stage and in such cases, it should go without saying, novelty and originality are very strongly associated. The great new ideas are not just new but original with a single person, who is either divinely inspired or in competition with the divine. In this theory as in most others, creation from nothing requires an essentially magical explanation.

Wiener's example of the telescope as the sort of material or technique that comes in at the second stage is fairly conventional,[94] and what he has to say about it is not very startling. But, in fact, the arrival of the telescope marks not just a stage in the process of invention but a very significant change in the nature of invention. As Wiener puts it a little later in the book, instruments like the telescope might even be said to have inverted the older process of invention. Instead of studying nature in order to produce a new mechanical means of affecting it, scientists actually study their own inventions—first of all to find out what they are capable of, and then to discover in their workings new and unexpected facts about nature. Science, in the sense of new knowledge, is not so much the cause as it is the effect of such new machines. As the historian Robert Friedel puts it in a recent history of inventions, "Science owed more to the steam engine than the steam engine owed to science."[95]

Wiener calls this very aptly "the inverse process of invention,"[96] but he does not note that in doing so he has also inverted the priority of his first two stages, deriving inspiration from technology and not from acts of grace. Nor does he acknowledge the fact that once inverted in this way, invention also at least begins to be separated from originality. This is one of the reasons why it is so difficult to assign priority for such well-known inventions as the steam engine or photography, because these were arrived at by a protracted process of studying and refining earlier machines, prototypes that made certain principles apparent without actually achieving a final product. Thus, as Friedel suggests, "the question, 'Who invented the telegraph?' does not make much sense."[97]

Of course, at the third stage Wiener's account of invention is openly social in any case. Though he still maintains, even in his account of this stage, that "new ideas are conceived in the intellects of individual scientists," he also warns that no such ideas are to be found where there is an insufficient concentration of intellects in collaboration.[98] This is the stage at which his account of invention sounds the most genuinely cybernetic, because he is emphasizing the importance of communicative networks in creating and testing ideas. Here Wiener also sounds the most like other influential accounts of innovation of this time, particularly the one by Kuhn, for whom scientific change is a matter of general paradigm shifts, not isolated individual moments of inspiration.

For Wiener, though, the newest and most up-to-date of his stages is the last, where economic interests come into play. Until about the time of the Civil War, as he tells it, the pure scientist could be regarded as a sort of "poet of industry"; but once the war was over, "a new element came into the game of invention."[99] That element was the industrialization of invention and its linkage to the patent system. Both aspects can be traced to Thomas Edison, whose greatest invention was "the industrial scientific laboratory,"[100] and whose most useful ability was his knowing how to file both protective and obstructive patent applications. Though it seems fairly obvious that the stage at which the scientist really could be a "poet of industry" is impossibly far back in time, since inventions have had to be exploited economically for many centuries, Wiener persists in writing as if this were a recent development. He calls it "a new phase," a "new age," a "new climate," and a "new step."[101] The language of novelty proliferates around this stage in what seems an ironic suggestiveness, as if to admit that the industrialization of invention is a new development that has canceled out the very possibility of novelty itself.

This is an effect not just of economic exploitation or of the patent system but also of automating the making of inventions. Not only is novelty severed decisively from originality, but its very status seems to change. At the first and earliest stage in the history of invention, as Wiener puts it, "the use of the human mind for evolving really new thoughts is a new phenomenon each time."[102] The beauty of this natural source of novelty is that it, in addition to throwing off new ideas, also alters the very nature of novelty itself. New ideas are not just new but new in a new way. Unfortunately, in the historical process of invention as Wiener has drawn it, the entry of technology means that the most significant change in novelty is that it ceases to be new. Innovation is routinized; inventions are cranked out by industrial processes; and the new comes to seem not just inevitable but also oppressive and boring. This is a tragic conclusion, insofar as the material technology necessary to Wiener's second stage, and the collaboration necessary to the third, have merged in this fourth stage to produce the very antithesis of inventiveness.

This tragic conclusion also bears some negative implications for information theory and cybernetics in general. Wiener's history of the process of invention is a story about increasing self-reflexiveness as an original inspiration comes to work on its own creations instead of directly on nature, and then to invest the very process of investigation itself in machines. Of course, this sounds very much like what Wiener was preaching as the creator of cybernetics. In part, he is able to claim here as he does elsewhere that soul-destroying automation and corporate control of new ideas represent the theft of his innovations and their application in nefarious ways. In other words, ill effects come from the obstruction of real information transfer, of "damming up . . . the freedom of flow of information."[103] Even when information is allowed to flow freely, however, its course is essentially circular, as it is fed back into the system that generated it, and this recursive circularity seems capable of modulating the new and different until it no longer exists.

As Wiener warns, "If we have so organized our flow of information that there are no minor leaks, we have probably channeled it so narrowly that the healthy internal growth of our own technique is hampered."[104] In other words, noise is necessary to and even definitive of invention itself. What seems so ominous in this account of discovery and invention in the modern situation, though, is that noise no longer seems inevitable. Organized as tightly as it is and dominated by powerful interests, science may prove too successful, so that whatever anomalies arise get worked back into the system too quickly to amount to revolution. The tight integration and automatic coordination that make cybernetics so powerful also turn it into an ironic replica of the rigid industrial domination that Wiener had hoped to supplant.

Wiener's fears in this respect are confessed most vividly in the novelized version of *Invention* that he published as *The Tempter* in 1959. The novel is presented in the form of a long letter from Gregory James, chief engineer at the fictional Williams Controls, to his namesake, Gregory Williams, son of the company's founder and one of James's oldest friends. The purpose of the letter is to lay out in straightforward terms the unscrupulous means by which Williams Controls acquired the patent rights to one of its most lucrative inventions. The letter is a personal as well as a corporate confession, for James charges himself with having betrayed George Woodbury, the cranky, isolated, and chronically poor scientist who actually formulated the mathematical ideas from which Williams extracted its profits. In these bare terms, the novel retells the story of Oliver Heaviside, whose work on long-distance phone circuits was allegedly appropriated by AT&T and formed the basis of its domination of communications in the United States.

Since the purpose of James's letter is to serve "the claims of truth," his own writing succeeds in the only way necessary, by being "easy to decipher."[105] In this way, it seems, he represents the characteristic literary virtues of the engineer, for George Woodbury also possesses a style "as sharp and incisive" as could be.[106] In a long letter quoted within the main account, James praises Woodbury for always preserving "the novelty and directness of viewpoint" that lead to "straight pieces of writing."[107] At the other extreme in the economy of language is the "jargon" of lawyers, who write with "a professional fondness for obfuscation."[108] So different are the basic styles of Woodbury and the legal department at Williams Controls that James often functions as translator between them, as if they were actually speaking different languages.[109]

Woodbury is even more effective as a speaker than as a writer, and in a revealingly self-reflexive scene he explains to the narrator some of the basic concepts of cybernetics. In form, this conversation between two scientists mimics its subject, which is the "conversation between man and the machine."[110] Insofar as Woodbury's words are fresh, vivid, and effective, he seems actually to be speaking "the language of machines," which is not a childish language but one "with a really difficult syntax to it."[111] Nonetheless, James begins to glimpse the "new world of engineering in which the principles of machinery and its subtle language would be understood and mastered."[112] What Woodbury offers, in other words, is a general theory of messages identical to Wiener's, and in such a committed and vivid fashion that the conversation itself illustrates the power

of information to do real work. It is in this sense that the plainness of
Wiener's own writing is supposed to transcend itself: vivid with commitment if not with literary sophistication, it works by making a direct connection between writer and reader, transmitting motivation like current
along a circuit.

The beauty of this vision makes it all the harder to assimilate the fairly
large number of instances in which Woodbury is characterized as distant,
illegible, and cryptic. The most notable personal characteristic of this isolated scientist is his deafness, which had not only kept him from rising
in the organizational and educational worlds but also "made it hard to
communicate with him spiritually."[113] A "crabbed, cranky fellow," Woodbury also puts his scientific work down in what often seems to others a
crabbed and cranky way: "He seems to take a malicious delight in not
crossing his t's and dotting his i's, so that not many of us can read his
stuff."[114] Isolated, unhearing, and illegible as he is, Woodbury has at least
one advantage, that his uncommunicativeness makes it hard to steal his
ideas. His originality is identified with and protected by his unwillingness
to communicate. In terms of information theory, Woodbury is a channel
almost obliterated by noise, but Wiener constructs his novel so that the
removal of that noise also fatally contradicts the principle of invention.

Removing the noise from Woodbury's messages and thus making them
useful to industry is the dramatic role of the narrator of *The Tempter*. It
corresponds, of course, in an uncanny way to his structural role, which
is to interpret for us as readers the words and actions of a man so anti-
social he cannot speak for himself. When James, on sitting down to dis-
cuss with Woodbury the language of machines, insists that "one always
gets a fresher impression . . . when one hears . . . from the mouth of the
author with his original emphasis,"[115] he enunciates a principle that his
own narration implicitly contradicts, since he is about to narrate to us at
one remove the words of his interlocutor. Structurally and dramatically,
then, James's role as narrator is deeply ambiguous, since it is both necessary and reprehensible. That Woodbury's ideas cannot express themselves is not just an unfortunate accident but an index of their originality,
and yet that originality is somewhat pointless if it cannot be expressed.
James performs the necessary task of interpreting, translating, and filtering Woodbury's ideas so that they can be communicated. Unfortunately,

this process of translation is coterminous with and more or less identical to the process by which Williams Controls steals Woodbury's ideas and patents them as its own. As Wiener puts it in *Cybernetics*, "*traduttore traditore*" (translator, traitor).[116]

Dramatically, James functions as a control device, performing the very function that Woodbury's formulas are to help him perfect. As he puts it himself, "Control devices are devices which take our orders and pass them on to a machine in a language which the machine can understand."[117] This industrial process of translation depends on the prior process of filtering and interpretation that James performs on Woodbury's formulas. But this process, the novel makes clear, is also a process of appropriation, even of theft. The control device, then, is not just a neutral translator but an inverter that traps power and reuses it in its own way. The control of communications on which Williams Controls makes its fortune is not just the antithesis of real and open communication but the theft of it.

In the telling, then, something dramatic has happened to this story of intellectual dishonesty and appropriation: it has turned into an indictment of cybernetics as such. The process by which noise is removed from and then fed back into a circuit appears here as the domination of individuals by corporate interests, but also as the erasure of novelty in the course of cybernetic transmission. Instead of amplifying the new, the cybernetic process dampens it out. In another sense, this sad conclusion marks the return of Wiener's early relativism, his sense, inherited from Royce, that any new phenomena must appear in the context of old presumptions. It is not just normal science, in Kuhn's terms, that stifles novelty, but also revolutionary science, as it feeds its accumulated anomalies back into a newly constituted normality.

In these late works, Wiener anticipates the criticisms that would later accumulate around the declining reputation of cybernetics, which are rather similar to the criticisms that have been more commonly attached to Kuhn's work as its initial notoriety wore off. In both cases, theories that once seemed excitingly progressive and even dangerously radical have come to seem implicitly conservative.[118] There was a time when Wiener's ideas were influential with new poets, as when Charles Olson modeled his poetry on Wiener's definition of a message as "a discrete or continuous sequence of measureable events distributed in / time."[119] In these same years, systems theory, "communications theory," and early notions about information had a powerful influence on the visual arts, such that quotations from Wiener could appear in the polemics of artists like Robert Smithson, side by side with bits from the composer John Cage and attacks on the visual art critic Clement Greenberg.[120] In short, Wiener's ideas seemed to provide a viable model for new work in literature and the arts, at a time when the nature of novelty itself was part of the dispute between old authorities and younger artists.

The shift in reputation that has made cybernetics seem militaristic and repressive has a good deal to do, of course, with the sheer passage of time, but it also exposes something about the odd structure of novelty in an era that is often said to be defined by it. If modernity sometimes looks like a situation in which nothing is fixed and there are no solid conventions to rely on, that very situation also seems to mean that even the most insubstantial and temporary convention must go unquestioned, since there is no external standard by which it can be judged. Though the new seems ubiquitous, it also seems impossible to establish that anything is truly new. The projects of Wiener and Kuhn, among many other things, are attempts to arrange this painful situation in a sensible way, so that convention and novelty can be seen to foster and inform each other. That their solutions do not always convince may mean that no viable solutions are to be had, or that our commitments are so inconsistent that they tend to re-create the same imbalances decade after decade, no matter what clever scientists may suggest. In either case, the confounding problems around novelty are persistent enough to appear in modern theories of the arts, much as they do in the philosophy of science.

6

MAKING IT NEW : NOVELTY
AND AESTHETIC MODERNISM

THE ARTWORLD OF THE NEW

Very shortly after the publication of Kuhn's *The Structure of Scientific Revolutions*, its influence outside the history and philosophy of science was demonstrated by the publication of a paper called "The Artworld" by the art critic and philosopher Arthur Danto. This paper, with its simple and yet sweeping title, is now famous for a number of reasons, most of them related to the fact that it records Danto's first encounter with the work of Andy Warhol. The Brillo boxes that Warhol had just shown for the first time became the chief exhibits in Danto's argument that a decisive shift to a new understanding of art had occurred, a shift so fundamental that it might almost be said to have marked the end of the history of art. In the years since the first publication of this essay in 1964, a tremendous amount of attention has been focused on this claim, and on its implications for art produced after Warhol—so much in fact that relatively little notice has been given to the essay's opening gambit, which is to present, in terms clearly derived from Kuhn, a thumbnail sketch of the beginnings of aesthetic modernism.

To see something as art at all, Danto argues, requires the supporting context of "an atmosphere of artistic theory, a knowledge of the history of art: an artworld."[1] What he had in mind at the time, he said many years later, was something like the meaning philosophers since

Ludwig Wittgenstein have given the term *world*. In this case, it would designate the world "populated by all and only artworks, much as The Animal World was made up of all and only animals."[2] In other words, Danto calls on *world* to do much the same duty done in Kuhn's work by *worldview* or, more famously, by *paradigm*. The artworld is not, Danto has always insisted, what has come to be known as the art world, the assembled social institutions that administer the production, exhibition, and analysis of artworks, but rather the collection of entities that fit a conceptual definition of art. The first example given in the essay is the collection of traditional artworks that fit a mimetic theory of art.[3]

In discussing the fate of what he calls the IT, the imitation theory of art, Danto follows out the implications entailed in calling it a world. Since it is a category that includes only and all those things considered works of art, it is total, complete, cohesive, and theoretically unchangeable; that is to say, if the collection is to be altered in any fundamental way, the theory must be changed. Of course, as exceptions present themselves, auxiliary hypotheses may be patched onto the main theory; but sooner or later, if new items demanding the designation *art* continue to occur, there must be a violent, abrupt, and complete redefinition, a revolution. Danto calls this sort of change a "conceptual revolution," and he cites as prototype "certain episodes in the history of science."[4] In art as in science, he says, in what is an obvious echo of Kuhn, to change theories is not just to change one's mind but "to exchange one *world* for another."[5]

Danto does even less than Kuhn to explain how a totality so complete it can be called a world could ever allow exceptions to appear, much less accumulate in numbers sufficient to foment revolution. He is content to note that this has happened, particularly when the IT was replaced by the new artworld of aesthetic modernism. As he explains this shift, "The artists in question were to be understood not as unsuccessfully imitating real forms but as successfully creating new ones, quite as real as the forms which the older art had been thought, in its best examples, to be creditably imitating."[6] Danto calls this new artworld RT, and the idea that modernism is to be defined by its pretensions to creating real things, not imitations, is crucial to the rest of his argument. This is actually a rather idiosyncratic choice for the defining characteristic of modernism, and even his own statement of it contains another, much more common alternative: novelty. Why not call the new artworld NT, since it is not only new but dedicated to creating new things?

The most immediate reason for Danto's choice, of course, is that he has seen in Warhol's Brillo boxes what seems to be a definitive tension between art and reality, and he is less interested in these works' threat to ideas of novelty and originality. But there is also a fundamental difficulty with the whole idea of an NT, one challenging enough that it may have discouraged Danto from even considering it. Can there be an artworld entirely populated by new things, a paradigm defined by resistance to paradigms? Royce had long since argued that this is not possible, since inclusion within the paradigm of the new requires that the individual novelty of the instance be sacrificed.[7] In respect to aesthetic modernism, Theodor Adorno says much the same thing. For Adorno, the new is a particular that cannot be fit into some preexisting conceptual category, an individuality that lives outside a paradigm. No more than Royce does he believe that this is actually possible in the current state of things, so the new remains for him a kind of rebuke, the impossibility of which figures forth the corrupt state of life as it exists.[8] A tradition of the new thus seems doubly prohibited by Adorno's reasoning—first because the new itself is unreachable, and second because the construction of a new category out of such things would neutralize all that is truly valuable in them.

In the "Artworld" essay, Danto avoids these difficulties by dropping the idea of "new things" as soon as he introduces it, and the concept of novelty does not play much of a role in the years of writing that follow. But this early essay may serve nonetheless as a valid introduction to the role of novelty in the theory of aesthetic modernism. For one thing, it demonstrates that the problem of novelty is one that art and literature of the modern period share with the science of the time. The specialization and subjectivity definitive of modernity, the way that *world* and *worldview* come to be synonymous, make the particular viewpoint as impervious to new things as the most hidebound tradition. Though it may be the cardinal virtue of modernity, novelty thus remains, as Adorno says, a semblance, a figure for itself. More ironically yet, the specific ways in which these figures of the new are realized are inherited from a tradition going all the way back to the beginnings of European philosophy. Danto's account of art has as its immediate source Kuhn's influential model, with its alternations of patient recombination and sudden revolution; but it follows the pattern so closely because these are apparently the only two ways of allowing for the possibility of novelty, given a closed and complete world. Backed by the example of Kuhn, which is itself backed by that of Darwin, Danto applies this dual model to the situation of aesthetic modernism.

By the time of Danto's essay, in fact, aesthetic modernism had come to be rather generally understood as a break with artistic tradition that led back to a refined and reestablished version of that tradition, a graph of progress and return shared by proponents such as Clement Greenberg and the opponents who were to establish postmodern theory. Thus modernism ended up in more or less the same bin with cybernetics, as another once-exciting innovation that had come to seem inherently repressive. One of the reasons it was possible to make either claim, to see modernism as drastic and uncompromising innovation or as conventional in its own right, is that the graph of change that had come to form modern thinking about the new linked these two possibilities so closely together.

THE IMPOSSIBLE NOVELTY OF MODERN ART

The idea that an artwork must have some measure of novelty in order to please is an old one. Striking and surprising effects have a basic appeal, and the ability to vary and invent has been considered one of the particular strengths of art virtually from its beginnings. Sometime in the course of the Renaissance, though, novelty graduated from its secondary status as an incidental effect to become a necessity, a quality without which no artwork could succeed.[9] Even writers like Joseph Addison and Samuel Johnson, who were great enforcers of decorum, felt that a work must be fresh even as it conforms to the rules.[10]

The status of novelty in periods such as the eighteenth century exposes a basic paradox: for much of recorded artistic history, novelty functions as a necessary deviation, a break in the rules that satisfies some other kind of rule.[11] It may be less of a paradox, then, or simply a paradox of a different kind, that novelty eventually becomes a rule of its own. Sometime in the nineteenth century, as it is often said, novelty was promoted from its old status as an attribute that an artistic work or style may have in some measure and became a style in its own right. To be "absolutely modern," it is necessary to create a work that conforms only to its own rules.[12] A whole set of associated virtues—originality, authenticity, autonomy—derive from the prime virtue of novelty. As the symbolist painter Odilon Redon put it in 1922, "Everything that is sincerely and humbly new . . . carries its meaning within itself."[13]

Thus it is that novelty comes to be the defining characteristic of aesthetic modernism, enshrined for good and all in the titles of popular works such as the art critic Robert Hughes's *The Shock of the New* and in the common wisdom as it is expressed in works such as the historian Peter Gay's *Modernism: The Lure of Heresy*. Art critics since Harold Rosenberg's *The Tradition of the New* have repeated this categorical claim: "The only thing that counts for Modern Art is that a work shall be NEW."[14] In so doing, though, they are only repeating a demand made innumerable times by writers and artists themselves, from Kasimir Malevich's relatively simple projection of a new art that will "build up a new world"[15] to Jackson Pollock's massively redundant claim, "New art needs new techniques. And the modern artists have found new ways and new means of making their statements."[16]

Anything said for so long with such unanimous conviction and certainty inevitably inspires contradiction, however, and so the value of the new and its status in the definition of modernism have also come to be questioned. Conservatives and reactionaries from the author Max Nordau to Adolf Hitler, opposed to novelty more or less by definition, have denounced what they see as the corrosive effect of it on all other values.[17] But a fair number of artists and writers with paid-up memberships in the avant-garde have also resisted the apparently universal imperative of their time, including Amédée Ozenfant: "What imbecility, this prejudice of the hideous called beautiful is, merely because it is new: as if every novelty necessarily meant something!"[18] Even more significant in a way is the number of modernists who renounced the claims of an absolute novelty in favor of one that is merely relative, artists whose motto, the literary scholar Antoine Compagnon says, "was 'redo,' not 'make new.'"[19] It is hard to imagine a modernist manifesto with the slogan Redo, but sometimes even the manifestos were candid about the actual status of their claims: "We know that the basic ideas of what we feel and create today have existed before us, and we are emphasizing that in *essence* they are not new. But we must proclaim the fact that everywhere in Europe new forces are sprouting like a beautiful unexpected seed, and we must point out all the places where new things are originating."[20] Knowing that nothing is ever actually new and announcing the advent of new things are not, in the context of the modernist manifesto, incompatible.

More considerable objections to the privileged status of novelty in the definition of modernism have existed from its very beginnings. Charles Baudelaire, it is often noticed, matched the fleeting and transient aspect of modern beauty to its necessary complement, "the eternal and the immovable."[21] The first comprehensive account of modernist poetry, published by the poets Robert Graves and Laura Riding in 1926, attacked the pretensions of those who "wanted to be *new* rather than to be poets."[22] Later, when postmodernism mounted its attack on authenticity, autonomy, and originality, all attributes strongly associated with the new, scholars such as Rosalind Krauss began to reread the founding documents of modernism so that they came to define an avant-garde that was constitutionally opposed to novelty.[23]

In some cases, these rereadings turn on the notion that the ambition to be new is inherently self-defeating, so that modernism faces the impossible task of establishing its foundations, over and over, on ground that it has itself undermined. This is the argument of the literary critic and theorist Paul de Man's classic essay, "Literary History and Literary Modernity," in which novelty is achieved only by a "deliberate forgetting," an erasure of the past in the hope of arriving at an absolute present. The more a writer renounces the past, however, the "greater the dependence on the past," especially on those forebears who had themselves attempted the impossible task of self-creation.[24] For very different reasons, Adorno also felt that modernism's ambitions to be new were intrinsically contradictory. Aiming at novelty in order to establish the autonomy of art runs into the unpleasant fact that novelty is itself one of the most basic requirements of the capitalist market. To be new is therefore not to be different, or at least to be different in a way that is not just anticipated but also necessary.[25] More recently, and for yet another set of reasons, the sociologist Bruno Latour has described modernism as a failed revolution, and not a noble failure but one that leaves behind a sour sense of self-betrayal and hypocrisy. The pretense to independence that is the basis of modernism clashes everywhere with the fact of dependence on the past, so that both the present and the past are devalued.[26]

In addition to all this, it might also be argued that the kind of novelty most commonly ascribed to aesthetic modernists is not particularly modern. If Norbert Wiener's analysis in *Invention* is correct, then the most common form of novelty in recent times is not the thunderclap of inspiration but the impersonal and dispersed process that perfected the steam engine or, to take one of Kuhn's favorite examples, distinguished oxygen at long last from the vaguer notion of air. If Randall Collins is right, then creativity, both intellectual and artistic, has always been a relative thing, a matter of "new combinations of ideas arising from existing ones, or new ideas structured by opposition to older ones." Novelty, in this analysis, is also a matter of networks, so that an individual "in isolation rarely develops a new issue or a new way of resolving it."[27] For Collins, this is just as true of ancient Greece as it is of contemporary Manhattan; but this very insight is obviously conditioned by a modern experience, long used to thinking of invention as a diffuse event shared among many equally responsible inventors. How different is this from the common cliché of the modernist as lonely rebel, still decked out in some old wardrobe left over from *La Bohème*?

Taken together, for all their differences these arguments form a convincing indictment of the very notion of intellectual or aesthetic novelty. Though it may seem a less daunting prospect to achieve a new work of art than to perform the ontological feat of creating new matter from nothing, the arguments against it seem just as sound. Artists have never been considered creators *ex nihilo*, and it has always been obvious that the thoughts and experiences on which they rely must preexist them as much as their materials do. The poet Guillaume Apollinaire did once insist that the modernist painter will invent new colors, just as the Russian futurists invented new words.[28] For the most part, though, artists and writers of the modern period are confined by the same realities first noticed by the pre-Socratics and by the constraints on new ideas adumbrated by Kuhn.

There is one additional irony, then, to attach to the project of modernist novelty: in describing how they intended to be new, modernist writers and artists had to rely on the traditional complement of models and metaphors in order to describe their goal. For all its rhetoric, for all its claims and promises to be new, aesthetic modernism did not have its own account of what it means to be new. In this, which would seem to be a crucial aspect of its self-definition, modernism's lack of autonomy was total. In a general sense, this lack of autonomy is freely confessed whenever modernist writers or artists claim that aesthetic novelty is required by the conditions of modern life. When the artist and polemicist El Lissitzky says, for example, "The new book requires a new *writer*. Inkwells and goosequills are dead," he makes it sound as though technological advance has created a kind of vacuum into which writers will be sucked despite themselves.[29] Aesthetic novelty, in other words, is often described in the context of the modern period as a secondary phenomenon, necessitated by developments outside the world of art. What is not so freely acknowledged or so often noticed is the rhetorical dependency of modernist polemic on the small set of terms for new things that had been doing that duty for centuries.

VARIETIES OF MODERNIST NOVELTY

Though modern art is supposed to be absolutely new and different without compromise, its advent is often announced as if it were the return of something long exiled in the past. The futurists, to take one obvious example, presented their movement as the "cultural resurgence" of Italy.[30] In much the same way, Apollinaire once described the new painting of the School of Paris as the rebirth of Gothic art, but he was conscious enough of a potential difficulty that he rather nervously insisted that it was "a rebirth wholly spontaneous and free of pastiche."[31] One way to avoid this problem is to deploy metaphors of rebirth as if they have to do with birth alone. The dawn that F. T. Marinetti descries in the first manifesto of futurism, issued in 1909, is not the old, shopworn dawn that shows up every twenty-four hours but "the very first dawn."[32] Thus the common cyclical novelty apparent in everyday life is stripped of its recurrent quality and presented as if it amounted to an origin.

The warrant for doing so is provided by the historical practice of Christianity, by the idea that religious renewal is in fact return to a different and better state, and some modernists with a spiritual bent relied on this history more or less openly. The painter Wassily Kandinsky may have summoned a spirit so general it was actually called the "Abstract Spirit," but the "new value in the human soul" that this spirit was to breathe into its acolytes was nonetheless a modern descendant of the New Testament.[33] Sometimes, even in what might seem the unlikeliest instances, modernist evocations of a "new man" actually seem to depend on the Christian prototype. The Dadaist Tristan Tzara's "new men," for example, are so ridiculous they "ride astride on hiccups," but they imply a new way of looking at God nonetheless.[34]

Even where there is no specific religious belief, there is often a kind of generalized spiritual idealism of the sort evident in the painter and filmmaker Hans Richter's "Towards a New World Plasticism," which starts out as a denunciation of capitalism and Christianity and ends with the proclamation of a "new spirit . . . the spiritual body of the new world."[35] Richter's manifesto is fervently revolutionary, and it draws very clearly on the original reformist zeal of the very religion he despises, but the appeal to spiritual values always has in it the countertendency toward the eternal and the changeless. The writer and literary critic Eugene Jolas wraps up both revolution and return in the same package when he insists, "Unless there be a perception of eternal values, there can be no new magic."[36] For Jolas, the eternal has fallen so far out of fashion that a return to it amounts to a new beginning, but it is still hard to ignore the implicit conflict emerging from these metaphors of spiritual rebirth, so long as they hearken back to a steady state that seems attractive insofar as it is not modern.

Thus there is an implicit conservatism in these metaphors of rebirth and renewal, one that emerges in all sorts of ways, from the traditionalism of T. S. Eliot to the primitivism of writers such as D. H. Lawrence, and even to the apparently neutral formalism of the futurist painter and sculptor Umberto Boccioni's "NEW PLASTIC IDEAS," which involve "the primitive purity of a new architectural structure of masses."[37] A return to original purity is the goal of these manifestos in favor of rebirth and renewal. Although this goal might be seen as utopian and forward looking, insofar as the true state of original purity has never actually existed on this earth, these writings can also very easily end up as flatly conservative, insofar as they are tempted by some imagined state of perfection located in the actual past or in some timeless present. It is perhaps for this reason that the Russian futurists Mikhail Larionov and Natalya Goncharova reject the whole opposition of old and new, which they see as itself a dead letter. The "argument with old art long since departed," they insist, "is nothing but a resurrection of the dead."[38] The wish to supplant the dead, in other words, becomes the act of replacing the dead, so that new art with no other aim than to be new simply ends up recreating the old system of precedence with itself on the throne.

Besides its religious motive, the rebirth of the cowed, tired citizen of modern times as a "new man" also has a political dimension.[39] When British writers of the 1930s put their efforts behind "the idea of a change of heart that should change society and the idea of a new society making a new man," they did so in concert with their commitment to communist revolution.[40] For writers and artists ranging from the novelist Émile Zola to the poet W. H. Auden, the link between artistic and political change was a natural one, and the call to revolution in their manifestos and works was at least to some extent literal. It is not hard to find such associations in the midst of putative or actual revolutions, motivated either by the idea, as the painter and architect Vladimir Tatlin puts it, that "revolution strengthens the impulse of invention,"[41] or by the symmetrical expectation that inventive artistic efforts can help motivate a political revolution. In and around the time of the Russian Revolution, to European leftist movements that followed or hoped to follow it—among these the surrealists under the French poet and critic Breton and the British writers of the 1930s under Auden—the term *revolution* when used in artistic situations also necessarily entailed some commitment to a political version.

It is necessary to insist on what might otherwise seem a fairly obvious point because revolution is so frequently little more than a metaphor, perhaps the favored one for modern artists and writers with advanced ambitions. When the critic Clive Bell speaks of the Second Post-Impressionist Exhibition as the work of a "revolutionary movement," he has nothing more in mind than art.[42] When the abstract expressionist painter Robert Motherwell maintains that "every consequential contribution to *l'art moderne* has been made by revolutionary minds," he is being equally figurative.[43] In fact, one of the great debates about modernism in the arts has to do with whether its revolution has anything at all to do with the political revolutions of the twentieth century.[44] On the other hand, it is easy to consider the idea of revolution in terms that are too narrow and literal. According to Karl Marx's *The Communist Manifesto*, which may be prototypical for the artistic manifestos to follow, revolution in modern society is a chronic condition, since the "bourgeoisie cannot exist without constantly revolutionizing the instruments of production."[45] In a situation in which revolution is constant and pervasive, use of the term outside politics can hardly be considered illegitimate.

Still, it is more than a little ironic that one of the very first manifestos associating the art of modernity with revolution is by the composer Richard Wagner, who makes all the reactionary possibilities of the association plain. For Wagner, the perfect artwork of the classical past "cannot be *re-born*, but must be *born anew*."[46] A revolution is still a return, but in this case it is a single return, one meant to stop history at the very instant of its new beginning. Wagner's terminology is classical and not religious, but the pattern he preaches is the Christian pattern: having fallen away from Greek perfection, modern man is in a position to revive it in a state more perfect than that achieved by the Greeks themselves. Restitution means purification, not just of the degraded present but even of the classical past, which had failed in the Garden of Eden and thus lost the chance to achieve real paradise.

The newness thus promised is ominous — not just because it actually means a return to the past, and not even because it actually means the end of history and change, but also because it is itself a totality, more perfect than anything to be found in any age. This is particularly the case for Wagner, whose new man to come is one of those rooted, as Alain Badiou says, "in mythic totalities such as race, nation, earth, blood and soil."[47] But revolutionary change is always total and thus implicitly violent. In the history of the twentieth century, as Badiou also says, these implications have often been realized: "The new world is born under the sign of the torment and death of the innocent."[48] Even the purely intellectual revolution imagined by Kuhn is characterized, according to Stanley Cavell, by "violence and irreversible change."[49]

There is also another, much less dramatic possibility inherent in the figure of revolution. As Latour puts it in his sarcastic indictment of the nonmodernity of the twentieth century, conceiving of social forms as homogeneous totalities means that they "could not be touched unless they were totally revolutionized."[50] If this leads to massive crimes on one hand, it can also yield utter stasis on the other, as the impossibility of total change stands in the way of incremental change. For Latour, the modern tendency to think only in terms of revolutions or complete epistemological breaks results in the mystification of history, so that actual change is misunderstood and reform is bungled.[51] If the necessary totality of revolutionary change makes history itself into an impossible effort, though, it also turns the continuation of historical time into something of an embarrassment. The new dawn turns into an old dusk unless it is replaced by another new dawn. However, as Badiou says, this means the reinstatement of repetition, only in this case the repetition of revolution, as one avant-garde after another comes forward with "yet another radical doctrine of beginning."[52]

Badiou and Latour are not very much alike, and yet they agree pretty completely in this analysis of the ill effects of the revolutionary model of change as it has been applied in the modern period. It is, in fact, a fairly familiar indictment of a belief in radical novelty that leads to the constant, pointless churning of fashion, where complete and total change is so familiar it is hard to distinguish from blank routine. Criticism of this syndrome often includes, in the same breath, criticism of modernism as an aesthetic movement, as if modernism and revolutionary novelty were more or less identical. But this is not by any means the case, since modernist polemic figured the new in a number of ways, some of them quite distant from the model of revolution.

Zola once called the development of naturalism "an evolution in the human mind" that had revolution as its inevitable conclusion.[53] In this, he combines slow, incremental development with sudden, cataclysmic change in a way that anticipates Kuhn and Danto. He also generalizes the meaning of *evolution* so that it is not just a scientific belief but a general metaphor, and thus he anticipates the range of meanings the term was to have for artists and writers after him. Of course, evolution enters modernist polemic most obviously as it does the novels of Zola, in the form of Social Darwinism.[54] Even the poet Jean Moréas's conviction that symbolism will supplant Zola's naturalism depends on the notion that "each new phase in artistic evolution corresponds with the senile decrepitude, the ineluctable end of the school just before it" —a notion he shares with Zola.[55] But evolution also served as a much more general model, aligning the development of aesthetic form with that of biological structures. According to the manifesto "Art-Evolution," issued by the painter and art theorist Joaquín Torres García in 1917, "Art has to concur with the course of life. So we have to be evolutionists."[56] What this meant varied a lot from case to case. When the poet Pierre Reverdy speaks of cubism as a "new adapted means" of making art, he is consciously speaking in the context of evolution, but he is not being very specific at all.[57] However, when Kandinsky says that "necessity creates form" and uses the example of fish in "lightless depths" losing the sense of sight, he is consciously constructing a theory of art from ideas and examples traceable to Darwin.[58] The most peculiar of these evolutionary theories of art is almost certainly the one offered by Ezra Pound in his postscript to the symbolist poet and philosopher Remy de Gourmont's *Natural Philosophy of Love*. In Pound's version, it is not the genome but the "cerebral fluid" that tries "all sorts of experiments," forcing matter into "all sorts of forms" until it gives to insects their diligence, to birds the power of flight, and to human beings a perfected version of the impulse to experiment itself.[59]

As ridiculous as this may be, it is an eccentric version of an idea that Pound also pursued in a more serious way, an idea he shared with artists such as Le Corbusier, who believed in an aesthetic and technological version of natural selection that might be called "mechanical selection." It is by means of this principle that the innumerable novelties incidentally thrown up in the process of an industrialized life are whittled down to the few that work, which are also, Le Corbusier believed, the few that are beautiful: "Both natural selection and mechanical selection are manifestations of purification."[60]

The implications of the evolutionary model of artistic change and renewal are obviously very different from those of the revolutionary model. Instead of cataclysmic and total change, there is slow, steady, incremental advance. And the prototype for artistic novelty comes not from religion and politics but rather from science, so that the motives and practices that foster novelty seem completely different—rational and dispassionate instead of inspired. In this role, modernism wears a white coat, and potters among its test tubes. Apollinaire, with his interests in such advanced scientific concepts as the fourth dimension, was particularly fond of the notion that the "New Spirit" in the arts would naturally "keep pace with scientific and industrial progress."[61] This sentiment was shared by the futurists in their truly futuristic mode, with their faith in "the triumphant progress of science."[62] Modeled on scientific discovery as it is in such cases, modernist art also seems truly modern, forward looking and progressive, and without the implications of return that haunt the revolutionary alternative.

It is in this context that works of art and literature come to be thought of as experiments. Walter Pater speaks of the necessity of "curiously testing new opinions and courting new impressions," running each of these under the "microscope of thought"; but he is also resolutely opposed to any "idea or system," any discipline that might reduce this curious sampling to a scientific methodology.[63] Zola, on the other hand, is adamant about the "experimental method" of the novelist, and between them they seem to have defined the limits of the odd tendency in the modern period to think of artistic work as if it advanced by way of experiment.[64] Writing in 1926, Robert Graves tried to distinguish these two extremes, "a delicate alertness directed towards the discovery of something" and the rigid pursuit of novelty according to some predetermined system.[65] The problem with the latter, of course, is that it cannot lead to anything truly new. But this did not discourage the many writers and artists who believed that the study or the studio could be a laboratory, and that works of art could be controlled experiments.

Scientific discovery and technological invention thus become privileged metaphors for new developments in the arts. The novelist John Dos Passos says so quite emphatically in "The Writer as Technician," where "discovery, originality, invention" are even described as products.[66] The apparently very different Salvador Dali extolls the "limpid mechanical process" of invention first made possible by the camera, then to be emulated by the artist's eye itself.[67] The poet Vicente Huidobro anticipates Danto's account of the coming of modernism, with scientific invention as the process that replaces traditional mimesis: "Man no longer imitates. He invents, he adds to the facts of the world, born in Nature's breast, new facts born in his head: a poem, a painting, a statue, a steamer, a car, a plane."[68]

Huidobro includes in his manifesto a simple and forthright statement of the principle that for many artists and writers of this time turns aesthetic invention into a scientific method: "The study of art throughout history shows us very clearly this tendency of imitation to move toward creation in all human productions. We can establish a law of Scientific and Mechanical Selection equivalent to the law of Natural Selection."[69] The beauty of speed as Marinetti saw it, the constructivist ideal of geometric forms in space, the industrial purism of Le Corbusier and Fernand Léger, are all based on this notion that industrial progress works like the principle of natural selection, streamlining and eliminating the useless and unnecessary until it reveals the beautiful necessity. When Léger speaks of the "evolution of the automobile," then, he is being literal as well as metaphorical, because he believes in an inevitable tendency toward utility in industrial progress that produces pure form.[70] A great deal of the art of the twentieth century was produced in conscious analogy to this process. "In a spirit as taut as a compass," as the sculptors Naum Gabo and Antoine Pevsner put it, "we construct our work as the universe constructs its own, as the engineer constructs his bridges, as the mathematician his formula of the orbits."[71]

In this way, by manipulating basic, standardized units, aesthetic modernism discovered for itself the regime of novelty that had characterized the scientific method since the sixteenth century. As early as the painter James McNeill Whistler, modern art identified as its general medium the building blocks, the "elements, in color and form," to which aesthetic experience can be reduced. The artist, Whistler says, "is born to pick, and choose, and group with science, these elements, that the result may be beautiful."[72] In the case of movements such as cubism, these elements become explicit, and the art of painting becomes the act of developing "new structures with elements borrowed, for the most part, from visual reality."[73] In the twentieth century, the implications of the word *element* are much the same as they were in classical times, so that inevitably the basic units of aesthetic invention come to be thought of as letters in an alphabet. What the artist Theo van Doesburg says of the constructivist poet, who "makes himself a new language with the alphabet," is also true of the constructivist artist, who makes his new creations with an alphabet of basic geometric forms.[74]

The implications for the theory of novelty of this dedication to pure manipulation are acknowledged at the outset. Whistler admits the obvious fact that inventing a new letter is as impossible as inventing a new geometric solid: "Neither chemist nor engineer can offer new elements of the masterpiece."[75] What the artist invents, then, are new relations, new arrangements of preexisting forms. Sometimes, these relations might be wild, random, and unanticipated, like the "fantastic juxtapositions" that the painter Luigi Russolo predicted for futurist music.[76] Or, they might be cool and obvious, like the "exact plastic of pure relationship" that Piet Mondrian imagined as the basis of neoplasticism in painting.[77] Of course, the more rational and necessary these pure relations are, the more they come to seem as predetermined as the forms themselves, so that it might seem that the work of the artist is merely that of discovery and revelation: "The work of art will bring to light a new order inherent in things."[78] At this point, though, the novelty of the new order may begin to seem more than a bit tenuous.

At the very least, it should be obvious how much this version of the novelty of modernism differs from the kind imagined in its more revolutionary moments. Conceived as the rearrangement of elemental forms, novelty occurs in a time completely different from the abrupt and apocalyptic time of revolution. For Kandinsky, the creation of the modernist work is not so much a matter of revolt as it is an exercise in home economics: "Matter here is simply a kind of pantry from which the Spirit, like a cook, takes necessary ingredients." If this is the case, then invention must be a slow simmering, a patient waiting for "the necessary conditions for the ripening of a particular form."[79] With the organic rhythms of agriculture transferred, quite naturally, to the human rhythms of the kitchen, and then to those of the studio, artistic creation is gradual and slow.

There is also a necessary symmetry between the construction of the artwork, assembled as it is from many preexisting elements, and the construction of the artist, whose creativity comes to be seen not as an individual expression but as the expression of something latent in the collective to which the artist belongs. As the sociologist Niklas Luhmann explains it, the model of evolution makes it harder to think of innovation as the work of exceptional individuals—not so much because such individuals don't exist, but more because their difference comes to seem the natural variation always present in any large population. Given a large-enough sample set, the exceptional comes to have a certain kind of statistical normality.[80] Even if it is literally the work of individual genius, then, and not the result of some group effort, creative novelty is still the product of the whole population, which generates the new and different in the very process of maintaining its continuity.

A novelty that is relational in so many ways is also more likely to be seen as relative, not absolute. Franz Marc was not the only modernist to accept and admit this possibility. Even a movement with such an uncompromising name as suprematism might acknowledge its limitations in this respect: "Suprematism did not bring into being a new world of feeling but rather, an altogether new and direct form of representation of the world of feeling."[81] Or, as the poet and playwright Vladimir Mayakovsky put it in 1913: "The new can be not some object that is still unknown to everyone in our grey-haired world but a change in looking at relationships between objects."[82] In this way, Mayakovsky owns up to what is for many critics of modernism one of its most egregious failings, which is the tendency apparent in collage, in cinematic montage, in the stylistic pastiche of *Ulysses* and *The Waste Land*, the historical borrowings of Pound's *Cantos*, to let rearrangement stand in for creation. Modernism fails, according to this critique, because it is *not* revolutionary, because it does not break with the past but simply turns it into a "great jumble sale," as the philosopher and literary critic Georg Lukacs has it, to be rearranged into a slightly different version of its existing disorder.[83]

On one hand, then, the recombinant model of aesthetic novelty suffers from a fairly basic defect. Dali confesses it in what seems a guilty afterthought: "Let's trust in the new imaginative means, born from simple objective transpositions. Only the things we are capable of dreaming lack originality."[84] In other words, a merely relative novelty, a novelty of "transpositions," is not much of a novelty at all, and certainly not much like the grand transformation promised by revolution. Modernist programs that depend on recombination of some kind are therefore vulnerable precisely where their great prototype, evolutionary biology, has been vulnerable, in exactly defining the nature of the novelty that is supposed to be produced by recombination.

On the other hand, however, there are some clear advantages to the evolutionary model. Most particularly, it does not require a special explanation for the new and different, which can be derived from the same processes that a complex society uses to preserve its continuity. This is one of the reasons why the evolutionary model appeals to Luhmann, why it informs a relatively positive chapter in his account of the role of art in the social system of modernity. As he says, the "sheer quantity of operations" in a complex system such as a modern society "allows variations to occur on a gigantic scale."[85] Some of these variations survive, and it is by their influence in general that structures become more complex and also different.[86] The improbable, the new, arises as a function of the probable, and the dynamic emerges from stability and then reinforces it in a different state.

Novelty of this description is not really exceptional, and thus it need not be cataclysmic. Thus it avoids the horrific consequences attached to the revolutionary model by Badiou and Latour. Certainly, it would be a relief, after a century in which modernist ambitions have been routinely associated with the very worst in modern politics, to believe in Kandinsky's version of the artist, bustling about in the kitchen, mixing up a stew. Unfortunately, the evolutionary prototype stands behind Pound's obnoxious model of creativity, with its continuous upjetting of seminal fluid, just as much as it stands behind Kandinsky's. And there remains, on the other hand, the possibility that Lukacs is right, and that without any really reliable notion of the new, recombination is inherently conservative, simply an abstract version of the classic cliché about rearranging the deck chairs on the *Titanic*.

For better or worse, though, this is not in fact a choice that modernism presents. As some of the examples cited previously have suggested, pleas for revolution and statements of gradual, evolutionary change often occur in the same voice. Certain movements, such as constructivism, which favored recombinant techniques, also believed in the necessity of revolution. Even Kandinsky's Abstract Spirit, ripening slowly over time, reaches a moment in which change must be total. Novelty, in other words, is not the simplest but rather one of the most complex features of aesthetic modernism, and the desire for the new did not always bring

clarity of purpose to the movement but often complexity and ambivalence. Most of all, concentration on the new tended to reveal the inherent impossibility of ever finding it in a pure state, uncompromised by a
return to the old, unadulterated by pastiche and rearrangement. Much of
this complexity is to be found, in fact, in what is the most popular expression of modernism's claims of novelty, one that appeals so universally because it seems so simple, being only three words long.

MAKE IT NEW

It should not be necessary to argue at any length that the slogan Make It
New is the most durably useful of all modernist expressions of the value
of novelty. In certain accounts, such as Gay's *Modernism: The Lure of
Heresy*, these three words are assumed to sum up most of what modernism stands for: "In short, modernists considered Ezra Pound's famous
injunction, 'Make It New!,' a professional, almost a sacred obligation."[87]
Scholars as eminent and yet as utterly different from one another as
Richard Rorty, Frank Lentricchia, Jackson Lears, Fredric Jameson, and
David Damrosch have used this phrase to make various points about
modern life, art, or literature.[88] Some of these citations are vague and
atmospheric, even anonymous, as the slogan is often used without specific reference to Pound. But this is perhaps an additional tribute to his
influence, as the slogan has become so ubiquitous as to have lost its
trademark status, like Kleenex or the Xerox copy.

The actual genealogy of the phrase "Make It New" has been established by Pound scholars and is well known to those among them who
specialize in Pound's relation to China, but it is so often misdated and
for that matter misquoted (tagged with a spurious exclamation mark)
that its genesis is worth recounting in some detail. The crucial fact to
begin with is that the phrase is not originally Pound's at all. The source
is a historical anecdote concerning Ch'eng T'ang (Tching-thang, Tching
Tang), first king of the Shang dynasty (1766–1753 BC), who was said to
have had a washbasin inscribed with this inspirational slogan.[89] According to the sinologist James Legge, it is not a commonly told anecdote,[90]
but Pound was fortunate enough to have found it in two sources: the *Da
Xue* (Ta Hio), first of the four books of Confucian moral philosophy, and

the *T'ung-Chien Kang-Mu*, a classic digest and revision of an even older classic Chinese history. That Pound coincidentally found the same uncommon anecdote in two different places may be explained by the fact that both texts were prepared by the neo-Confucian scholar Chu Hsi (1130–1200 AD), who has perhaps the best claim as true originator of the slogan Make It New.[91]

Pound first became interested in the Confucian texts in October 1913, at about the time he received from the widow of the art historian Ernest Fenollosa the materials that would lead to *Cathay* and *The Chinese Written Character as a Medium for Poetry*. Inspired by the poet Allen Upward, who had published some translations from the *Analects* in the *New Freewoman*, Pound started reading Confucius, first in Upward's English selection and then in more complete versions in French.[92] Sometime in the later 1920s, he began preparing his own translation of the *Da Xue* (Ta Hio), a text that Legge had called *The Great Learning*. It seems clear that at least toward the end of his work on this text, Pound had a copy of Legge's English version, almost certainly in an edition that included the Chinese original.[93] For reasons of his own, however, he chose to work primarily from the French version he had owned for some time: M. G. Pauthier, *Confucius et Mencius: Les quatres livres de philosophie morale et politique de la Chine*, published in Paris in various editions beginning in the 1850s.

Pound's translation of the *Da Xue*, entitled *Ta Hio: The Great Learning, Newly Rendered into the American Language*, was published by Glenn Hughes as a University of Washington Bookstore Chapbook in 1928. As is explained in an opening note to this translation, the *Da Xue* is the first of the traditional Four Books of Confucian wisdom, but only the very first part of the *Da Xue* itself is attributed to Confucius (only forty-six characters in the original, Pound adds in an interpolated comment).[94] The bulk of the work comprises commentary and annotations by a disciple that Pound calls, after Pauthier's French, Tsheng-tseu. It is in these annotations, further refined themselves by the subsequent editing of Chu Hsi, that the first published version of Make It New is to be found.

The subject of the *Da Xue* (Ta Hio) at this point is good government, which is to be achieved by renewing the virtues of the sovereign and enlightening the people. As an illustrative anecdote, Tseng Tze (Tsheng-tseu), the commentator, notes the story of King Ch'eng T'ang (Tching-thang), who was said to have a bathtub or washbasin with the following inscription engraved on it:

Renouvelle-toi complétement chaque jour; fais-le de nouveau, encore de *nouveau*, et toujours de *nouveau*. (Pauthier's French)[95]
If you can one day renovate yourself, do so from day to day. Yea, let there be daily renovation. (Legge's English)[96]
Renovate, dod gast you, renovate! (Pound's American)[97]

Pound's version has at least the virtue of brevity, but he spoils the effect somewhat by adding a long footnote, which actually translates the French again: "Pauthier with greater elegance gives in his French the equivalent to: 'Renew thyself daily, utterly, make it new, and again new, make it new.'"[98] "Make it new" actually seems a fairly willful translation of "fais-le de nouveau," which might just as easily be rendered "do it again." Had Pound translated it so, the whole history of modernist scholarship would presumably have been quite different. Moreover, "make it new" seems to remove the reflexive sense present in all these translations and thus to turn the aphorism away from its obvious topic of self-renovation.[99] But Pound is clearly a little transfixed by the italicized *nouveau*, attracted to it and oblivious to the possibility that its force might not be augmented but rather diluted by repetition. In any case, his footnote also shows another influence when it refers to a second translator, who testifies that "the character occurs five times during this passage." In his excitement, Pound neglects to tell us *which* character, but the translator he is referring to here is Legge, who says in his commentary on this passage that "the character 'new,' 'to renovate,' occurs five times."[100] Additionally, Pound's footnote goes on to make it clear that he has an edition of Legge with the Chinese, for he maintains that "the pictures (verse 1) are: sun renew sun sun renew (like a tree-shoot) again sun renew."[101] In other words, Pound has identified the Chinese character that Legge translates as "new," "to renovate," and has allowed it to drive his footnoted retranslation. When Pound's *Ta Hio* was republished by Stanley Nott in 1936, it included this character, *xin* (hsin), in the place of pride on the title page.

It is actually this character, sometimes with its companion, *jih*, the

character that Pound took to represent the sun, that is included sporadi-
cally in his later work. Usually, the Chinese is shadowed somewhere in
the text by an English equivalent, though Pound is not always very care-
ful to link the two securely together. But he never publishes the English
without the Chinese, which is to say that he always represents his phrase
as a translation of the motto of an ancient Chinese nobleman. In short,
Pound does not offer Make It New as his own words or in his own voice.
It is a historical artifact of some interest, to be sure, but it is not to be
understood out of context, as if it were being delivered by Pound himself
to the present-day reader of Pound's own text. One of the main reasons
to keep this context in mind, even now, is that it restores the full complexity of Make It New, which is in fact a dense palimpsest of historical
ideas about the new.

Even the oldest and most basic layer, that of the original Chinese, is not
simple or undifferentiated, since the *Da Xue* (Ta Hio) as Pound came to it
was the product of neo-Confucian interpretation of a text compiled from
various sources. But Pound clearly felt that he had found in this ancient
text a model of novelty that was itself ancient and even foundational. The
Chinese indicates, as he says in the relevant footnote to his first translation of the *Da Xue*, "daily organic vegetable and orderly renewal." Thus
his notion that the character for "renew" is to be glossed with the modification "like a tree shoot."[102] Regardless of whether this is actually to be
found in the Chinese, it does correspond to the most ancient definitions
of novelty available in Europe, which were based on the obvious models
in nature. One of the innumerable possible examples of this conventional
notion is to be found in Ovid: "Ever inventive nature continuously produces one shape from another. Nothing in the entire universe ever per-
ishes, believe me, but things vary and adopt a new form."[103]

This very ancient version of novelty, if it is in the Chinese text at all,
does not come to Pound directly but as mediated through the interpretations of the first English translation he turned to, that of James Legge. In
helping Pound to discover an organic model of novelty in his text, Legge
also layers over that another and slightly more recent one. A Christian
missionary as well as a scholar of Chinese, Legge believed, almost as an
article of faith, that the wisdom to be found in the Confucian classics
could be related to that in the Christian scriptures. The Bible in fact be-

came his model for the organization and interpretation of what were called the Five Classics and the Four Books, which Legge saw related to one another as Old to New Testament.[104] It is not at all odd, then, that his version of the *Da Xue* (Ta Hio) should often sound a lot like the King James Bible. His version of Ch'eng T'ang's bathtub inscription, which reads, "If you can one day renovate yourself, do so from day to day. Yea, let there be daily renovation," seems to have been based at least in part on 2 Corinthians 4:16: "Though our outward man perish, yet the inward man is renewed day by day." In fact, Pound's own formula, seemingly so simple and so modern, is constantly anticipated in the New Testament, especially Revelation 21:5, which promises, "Behold, I make all things new."

Pound's own Presbyterian background may be at work here, as well as the influence of Legge's translation. In any case, what happens is that a new layer is added to the base model of organic change occasioned by the Chinese original. The model on this layer, Christian rebirth, is based on that of organic change but brings with it certain significant differences. As the medievalist Gerhart Ladner explains it, when Paul uses terms such as *neos* to describe the "new man" to be achieved in Christian conversion, he not only introduces a significant religious concept but also changes the meaning of the term *new*.[105] What had ordinarily been used in a merely temporal sense, often with a pejorative connotation, now acquires a meliorative and redemptive significance. Though the basic concepts of renewal, regeneration, and rebirth all imply a return to some earlier state, Christian theologians defined these terms so that they could also mean return to something better than what had existed before. Thus humankind need not merely return to the state of nature, even in its perfect form in Eden, but to a resemblance to the creator even truer and closer than that of Adam. Thus Paul says in 2 Corinthians, "If any man be in Christ, he is a new creature: old things are passed away; behold, all things are become new," implying that the new does not just return to but also surpasses and supplants the old.

The fact that Pound left the Presbyterian Church far behind as he moved through the avant-garde movements of Europe does not necessarily mean that the echoes of the New Testament in Make It New are merely verbal. His own most constant model of change, that of renaissance, begins with and is based on the two earlier versions of novelty.

The dependence of this model on that of organic change is obvious in the term itself. When Pound's favorite Renaissance theorist, Jacob Burck-hardt, speaks of "the resuscitation of antiquity," he brings out a latent link between the notion of rebirth and that of resurrection.[106] As Ladner puts it, the metaphorical meaning of *renasci* is closely linked to horticulture, to the new growth that sprouts from the act of pruning, a meaning that is expanded in Christian times to relate to spiritual rebirth, "with conno-tations which could range all the way from vegetative to cosmological re-newal."[107] Consequently, when Pound chooses *Make It New* as the title for his collection of essays on the troubadours, Elizabethan classicists, and translators of Greek, he is being consistent with the tradition of cultural rediscovery and rebirth exemplified by the Italian Renaissance. In the later cantos, where he tends to attach the Chinese characters so closely to quotations from and references to Ocellus that it is easy to imagine that this ancient Greek philosopher is actually a Confucian sage, Pound is re-imagining the *Da Xue* (Ta Hio) as if it were the first in a series of spiritual bursts of light, flashing again and again as ancient learning is revived by one renaissance after another.

Even the more sinister applications that Pound developed for the motto have a significant relationship to this history. In 1935, Stanley Nott published *Jefferson and/or Mussolini*, one of whose many subtitles was *Fascism as I Have Seen It*. In this text, Pound summarizes the *Da Xue* (Ta Hio) in two pages, including again the Chinese characters. In this case, he translates the characters as "Make it new, make it new as the young grass shoot."[108] But he also includes a footnote, which claims that the first ideogram, *xin* (hsin) or "renew," "shows the fascist axe for the clear-ing away of rubbish."[109] This vivid pictographic interpretation is derived from a Chinese dictionary, compiled by the Protestant missionary Robert Morrison, that Pound had owned since 1915. Morrison gave Pound the idea that the right-hand side of the *xin* (hsin) character represented a "hatchet," shown hacking away at the wood supposedly represented on the left.[110] It was Pound's own inventiveness that associated the ancient Chinese hatchet with the Fascist axe and his own increasingly vindictive hatred of complications that provided the rubbish, which is not present in the Chinese original.

Pound had in fact taken his slogan quite a way from its Chinese origins, which emphasized the necessity of self-renewal, not the forced renewal of others, and he had removed it even farther from any association with avant-garde agitation. The renovation demanded by the slogan was now the dictator Benito Mussolini's "rivoluzione continua," and the "rubbish" to be cleared away was not excess verbiage but a whole people.[111] What appears to be a paradox in the Fascist slogan of "rivoluzione continua" is in fact the remains of the earliest meaning of *revolution* preserved within a modern travesty of it. At this time, Pound begins to show particular interest in the "young grass shoot" supposedly represented in the *Da Xue* (Ta Hio) because it resonated with parts of the Italian Fascist program, but he also asserts and exaggerates its presence because it ties Mussolini's drastic plans for Italy back to an apparently natural process of destruction and renewal. The "continual" or constant nature of the revolution thus appears as part of the older meaning of the term, in which *revolution* merely meant a complete turn in the course of events.

With this history, running from ancient China to Fascist Italy back in place, Make It New can be seen to imply a complete history of the concept of novelty. Of course, the explicit emphasis of this history is on models of recurrence, from organic renewal to Fascist revolution, and there is no doubt that Pound felt the appeal of the total transformation that such models promise. But it is also hard to miss the fact that Pound's actual practice in his successive repetitions of this slogan is one of quotation and combination. Pound habitually worked by arranging and rearranging certain bits of knowledge that had been canonized within his own idiosyncratic system, and the ancient Chinese saying is but one of many nodes in this system, attracting to itself over the years bits of Mussolini and bits of Neoplatonism and even bits of modern anthropology. The form, then, of Make It New is recombinant, as it comes to signify a whole anthology of Pound's efforts and interests. As he says himself in "The Serious Artist," major poets "heap together and arrange and harmonize the results of many men's labour. This very faculty for amalgamation is a part of their genius."[112]

The most significant fact to emerge from this history, though, is also the most obvious: Make It New was not itself new, nor was it ever meant to be. Given the nature of the novelty implied by the slogan, it is appropriate that it is itself the result of historical recycling. This was a fact that

Pound himself always tried to keep in the forefront by using the original Chinese characters and letting his own translation tag along as a perpetual footnote. The complex nature of the new—its debt, even as revolution, to the past, and the way in which new works are often just recombinations of traditional elements—is not just confessed by this practice but insisted on. This is what makes the slogan exemplary of the larger modernist project, that by insisting on the new it brings to the surface all the latent difficulties in what seems such a simple and simplifying concept. It was only later, as critics and scholars tended to the endgame of modernism, that the new was simplified again, a process in which Make It New was to play a crucial role.

THE MAKING OF MAKE IT NEW

Make It New is now such common shorthand for modernist novelty that it is easy to assume that it was always so. Yet these three words did not appear in Pound's work, it should be remembered, until 1928, well after the appearance of the major works of modernist art and literature, and the words did not become a slogan until some considerable time after that. Just how utterly obscure the phrase remained even in the middle 1930s is evident in the reaction at Faber when Pound proposed it as the title for a collection of essays. Eliot informed him that Faber was not "altogether happy about your new title MAKE IT NOO we may have missed subtle literary allusion but if we do I reckon genl public will also."[113] The general public did miss the allusion and, in fact, the larger significance of Pound's reference, which quite escaped the reviewers when the collection appeared. Of thirteen contemporary reviews of *Make It New* consulted for this study, only two so much as mention the title, and both make it the target of sarcastic comment.[114]

In fact, it seems safe to say that no particular significance was attached to Make It New until 1950, when Hugh Kenner called attention to its reappearance in a new translation that Pound had prepared of the *Da Xue* (Ta Hio), which he now called *The Great Digest*. When Kenner notices "the 'Make It New' injunction in the *Great Digest*,"[115] not only does he pick this phrase out of the welter of Pound's prose for the first time, but he also nominates it for the role it was later to play. Even here, though, Kenner refers to the "injunction" not as Pound's but as belonging to the

Great Digest; and when he glosses the injunction, he links it not to imagism or free verse or insurrectionary art in general but to "Pound's translating activities."[116] Thus the emphasis is not on novelty at all but rather on "the sense of historical recurrence that informs the *Cantos*."[117] Even at this stage, though it had at last been recognized as an "injunction" of sorts, Make It New had not acquired either the meaning or the status that now seems inevitable.

Only six years later, the literary critic Philip Rahv refers in the *Kenyon Review* to "the well-known avant-garde principle of 'make it new.'"[118] Somehow, in the course of these few years, the quotation that had been obscure even to Eliot in 1934 and that had meant "recurrence" to Kenner in 1950 has become the all-purpose label for modernist novelty. In the course of the later 1950s and the early 1960s, writers for the literary quarterlies would make it into a catchphrase. The literary critic and theorist Northrop Frye, for example, writing in the *Hudson Review* in 1957, associated the "anti-'poetic' quality in Stevens" with "his determination to make it new, in Pound's phrase."[119] The literary scholar Roy Harvey Pearce, writing in the same journal two years later, said that any American attempting an epic poem "would indeed have, in Pound's phrase, to make it new."[120] By 1966, the literary critic Marvin Mudrick had turned the phrase into a single word: "make-it-new."[121] Writing in these years and in these journals, literary scholars such as Roy Harvey Pearce and Richard Ellmann established a dogmatic belief in "Pound's determination to make it new,"[122] and by way of Pound an association of modernism with novelty per se.

In the course of this remarkably brief transformation, Pound's three-word phrase loses its ancient Chinese context, its debt to the devotional program of Legge, and its involvement in Mussolini's Fascism. The bibliographical facts of its appearance in Pound's work are so thoroughly obscured that it becomes possible for scholars such as Peter Gay and Alfred Appel to misplace it to 1914, where it can seem influential and even foundational instead of obscure.[123] In the process, the role of novelty in the development of aesthetic modernism is distorted, and the nature of novelty itself is simplified. The vast array of different positions that can be identified among the practitioners of modern art and literature shrinks to the size of a simple, three-word slogan, and the complex history of novelty is subtracted even from that, so that modernism loses a crucial part of the debt to tradition that it owes, paradoxically, through its devotion to the new.

One of the reasons this happens in this particular way, it seems certain, is the sheer passage of time and the requirement of retrospective accounts of modernism for a quick and easy version of its defining characteristic. But this also happens, it is interesting to note, at just the time Kuhn was publishing *The Structure of Scientific Revolutions* and Danto was using his ideas in an effort to assimilate the Pop art of Andy Warhol. Pound's translated phrase achieves its canonization as a modernist slogan at this crucial moment, it seems, because novelty is being redefined under a certain amount of pressure. The aging and presumptive passing of modernism lead to a crisis in the concept of novelty that is felt and fought out at just this time.

MODERNIST NOVELTY AND THE NEO-AVANT-GARDE

7

TRADITION OF THE NEW?

By the time Make It New finally became a catchphrase, in the late 1950s and early 1960s, the sheer persistence of novelty itself in twentieth-century art and literature had come to seem something of a problem. As Harold Rosenberg put it in 1959: "The famous modern 'break with tradition' has lasted long enough to have produced its own tradition. . . . The new cannot become a tradition without giving rise to unique contradictions, myths, absurdities— often, creative absurdities."[1] Just a few months later, the literary critic Lionel Trilling delivered the first version of a lecture to be published in *Partisan Review* in 1961, as "On the Modern Element in Modern Literature." Trilling's concern, the teaching of modern literature, was rather different from Rosenberg's, but the cause of anxiety was much the same: "The process by which the radical and subversive work becomes the classic work" and what happens to the very notion of modernist subversion when it becomes an accepted part of the orthodox curriculum.[2] Both critics are troubled by the paradox immortalized in the title of Rosenberg's book, *The Tradition of the New*. Both wonder how the new can persist in the arts without wearing out its welcome.[3]

Questions like these were at the heart of the contest in the 1960s between a modernism just then being brought into high definition and the artists who aimed to supplant it. In these years, several still-influential accounts of modernism were first published: Clement Greenberg's *Art and Culture* in 1961; the art historian and critic Michael Fried's "Modernist Painting" in 1964; and Stanley Cavell's "Aesthetic Problems of Modern Philosophy" in 1965. But this was also the time of Arthur Danto's "Artworld" essay, first published in 1964, which was meant to mark the end of the very movement that Greenberg, Fried, and Cavell were in the process of solidifying. For both arguments, the model of historical change offered by Kuhn in 1962 was useful: it appears implicitly in the structure of Danto's argument, and it is cited explicitly by Fried and by Cavell, who was a friend and colleague of Kuhn's.[4] The example of *The Structure of Scientific Revolutions* was so important to these other writers because the midcentury struggle over generational change in the arts was also a debate about the nature of novelty and its status after fifty years of modernism.

The rough shape of this debate is apparent in the controversy, still rather lively, over Fried's decision to open his essay "Art and Objecthood" (1967) with a quotation from the eighteenth-century theologian Jonathan Edwards: "It is certain with me that the world exists anew every moment; that the existence of things every moment ceases and is every moment renewed."[5] On one level, this is Fried's version of Make It New, drawn from the same Christian model of renewal that motivates Legge's translations of Pound's Chinese source. And there has always been a great deal of irate opposition to the quasi-religious tone of what follows, especially the pious assurance that "presentness is grace." The unfriendly response to Fried's argument is, in part, that it preaches an ahistorical stillness in which change is impossible.[6] In placing so much emphasis on renewal, though, Fried is also using Edwards to offer a particular definition of novelty, to give it a traditionally circular shape that guarantees its continued existence and relevance. Recasting the new in the form of renewal is the time-honored way of resolving the apparent conflict between tradition and novelty, of forming them into an interdependent system that sustains itself. In this sense, Edwards is not so far from Kuhn, to whom Fried also appeals at this time.[7]

What Fried's epigraph contains, then, is one solution to the crisis identified by Rosenberg and Trilling. Tradition and the new need not be at odds, and there can be a tradition *of* the new, if history assumes the shape determined for it by the Christian model of reform to a better state, which is the model at the base of later revolutionary solutions such as Kuhn's. In fact, a great deal of writing about modernism and the art to follow is still conditioned by a version of this model worked out in the 1960s, one founded on fairly narrow grounds by Greenberg and then modified by reference to Cavell and, through him, to Kuhn and Wittgenstein.[8]

What is currently believed about modernism as a general movement in the arts is still largely dependent on the work of these few years at mid-century. Moreover, the relationship between the historical avant-garde, modernism, and what the literary critic Peter Bürger damned as the neo-avant-garde is still understood in terms established at this time.[9] Thus the basic positions of Greenberg and Fried, especially in relation to the status of art and its autonomy in modern society, are almost painfully familiar.[10] It may still be possible, though, to reread much of this material in the context of the actual tradition of the new, the history of solutions to the problems of novelty, and thus to understand in a different way the contest between the theorists of modernism and the artists of the neo-avant-garde. It should also be easier, then, to see the 1960s as a major episode in the history of novelty itself, a time when concerted thought about the status of art returned novel solutions to puzzles that had existed since the beginnings of organized thought.

GREENBERG AND THE STRUCTURE
OF ARTISTIC REVOLUTIONS

Clement Greenberg still compels the respect of critics and scholars, though most of his influence has evaporated, because he could make a convincing case for the new art of his time. He did this, in part, by explaining and justifying "those features that counted as new in the postwar art he admired," most particularly the "allover" quality exemplified by Jackson Pollock's famous drip paintings.[11] And it also seems clear that Greenberg admired such techniques *because* they were new. He was consistent throughout his career in insisting that the important art of any time is that "which wins new experience for human beings,"[12] and that the best art of any time is the new art, which is best precisely because it does in some way what art before it had not done.[13] But Greenberg had high standards in this respect, as in all others, and he found it fairly easy to differentiate the truly new from what he frequently damned as mere "novelty."[14]

In fact, the distinction between *new* and *novelty* becomes one of the most important in a career dedicated to making distinctions. It appears at the very outset, in Greenberg's differentiation between the avant-garde and kitsch, which is also his differentiation between the "genuinely new" and the spuriously new.[15] And it becomes something of an *idée fixe* in Greenberg's later years, when he hit on "Novelty Art" as an all-purpose dismissal of the contemporary art he did not like. In one sense, novelty art is art that is self-consciously aimed at newness for its own sake, and in another sense it is new art that has outstayed its welcome, art in which the impulse to change has degenerated into fashion.[16] In other words, novelty is the new become routine, habitual, old, and so the problem represented for Greenberg by the specter of novelty is the same one identified by Rosenberg and Trilling: the continuation in time of an art defined by its difference from the past. Greenberg, like Pound, defined modernism as news that stays new, and thus he had to work out how staying new could be distinguished from simply staying.

The model that Greenberg devises for the proper newness that defines important art is quite similar to the model that Kuhn was to make so famous, but this is not the result of influence, nor is it mere coincidence. A good deal can be explained by the fact that Greenberg's foundational assumptions about the creation of art are highly similar to Kuhn's in regard to scientific investigation. For Greenberg, there is simply no such thing as art created in perfect freedom, by purely spontaneous methods.[17] Art is "impossible without the observance of norms and conventions,"[18] just as science for Kuhn is unimaginable outside a paradigm. In Greenberg's usage, though, norms and conventions are primarily formal and have their basis in the physical requirements of a particular medium. Conventions are restrictive, to be sure, but only because, on a more fundamental level, they are constitutive: the combination of pigment and a flat support determines what is to count as the activity of painting.

If norms and conventions are not just socially or psychologically restrictive but also logically definitive, then it is hard to see how very much novelty can fit in. Greenberg's response to this conundrum is to postulate a kind of art so much like Kuhn's normal science that it might almost be called "normal painting." The paradigms of a particular kind of art having been established, workers within a paradigm proceed to tidy up loose ends and solve remaining problems. The impressionists and post-impressionists, for example, "left behind many loose threads the tying up of which has provided later artists with tasks whose performance asks more than unadventurous repetition."[19] Despite the rather backhanded phrasing, Greenberg genuinely sees this as creative work. Even Matisse clarifies and perfects what was left implicit by Gauguin.[20] And cubism, according to Greenberg, succeeds in part because Cézanne offered it "all the resources of a new discovery without requiring that much effort be spent in the process itself of discovery."[21]

Problem-solving art of this kind can be creative, but only in a particular way. The novelty achieved in times of "normal painting" is often to be found mainly in the aggregate — not as much in the individual effort as in the combined achievements of a school or movement.[22] Greenberg came to dislike the notion of experimental art, perhaps because it sounded too much like trial and error, but he did feel that the production of valid and interesting art within a healthy paradigm could be almost automatic.[23] Artists use the generative conventions left them by some great precursor, working through their implications and producing new art in a steady, incremental, and unspectacular way. In fact, it is characteristic of "normal painting" as it of Kuhn's normal science to resist fundamental innovation. Even painters such as Picasso and Matisse were, according to Greenberg, "reluctant innovators, cherishing the very conventions they felt themselves forced to go against."[24]

How does it happen that certain artists are compelled to invent, to break with the convention that has heretofore defined the very activity of art? In Kuhn's model, the accumulation of anomalies ultimately topples the paradigm, and though it does not seem very likely that anomalies can exist in the world of art, something similar must happen in Greenberg's version of things, since he sees artists as constantly discriminating between essential and unnecessary or spurious conventions.[25] Whatever is dispensable and useless in convention is rejected so that art can continue within the confines of a newly validated paradigm. This is the revolutionary moment in Greenberg's model of aesthetic innovation.

For Greenberg, revolution once had a literal significance within a roughly Marxist theory of art and society, and it functioned for him thereafter, as it did for many artists, as a useful and impressive rhetorical trope. In the space of a few years, he speaks of the revolutions fomented by impressionism, by Cézanne, and by the School of Paris.[26] In his later years, though, he became rather cranky about the whole idea of revolutionary art, and he complained about the absurdity of anointing every new turn "as a revolutionary break with the past."[27] But this is not perhaps as inconsistent as it may seem, for even when Greenberg was himself anointing various movements as revolutionary, he did not mean that they were breaking with the past. He silently restores to *revolution* its original and more literal sense, so that it means a dramatic return to a prior state, or, as in the Christian model, to a more perfect version of that state.[28]

In its revolutionary moments, then, art does not really break with the past, as it may appear to, but returns to it in a spirit of "rediscovery" and "revaluation."[29] The purpose of revolution is "to establish a new order, not anarchy,"[30] or, as the art theorist and critic Thierry de Duve puts it, "to seal a new pact around the broken one."[31] It is in this sense that Greenberg is able to make the apparently preposterous claim that modernism "remains continuous with the past."[32] "The Case for Abstract Art," as he says in the famous essay of that name, is that it confirms "instead of subverting tradition,"[33] and he is not just putting on a brave face for the readership of the *Saturday Evening Post* or compromising beliefs from the old days when he had thought of modern art as truly revolutionary. For the purpose of revolution is, as Greenberg sees it, to confirm a tradition that is actually sounder than it has ever been, now that the avant-garde has purged from it those conventions that are faulty or inessential.

In fact, it can sometimes seem as though revolutionary time runs backward for Greenberg. In his later years as an active critic, he did become fond of the term *devolution*, which he used to describe a historical arc in which Manet's reaching back to Velasquez leads through a series of stages until Mondrian finally arrives "back where the Renaissance began."[34] The formal counterpart of this history in reverse is the rigorous process of reduction, by which everything inessential is gradually removed from painting until artists finally find what they cannot do without: the blank support itself. This takes a fairly long time, according to

Greenberg, because painting has so many inessential conventions to dispose of—which is perhaps why there is a history of art at all.[35]

Greenberg's understanding of the shape of innovation in the arts therefore differs from Kuhn's similar theory of science in a couple of important ways: it is teleological where Kuhn's is not; and that teleological process leads backward through history, whereas science, as Kuhn sees it, does not regress. Where Greenberg sounds most like Kuhn, though, is in the curiously symbiotic relationship he discerns between "normal," problem-solving art and its revolutionary counterpart. For the purpose of revolution in both cases is to reestablish the paradigms that nourish and sustain "normal" work. When Greenberg arrived at a compact explanation of the whole cycle late in his life, it had all the inevitability of cliché: "A tradition of art keeps itself alive by more or less constant innovation."[36] Behind the banality, however, lies the somewhat more surprising notion that the effect of novelty is to maintain convention, which at the very least makes it difficult to see where the novelty comes from in the first place.

The model of artistic innovation that Greenberg presented in piecemeal fashion in the essays collected as *Art and Culture* in 1961 thus resembles in some intriguing ways the model of scientific discovery that Kuhn published as a coherent theory in 1962—though there was apparently no actual contact between the two men. Some of the overlap between the two accounts might be explained by Greenberg's general envy of the rigor of science and his specific belief in an "affinity between the new style in the visual arts and modern physical science."[37] Some critics have also argued that Greenberg owes an intellectual debt to the same logical positivism from which Kuhn emerged, and which he was originally seen to have challenged from within.[38] Farther off in the background for both men, though, is the example of evolution, which is surely the master template for all later models that link recurrence and recombination together in a recursive system, and to which Greenberg refers in both casual and pointed ways.[39] But the notion that "history is creative, always evolving novelty out of itself"[40] has a broader and more general reference than Darwin, for the recursive development of the new out of the old is one of the solutions to the problem of novelty that has persisted long enough to become part of tradition itself.

In his own context in the world of the arts, and especially that within which *Art and Culture* was first published, Greenberg's model of the new must have appealed, because it addressed the very conundrum identified by Rosenberg and Trilling. In Greenberg's analysis, an institutionalized modernism is not only not a contradiction in terms; it is a logical fulfillment of the purposes of artistic innovation. At the same time, he showed how it might be possible to square the revolutionary rhetoric of some modern artists with the purely technical reorganization of others, thereby gathering into one more or less coherent bundle all the wildly different ambitions to different kinds of newness inherent in the very different groups of artists active in the first half of the twentieth century. In short, Greenberg helped to establish the category of modernism by codifying one of its most important defining characteristics.

CAVELL'S MODERNISM

Though Greenberg and Kuhn published their most prominent works just a year apart, and though many readers in the early 1960s must have picked up both of these influential books, they do not seem to have been discussed in the same conversations, except perhaps by one or two with accidental connections to both men. When Stanley Cavell turned his thoughts to modern art in the early 1960s, it was partly in response to Greenberg, whose criticism he had been "assigned" to read by Michael Fried.[41] More or less respectful references to Greenberg show up in Cavell's published work as early as 1967,[42] though he was to speak of himself some forty years later as having been dissatisfied with Greenberg's ideas from the first.[43] For many reasons, he was much more likely to be sympathetic to Kuhn, with whom he had been a virtual collaborator in the late 1950s, when they were both young professors at Berkeley.[44] Kuhn is credited by Cavell with having forced a rewriting of his influential essay, "Must We Mean What We Say?"[45] And Kuhn pays a moving tribute to Cavell in the preface to *The Structure of Scientific Revolutions*, where he calls him "the only person with whom I have been able to explore my ideas in incomplete sentences."[46]

One of the ideas they explored together was that of the paradigm, which Kuhn had found in the work of Wittgenstein, where it bothered him for two different reasons: because it seemed to qualify freedom of thought by confining it within a particular context, and because it seemed to undermine the objectivity of science by putting all contexts on the same footing, with no independent way of deciding between them.[47] Cavell was to devote a good deal of his later work as a philosopher to elucidating what he tried to explain to Kuhn then, how the later philosophy of Wittgenstein resolves these issues. For Wittgenstein, as Cavell explains it, paradigms are not mere conventions in a social sense, meant to constrict or control behavior. They are like the rules of grammar or the criteria used in judging the appropriateness of human behavior, "forms I rely upon in making sense."[48] To focus on what they prohibit is to miss the much larger fact of what they make possible, as if the limitation of the base paths in baseball to ninety feet were a restriction on the freedom of the runner. It is true, of course, that the runner may not proceed indefinitely into the outfield without being tagged and possibly humiliated, but the fact that he may not do so is one of the things that make his running purposeful and therefore desirable in the first place.

The rules that determine what can and can't be done, what can and can't be thought, are therefore not merely restrictive, though they are that, but also constitutive and therefore enabling. They are "human forms of life which alone provide the coherence of our expression."[49] Cavell takes the phrase "forms of life" directly from Wittgenstein's *Philosophical Investigations*, where the examples are drawn from language, from the implicit grammar that Wittgenstein painfully teased out of everyday expressions.[50] Since this grammar is worked out in practice, it is variable and open to change. The standards that constitute a "form of life" must have been established by some sort of agreement, though an implicit and improvised one, and therefore they are, by definition, subject to contestation and even repudiation.[51] Just exactly how this might happen—how a rule or criterion that is constitutive of a particular practice might be changed from within that practice—is still a bit of a mystery in Cavell and in Wittgenstein. The amount of work that it takes in *Philosophical Investigations* just to bring a grammatical rule to full attention is such as to make purposeful change seem very difficult. In Kuhn's account of science, of course, such change is rare and traumatic enough to warrant the term *revolution*.

Nonetheless, Cavell's adaptations of Wittgenstein's later philosophy bring into the midcentury discussion of modernism and modern art a significantly different model of novelty. When Greenberg describes the problem-solving work of "normal" painting, he often makes it sound like the mere rearrangement of preexisting parts. He even uses the phrase "atom units" in discussing the logic of impressionism.[52] In this he harks back, almost certainly without knowing it, to the model first offered in the *Theaetetus* of a combinatorial novelty based on the example of the alphabet. As Wittgenstein came to see it, this model was also the precursor of the logical atomism of the *Tractatus*, with its belief that thought could be reduced to a few "primary elements."[53] In the *Investigations*, Wittgenstein is harshly dismissive of this idea, "for experience certainly does not show us these elements."[54] Language does not extend itself merely by rearranging elements present to it from the outset, a situation he symbolizes in the form of a machine that already contains within it all the movements it can make.[55] Instead, language extends its paradigms to include new situations, generating unprecedented meanings from the same old words.

There is obviously a bit of a mystery here, one that Wittgenstein puzzles over at some length, since the future uses of a word must exist in it in some way and yet they really are unanticipated and unpredictable.[56] The analogy he uses is one that obviously conditions Kuhn's discussion of the same problem in scientific investigation—seeing a diagram or a figure like the duck-rabbit picture in a new way: "If someone searches in a certain figure (call it Figure 1) for another figure (call it Figure 2), and then finds it, he sees Figure 1 in a new way. Not only can he give a new kind of description of it, but noticing the second figure was a new visual experience."[57] Instead of focusing on the epistemological limits suggested by the duck-rabbit picture, the fact that it is impossible to see both animals at the same time, Wittgenstein focuses on the possibilities suggested by it, what Kuhn calls the revolutionary moment in which the scales fall from the eyes and a new picture appears suddenly in the space of the old. But the visual example is mainly an analogy meant to illustrate the way in which new meanings are generated from the same old words, staring us in the face, thereby becoming the model for a kind of novelty that is much more flexible and open-ended than the recombination of simple elements could ever be.

As Cavell puts it in *The Claim of Reason*, language offers "an endless field of possibility" because it has "an indefinite number of instances and directions of projection."[58] The extensions of language are not arbitrary, because they are constrained by the criteria that determine what can make sense in particular situations; but they are still, in principle, unlimited. It is, therefore, possible for Cavell to see a good deal of human life as work within a paradigm without necessarily seeing it as mere paper-shuffling. The testing of criteria, finding the limits of what a particular language-game allows, becomes for him an act of communication with the other human beings whose lives have constituted those particular rules, and an act of self-discovery as well. Acting within a paradigm is an acknowledgment of others and thus, in some sense, a kind of submission; but it is also a process of growth insofar as the limits of the paradigm, and of the claims that can be made on the basis of it, can never be fixed.

In fact, it might seem that with a paradigm as flexible as this there would never be any need for revolution, so that Cavell could avoid those somewhat embarrassing episodes in Kuhn's account of science. As it turns out, though, revolution plays just as important a role in Cavell's work as it does in Greenberg's and Kuhn's. For one thing, paradigms as Cavell sees them do not always seem to be flexible enough to change without breaking. The twentieth century itself has seen so much dispute about particular conventions that the whole concept of convention has come to a kind of crisis. The modern is that situation in which "history and its conventions can no longer be taken for granted,"[59] when convention "as a whole" is looked on "not as a firm inheritance from the past, but as a continuing improvisation in the face of problems we no longer understand."[60] Another way of putting this would be to say that the modern sees as mere convention what had hitherto been unnoticed and unquestioned contexts of meaning.[61]

This sense of modernity as a crisis of confidence in norms and conventions is itself conventional enough to also appear in virtually identical terms in Greenberg.[62] In this light, it might really be said that modernity is the time in which anomaly becomes the norm and revolution, therefore, a constant condition. Cavell's version of the role of revolution in this situation is even more extreme in a certain sense than that of Greenberg or Kuhn, for he has purified it to the point at which it means nothing but return. The word *revolution* itself does not play a very great role in Cavell's work, but he has said that he sees himself as living through a revolution in philosophy, and that Wittgenstein had revolutionary things to say about philosophy, though he did not himself use the word very much.[63] Wittgenstein provides for Cavell a model in which entry into "a new form of life, a new world" is effected by way of a return, a reconception, which Cavell calls "a specific sense of revolution."[64] The "specific sense" he has in mind here is explicitly that developed by Hannah Arendt, in which *revolution* has its older and more traditional meaning of a full turn.[65] The more usual, contemporary "sense of revolution," he says in "Aesthetic Problems of Modern Philosophy," may give a feeling "of the past escaped and our problems solved,"[66] but this is illusory, since a real revolution returns us to the past, bringing us back to "a world lost."[67]

Hence modernism for Cavell is the revolutionary process by which art returns us to the world lost when modernity calls all norms and conventions into question. It is the purpose of modernism, he says in "Music Discomposed," to make "explicit and bare what has always been true of art."[68] Each artwork does this by searching out "the limits or essence of its own procedures,"[69] "asking exactly whether, and under what conditions, it can survive."[70] The purpose of this self-investigation is to find again what has been obscured in the course of time, to rediscover convention in its original strength and purity. The purpose of novelty, then, is not to defeat but to reinstate tradition: "The unheard of appearance of the modern in art is an effort not to break, but to keep faith with tradition."[71]

If this sounds very similar to Greenberg's notion of a novelty that reinforces tradition, it may not be entirely coincidental, for Cavell composed the key essays on modernism in *Must We Mean What We Say?* while in close conversation with Fried, who had come to him full of an early enthusiasm for Greenberg's criticism.[72] When Cavell sounds the least like himself in these early essays, and the most like the more caustic and combative Greenberg, it is when he takes on the "modernizers" for "finding new bases for aesthetics and a new future for art in every new and safe weirdness or attractiveness which catches on."[73] The word *new* becomes a kind of flail, as it sometimes does for Greenberg. But this captious tone persists in Cavell's later work as well, appearing whenever it encounters the "modernizer," who, unlike the true modernist, "is merely blind to the power of tradition, mocking his chains."[74] Together with Greenberg, he passes on to a later generation a definition of modernism in which it very nearly means the defeat and dismissal of the new.

THE PERSISTENCE OF THE PARADIGM

Greenberg now enjoys the kind of inverted devotion usually reserved for deposed dictators. The way he can't be killed is stylistically represented by the repetitive description of him as a kind of shadowy Moloch in Rosalind Krauss's *Optical Unconscious*.[75] That his ideas have survived in something other than a phobic form, so that they still very largely determine what is meant by the term *modernism*, is partly due to the way they have been filtered through the moderating influence of Cavell.[76] Fried makes this fairly clear in the introduction to his early work that appears at the beginning of *Art and Objecthood*, where he links his criticism of Greenberg to the influence of Wittgenstein and Cavell.[77] Greenberg had been the earlier influence,[78] the interest and excitement of which he had shared with Cavell.[79] But it was Cavell who tutored him in Wittgenstein and introduced him to the work of Kuhn.[80]

Fried thus comes to operate with a definition of convention that is much less literal than Greenberg's. The conventions that Anthony Caro explores in his sculpture, for example, are not just the material practices of past sculpture, such as the demand for a pedestal, but also deeply felt, experiential consistencies in human life, of the kind subjected to such scrutiny by Wittgenstein.[81] Fried's early essay on the artist Jules Olitski begins with a quotation from Wittgenstein, distinguishing "mere convention" from the kind of practice that expresses a deeply felt human need.[82] In many cases, this overt shift from mere social convention, or conventional artistic practice, to something more like a Kuhnian paradigm or Wittgensteinian form of life is managed by direct reference to Cavell. Fried's essay first published as "Modernist Painting and Formal Criticism," which reformulates the standard notion of artistic medium in light of what Wittgenstein says about grammar, cites Cavell twice,[83] and the essay on Olitski cites him in the same connection.[84] Thinking about convention less as a set of restrictive rules or repetitive practices and more as a generative grammar is a habit Fried ties directly to Cavell.[85]

Normally, then, art as Fried sees it will work within the flexible confines of a tacitly established grammar, much as normal science does for Kuhn, and new works will emerge in the form of expressions made possible by the paradigm. The works of the abstract painter Kenneth Noland, for example, "signify related transformations of syntax in the interest of saying something new."[86] Yet revolution will arise in the art when some artists feel that the paradigm has been stretched too thin, when "the range of solutions to a basic problem" has apparently been exhausted.[87] Kuhn concentrates on specific instances of this exhaustion, but modernity, for Fried as for Cavell and Greenberg, is a time when convention as such has come to seem exhausted. This is perhaps why all three feel justified in promoting the aesthetic response to another level, as if the "perpetual radical criticism"[88] to which modern art subjects its own conventions were an interrogation of convention in a much broader social sense.[89] In any case, the way Fried describes this "perpetual radical criticism" makes it sound like a cross between a Kuhnian scientific revolution and philosophy as practiced by Wittgenstein.

Another term for *perpetual radical criticism*, Fried says in the introduction to his early work, is *perpetual revolution*.[90] In the essay that first appeared as "Modernist Painting and Formal Criticism" in 1964, Fried defined *perpetual revolution* as the "principle by which painting can change, transform and renew itself."[91] Any revolution, as defined in the way agreed on by Kuhn, Greenberg, and Cavell, has this power of renewal, because revolution leads back in a circular fashion to the site of a lost origin. But perpetual revolution offers a particularly potent version of this pattern, because it makes revolution into a convention in its own respect. Fried's model of perpetual revolution, in which radical self-scrutiny is so intrinsic to modernist art that it comes to be its definitive practice, is his response to the problem debated at this time under the rubric of the tradition of the new. Modern art, he often says along with Cavell, leads back into tradition and reestablishes it—but in a sense this is unnecessary, insofar as modernist art has made the practice of self-interrogation and return into a tradition of its own. As in Kuhn, but in a much more perfect and overt way, the paradigm and the breaking of the paradigm collapse into each other and become the same thing.[92]

Fried perfected this formula for the new in modern art almost fifty years ago, but it remains influential, and not just because Fried himself continues to insist on it. In the recent work of Rosalind Krauss, for example, the "brute positivism" of Greenberg is civilized by reference to Cavell, and the relatively limited notion of an artistic medium is expanded by similar reference until it comes to mean a logic or a paradigm.[93] This word, made so familiar by decades of debate about Kuhn, has all sorts of implications for Krauss, particularly that of change and renewal, as artists who interrogate the current paradigms of art also create new paradigms within it.[94] Krauss is concerned to eliminate from this account any idea of recursion, but the art critic and historian Hal Foster quite explicitly repeats a theory of historical repetition he finds in Greenberg and Fried, only applying the idea of return to the neo-avant-garde of the 1960s and 1970s instead of the late modernist avant-garde favored by his teachers. But his avant-garde also "turned to past paradigms to open up present possibilities," distilling the new from an intent examination of the old.[95] The apparently flexible notion of the paradigm replaces an excessively specific and literal definition of the medium as it appears in Greenberg, and his intent concentration on the reductive self-definition of a particular medium becomes a more fundamental self-criticism of art in general, and beyond that of the conventional itself. But this happy wedding of the paradigm, or what used to be called tradition, with a recursive revolution, or what used to be called the new, doesn't really resolve some basic problems.

The problem with the paradigm has always been the way it seems to make impossible whatever it does not make possible. Thinking or practicing what is merely prohibited does not seem very daunting compared to the difficulty of thinking or practicing outside the conditions defining such activity itself. The mundane version of this problem that is encountered in the criticism of Greenberg and those to follow is the incorrigibility of taste, which can neither be justified nor disputed. The larger version of the problem to be found in criticism of the last half century is the hermeneutic circle, which is, the philosopher Giorgio Agamben says, really a "paradigmatic circle."[96] If a particular gets its meaning from reference to the paradigm, then how could any particular ever violate, or even substantially change, the paradigm? The difficulty of doing this is the subject of the literary theorist Roland Barthes's late lectures on "the neutral," which he both laboriously and playfully attempts to set up as a counterweight to the tyranny of the paradigm.[97]

The other half of the model developed by Kuhn, Greenberg, Cavell, and Fried, the revolution that reconfirms tradition, seems problematic on the very face of it. If an activity, such as the making of art, is a whole that perpetually reconstitutes itself so as to remain the whole, then it is a bit hard to see how the new can ever matter very much, in the split second between its miraculous appearance and its instantaneous reabsorption into the whole. Does it resolve the paradox behind the tradition of the new to call it a perpetual revolution, or does it merely restate the paradox? This abstract problem receives practical expression in the intense hostility of Greenberg, Cavell, and Fried to the newest art of their time, which managed somehow to fall outside the cycle of revolution and return. Why isn't the paradigm of modernist art flexible enough to embrace Pop, minimalism, or conceptual art? Was the whole notion of the paradigm merely a way to reject the work of the neo-avant-garde by definition, en masse instead of piece by piece?[98]

"NOVELTY ART"

At the same time that they were establishing and defending their definition of modernism's self-renewing novelty, Greenberg and Cavell were also stigmatizing a series of contemporary art forms because they were new in all the wrong ways. Pop, minimalism, and conceptual art, which began to stir up the art world at the very time that modernism was being formalized by Greenberg, all felt the back of his hand, swept aside under a blanket condemnation as "Novelty Art."[99] One of the sins of the artists behind these movements is that they were "eager" to innovate, whereas the modernists had all been "reluctant revolutionaries."[100] Greenberg had always felt that sincere and honest artists struggled to stay within convention as long as possible, succumbing to innovation only when it was absolutely unavoidable;[101] and as he got older he spoke more and more intensely of the great modernists as "reluctant innovators, cherishing the very conventions they felt themselves forced to go against."[102]

What he called premature innovation was the work of those who favored experiment for the sake of experiment,[103] or, worse yet, revolt for the sake of revolt, and nothing "sinks so low as revolt for the sake of revolt."[104] In this, he was of one mind with Cavell, who also disparaged artists "bent merely on newness."[105]

Greenberg's first and most influential term for the art made when "the new is looted for new 'twists'" was *kitsch*,[106] but he came to favor *Novelty Art*, almost always with the added stigma of the capital letters, a term that situated such art in a very particular context. When he self-consciously defined this term in 1968, he said it meant novelty "in the old-fashioned sense of novelties sold in stores."[107] He meant, in other words, to put Pop, minimalism, and conceptual art on the same dusty shelf with the whoopee cushions, the joy buzzers, and the dribble glasses. He felt as if his leg were being pulled, and he did not like the sensation. Cavell apparently felt the same way when he compared Pop art to "pin ball games or practical jokes or starlets."[108]

Greenberg and Cavell agree in applying to the neo-avant-garde of the 1960s the most recent—which is also the most puerile and degraded— meaning of the word *novelty*: as defined in the *Oxford English Dictionary*, "An often useless or trivial but decorative or amusing object, esp. one relying for its appeal on the newness of its design. Also (in later use): spec. a small inexpensive toy or trinket." As an adjective, the *OED* indicates that this sort of novelty appears in compounds such as *novelty item*: "something which has never been encountered before (with the implication that it will quickly disappear); spec. a frivolous thing, which has a certain amusement value, but usually little else to recommend it." Other such compounds include *novelty act* or *novelty song*, both of which share with *novelty item* a disapproving sense of ephemerality and mindless triviality that seems to have been preserved from earlier eras, when all newness was suspect. This automatic anathema, once pronounced on large and important innovations in science or religion, now seems to have been restricted to specialized arenas such as the stage, radio, and pulp literature.

This particular application of the word *novelty* bears the additional stigma, in English usage, of having come originally from the French, and, what is worse, from a commercial context. The earliest example provided by the *OED* of *novelty* used in this sense is in fact a translation from the

French, found in *Appleton's Journal* in April of 1874: "The great novelty-stores, to translate literally their title of *magasins de nouveautés*, are comparatively recent institutions in Paris." It is apparently through this side door that the term *novelty*, which had first come into English with the Normans many centuries before, acquired this additional sense. In its original form in the 1840s, the *magasin de nouveautés* stocked mainly dry goods: fabrics; sewing supplies; simple items of ready-to-wear clothing such as shawls and lingerie; and occasional oddments such as umbrellas. The novelties in stock were, in other words, quite ordinary, though they were understood as being a bit specialized and optional. In English, the miscellaneous nature of such stock is preserved in the word *sundries*, while its optional and perhaps frivolous quality is represented by *notions*. The essential innovation of the *magasin de nouveautés* was in fact to make this loose and undefinable collection of elective purchases into a category at all, bringing together in one place items that had been made and sold in separate shops.[109] If the new stores were not quite as new as they pretended, however, it is still the case that their claims were new, that their desire to appear new and to provoke in their customers an insatiable demand for novelty was not shared with the boutiques and specialty shops they gradually drove out of business. As the scholar Rachel Bowlby puts it, the most important innovation of the great department stores was "less the selling of the new . . . than the selling of 'the new' as a value in itself."[110]

The particular claim of this kind of novelty is made explicit in a catchphrase that has apparently accompanied notions, sundries, knickknacks, and doodads ever since they came to be represented collectively by the name of novelties: "no two alike." The earliest nonfictional example given in the *OED* of the term *novelty* used to mean a trivial or useless artifact comes from a print ad that ran in the Victoria, British Columbia, *Daily Colonist* in 1901: "Sterling Silver Novelties. An English manufacturer's range of samples: no two pieces alike. Puff Boxes, Tooth Brush Boxes, Vases, Cigarette Cases, Match Boxes, Napkin Rings." Useless and unnecessary items such as puff boxes and napkin rings become novelties only in combination, when their dissimilarity from one another can stand in for their otherwise utterly specious uniqueness in time. This is why the term *novelty* used in this way is, as the *OED* puts it, "Freq. in pl.," because this sort of novelty is inherently multiple. In this sense, the uniqueness of the new exists in a tense and apparently paradoxical relationship with its obvious multiplicity and standardization.

In part, then, the rhetorical strategy behind calling the new art movements of the 1960s "Novelty Art" is meant to place them in invidious association with commercial products of the lowest kind and thus to accuse them of having primarily mercenary motives. This is the first salvo in what will become an interminable battle over the commodity status of art, which was actually embraced with various admixtures of irony by many of the artists Greenberg and Cavell disdained. But this is also the first engagement in another debate about the nature and status of novelty, in particular whether it can exist in the absence of all the other qualities usually associated with it: originality, autonomy, uniqueness. Can something be new if it is also a reproduction, and, if so, does its novelty work in a way that is fundamentally different from the quality as it appears in earlier art? Finally, since novelty of this kind exists only in the multiple and preferably in a series, it presents a stark contrast to the model developed by Kuhn as well as Greenberg, Cavell, and Fried. In short, there is no revolution to return the series production of normal art or science to its origin and thus to give the entire system the unity and purpose of a cycle. The novelty of novelty art is open-ended and endless — and thus, as Arthur Danto maintains, ahistorical, since a mere process of endless substitution, just one damn thing after another, is not a history. In these various ways, then, the controversies about art in the 1960s were about "the vexed questions of how novelty might be described, and what it could be said to mean."[111]

"NOVELTY ART" STRIKES BACK

The accusation contained in the label "Novelty Art" evidently struck a nerve, for artists were still wincing as late as 1975, when the conceptual artist Joseph Kosuth complained about the "Greenberg gang" and its hostility toward "us 'novelty' artists that didn't happen to fit into the prescribed historical continuum."[112] There was, of course, a great deal of general back-chat against Greenberg's criticism in these years, but Kosuth was not the only artist-critic to fasten on the "Novelty Art" label in particular. Charles Harrison also charged that "Greenberg's concept of Novelty Art movements . . . acts as if to obfuscate ideas which operate within the context of art but outside Greenberg's concept of 'Modernism.'"[113] The label was seen, in other words, as a ploy to restrict in advance what might count as genuinely new, and thus to control what sort of art might be accepted in the future.

These reactions to this particularly egregious example of Greenberg's rhetoric also focus the much more general discussion about novelty that his criticism seems to have made necessary. One way of dealing with Greenberg's charge was to disclaim the new as such, and it is hardly an accident that some younger artists of this time vowed to "abandon the search for a new form at any price."[114] The conceptual and minimalist artist Sol LeWitt extended this critique of "the need to invent new forms" so that it also included the drive to find "new materials."[115] And some artists, including Douglas Huebler, vowed to stop adding to the world's store of new objects.[116] Of course, a fair amount of this reaction against what the art critic Lucy Lippard called "a public greedy for novelty" was motivated by the rapid succession of art movements themselves, which appeared even to those involved as disturbingly like the succession of new product lines.[117] To refuse to play the game of novelty was, for some artists, to resist the way the "market capitalizes on 'innovation' for its own sake," and to prevent the artwork from being turned into another commodity.[118]

Another way of dealing with the same situation was to play it *as* a game, to ironize the difference between old and new, as Robert Smithson did when he maintained, "Nothing is new, neither is anything old."[119] Where Smithson was still a bit intense about his indifference to the new, though, Warhol was famously blasé; at times, he could sound as if he were committed to the new with something like ordinary sincerity. He often spoke of his own career as if it had to progress from innovation to innovation in the most conventional way: "I knew that I would have to move on from painting. . . . I knew I'd have to find new and different things."[120] Having moved on from painting to film, Warhol then moved on to TV, which appealed because "it's the new everything. No more books or movies, just TV."[121] To some extent, this commitment to endless novelty was the pose of a person who wanted to be identified with complete contemporaneity, whatever it was; and to some extent it was the expression of a real emotional aversion to the old. In positive terms, this expressed itself as a fancy for whatever looked or felt "modern."[122] In negative terms, it emerged as a querulous fear of becoming old and dowdy: "I can't face my old work. . . . It was old."[123]

On the other hand, the same person who solidly announced, "What I like are things that are different every time," also maintained, "I don't want it to be essentially the same—I want it to be *exactly* the same. Because the more you look at the exact same thing, the more the meaning goes away, and the better and emptier you feel."[124] The artist who wanted to move on to new and different things also complained, "We're so programmed to that idea that you have to go onward and upward to something new and something advanced. It's really getting boring, so you want to do something old."[125] But even this determination, so apparently similar to the genuine feelings of a principled person, was too much for Warhol to sustain. The best expression of his studied indifference to the whole issue is this damp testimonial: "Oh, I like all paintings; it's just amazing that it keeps, you know, going on. And the way new things happen and stuff."[126]

In this way, Warhol managed to ironize the difference between irony and sincerity, with respect to novelty, as he had done with respect to so many other topics. But even this unfathomable blandness about the new can be seen as part of a reaction against it, insofar as Warhol's indifferent irony established his distance from a set of qualities, such as authenticity, originality, and autonomy, usually associated with the new. Inventiveness and individuality have always helped to sustain each other, so that artists like Warhol or like the minimalists who wanted to "clear away the boring display of personality"[127] also inevitably cleared away the overtly new and inventive. Thus the determined anonymity of minimalist art, "the blank, neutral, mechanical impersonality" of it, to take the art historian and critic Barbara Rose's early description, also seemed to imply a lack of originality, and there were scandalized stories of artists who did not actually contrive their own works but simply ordered them up by telephone.[128] Daniel Buren, among many other conceptual artists, overtly confronted the expectations behind such stories, purposely confusing his work with that of his collaborators, reiterating the same basic shapes from work to work, and generally doing whatever he could to cancel out "an identity which is constant by virtue of its difference in relation to a sameness."[129]

For such artists, in fact, novelty seems merely a secondary effect, a difference in time that is cleared away along with more fundamental differences in personality, style, and medium. For the Pop artist James Rosenquist, to take just one more example, the determination to choose for his work everyday objects "common enough to pass without notice [and] old enough to be forgotten" puts the common first and lets the old arrive as a necessary consequence.[130]

In any case, the new is surrounded on all sides and driven back on itself to such an extent that even such apparently fundamental aesthetic qualities as formal innovation come into question. What is particularly striking, considering the time period, which includes both the civil rights and student movements, is the number of statements against the notion of revolution in the arts. The artists Carl Andre, Robert Barry, and Lawrence Weiner recorded a discussion in the eventful year of 1968 in which they decided that "revolution never has to do with anything new," and in the same year Buren writes from Paris that "in regard to art, the artist is reformist, he is not revolutionary."[131] Of course, Buren often said exactly the opposite, as did quite a few other artists of this time.[132] What seems to require some explanation is the skepticism that sometimes attaches to the idea of revolution in the arts, a skepticism that arises when revolution is seen in the context of fashion and planned obsolescence or when it is identified with Greenberg and his followers. Thus the conceptual artist Ian Burn defies the "popular idea of a 'permanent revolution'" as a dodge meant to trap artists into "a set of empty gestures which threaten none of the market requirements and end up being a sheer celebration of the new individuality."[133] Thus the new in all its bogus forms is associated with Fried and the definition of modernism as a permanent revolution, and the anticommercial bias behind the term *Novelty Art* is turned back on itself.

In this respect, the 1960s appears to be a time not just of controversy but also confusion where the new is concerned. It was a time in which the ordinary succession of new art movements notably accelerated, and a complete aesthetic revolution seemed to be occurring every few months. The movement that came to be known as Pop Art was branded as the New Realism for a brief period, and works associated with it were frequently shown under the bland but significant rubric of The New Art.[134] The similarity of this to ordinary commercial rhetoric appears quite clearly in a spread that Warhol did for *Harper's Bazaar* in 1963 called "New Faces, New Forces, New Names in the Arts," for which he served as designer and subject at once. What came to be known as minimalism also existed for a brief time under the rubric of the New Sculpture.[135] And the enthusiastic artist and critic Gregory Battcock published within just a few years anthologies under the titles *The New Art, The New American Cinema, New Artists' Video*, and *New Ideas in Art Education*.[136] Artists who virtually defined their work in terms of its resistance to a seemingly endless treadmill of innovation found that they were advertised and appreciated as if sheer novelty were their only claim to fame. Novelty for its own sake was disavowed on all sides, by Greenberg and his opponents, yet it still seemed to define art and determine the way in which it developed through time.

Some of the most pertinent examples of this paradox are to be found in the vicinity of Warhol and his work. Warhol's basic techniques—appropriation of existing imagery, serial repetition, the use of reproductive processes such as silk-screening—all contributed to an image of art as product and artist as machine. Warhol apparently did not refer to his various establishments as the Factory, the name they made famous, but he did call himself a factory, as well as express a frequent ambition to become a machine.[137] He certainly meant by these remarks to provoke the sort of grim disapproval that comes through in essays such as the critic Paul Bergin's "Andy Warhol: The Artist as Machine," which first appeared in 1967.[138] And he certainly meant, by insisting that art could become an automated process, to defy a demand for novelty traditional in the world of fine art: "You see, the way I do them, with my technique, I really thought I could do four thousand in a day. And they'd all be masterpieces because they'd all be the same painting."[139] Here the idea that mechanical reproduction demolishes the aura of the unique masterpiece is turned inside out, so that distinction comes to depend on sameness.

Still, it has rather frequently been argued from various viewpoints that repetition in Warhol's work is not really repetition; it somehow transcends itself and becomes new and unique again at another level. The art critic and curator Henry Geldzahler argued very early on that Warhol's appropriations present their subjects "freshly, with immediacy," so that hackneyed and formulaic images "regain their vigour."[140] Recently,

Danto has argued that repetition in Warhol's work is actually "a sign of significance," investing the commonplace and everyday with meaning.[141] Even Rosalind Krauss, who has written with great conviction on behalf of avant-garde seriality, sees Warhol's repetitions as part of an "endless insistence on the fact of difference within the same."[142] Novelty, freshness, vigor, and difference, all qualities that Warhol's work seems to ironize out of existence, turn out to have been preserved and even elevated to a new level of significance. It was Warhol's purpose as an artist, according to the philosopher and cultural theorist Hugh Silverman, to expose the pretensions of aesthetic modernism, the hallmark of which was supposedly "to produce something new, to break with tradition, to come up with a new expression, or a new style, or a new object."[143] And yet the first exhibition of his Brillo boxes constituted such a striking innovation that Danto proclaimed it "the discovery of a whole new class of artworks," requiring from critics and scholars a whole new theory of art.[144] In Danto's writing ever since, the appearance of the Brillo boxes in New York City's Stable Gallery has epitomized a "conceptual revolution," a "transvaluation of values" so profound it has led to the end of the history of art itself, at least as the European world had conceived it.[145] The most obvious and consistent way of unraveling this paradox, by arguing with Danto that a landmark has been reached now that novelty has been disavowed for the first time in European art, conflicts dramatically with the analysis of Greenberg and Cavell, who believe that the very same art has installed novelty itself as the only norm that art must respect.

LANGUAGES OF THE NEW

Another way out of this impasse was suggested by one of Kosuth's first rejoinders to Greenberg: "What is called 'Novelty Art' by the formalists is often the attempt to find new languages."[146] If taken metaphorically, this is a fairly nondescript statement, echoes of which might be heard all across the neo-avant-garde, and Kosuth himself sometimes protects the idea of "art's 'language'" with scare quotes.[147] But he also believes that "a work of art is a kind of *proposition* presented within the confines of art as a comment on art," and that "the very stuff of art is indeed greatly related to 'creating' new propositions."[148] Among Kosuth's colleagues in the conceptual art movement, the idea that the work of art is a kind of proposition was a common one, though there was a good deal of divergence as to exactly what kind. For some, the work was embedded in linguistic statements and thus uninterpretable outside some linguistic context, while others made art quite literally out of linguistic materials.[149] But this equivocation is not quite so important as the one visible in the scare quotes that Kosuth attaches to the all-important word *creating*. Here Kosuth suggests that conceptual art makes new things in much the same way that language does—which would be helpfully illuminating if we really understood exactly how language creates itself anew. Still, in the context of the controversy between Greenberg and the neo-avant-garde, this is a useful statement, since it admits that the new art aims at novelty, but with the proviso that it also aims to redefine what that term has meant in the arts, with language as a model.

One trait that has always been said to mark the major art movements of the 1960s—Pop, minimalism, and conceptual art—is their common tendency to work in series. The series as such was already familiar from abstract expressionism, but in a form, Krauss argues, that managed to reinforce the status of the individual work. The numbered, nearly monochrome paintings of Ad Reinhardt, she says, make "every pure painting the 'ultimate' or last work of its kind, the final, culminating member of a progressive series, or alternatively, as a peculiar extension of this logic, the first in a completely new type of art whose history is yet to be written."[150] In contrast, the artists who followed Reinhardt clearly meant the series to qualify, at the very least, the novelty along with the uniqueness of the individual instance, but also to substitute for this vanished new another kind, derived from the very multiplicity of the series.

What this means in some cases is that artists embraced and exploited the logic of the novelty store in the very form in which it had been denounced by Greenberg. When the sculptor Claes Oldenburg, to take one outrageous example, started up the "Ray Gun Manufacturing Company" late in 1961, he established its headquarters in a part of New York full of dime stores, and he consciously duplicated not just their stock but their peculiar method of making that stock seem new.[151] It was the novelty of the *magasin de nouveautés* all over again, with disarrangement and multiplicity suggesting a nearly infinite number of options. In much the same way, and perhaps with Oldenburg in mind, Warhol first displayed his *Campbell's Soup Cans* at the Ferus Gallery in an array of thirty-two, an arrangement John Klein traces to "the marketing practices of the nineteenth-century department stores." It is important, Klein insists, to see all thirty-two of the paintings together, as they were first displayed. In the store or on the wall, "having them all there before you—cans or paintings—contributes to the generation of desire for one."[152] That the effect of one painting can be augmented, not diminished, by many others nearly the same seems a paradox only if the debt of such display techniques to the *grand magasin de nouveautés* is unknown.

In a very different context, Robert Smithson comes to celebrate urban sprawl, especially the "discount centers and cut-rate stores" that cluster near superhighways. Within such places, he finds "maze-like counters with piles of neatly stacked merchandise; rank on rank it goes into a consumer oblivion. The lugubrious complexity of the interiors has brought to art a new consciousness of the vapid and the dull. But this very vapidity and dullness is what inspires many of the more gifted artists."[153] In his rhapsodies of this kind, Smithson is not just romanticizing the down-at-heel. He also finds a viable aesthetic principle in the bins of the discount store, a kind of disarranged multiplicity that has for him a generative potency much like the vocabulary and grammar of a language. Implicit in these recuperations of the novelty store is an argument about the kind of novelty to be found there, an argument to the effect that it is not just the rearrangement of preexisting units but something more, something with the power of *creating* "new propositions."

Conceptual artists such as Mel Bochner were the most self-conscious in articulating the redefinition of series as grammar. Bochner's essay "The Serial Attitude," for example, is a collage of statements from other artists and programmatic announcements from Bochner himself about the power of language as a model for art: "Language is often considered as a system of elements without assigned meanings ('uninterpreted systems'). Such systems are completely permutational, having grammatical but not semantic rules. Since there can be no system without rules of arrangement, this amounts to the handling of language as a set of probabilities."[154] Language, in other words, works by rearranging standardized units, but since those units operate only according to probabilities, not certainties, the systems generate truly new possibilities. This is also the reasoning by which Kosuth insists that art can generate new propositions.

Thus it is by reference to language that the repetition of ordinary seriality is transformed into something capable of actual creativity. In her essay on Sol LeWitt, Krauss differentiates between the determinism of a mathematical series and the randomness, the babble, of a linguistic series, which is continued and extended by what she calls "the notion of *etcetera*."[155] What she has in mind here must be something like the distinction Wittgenstein draws in *Philosophical Investigations* between "the 'and so on' which is and the 'and so on' which *is not* an abbreviated notation." To make this distinction clear, he says, "Teaching which is not meant to apply to anything but the examples given is different from that which *'points beyond'* them."[156] In other words, there is in the rules of language an implied extension, an "and so on," the size of which is always unpredictably bigger than any series we can write down. The extension is determinate and even rule-bound, but it still cannot be specified in advance or exhausted.

In much Pop, minimalism, and conceptual art, a good deal is staked on the notion that units other than words can be found and arranged in series that might display this sort of unlimited extension. The conceptual artist John Baldessari, for example, matches strings of words to grids of photographs as a way of suggesting equivalent ways of generating meaning. The open-ended possibilities suggested by a few photographs could thus provide "all the meaning a person would need to give life value."[157] Thus the conceptual artist Douglas Heubler, who wanted to avoid cluttering the world with any more new objects, worked by assembling photographs, each of which was meant to "represent one of an infinite number of incidental moments."[158] Ultimately, Huebler dedicated himself to the "Everyone Alive" series, which was supposed to document by selective implication "the existence of everyone alive."[159] The potential of a project like this apparently lies in its randomness, in the notion that choosing as randomly as possible will make the resulting collection as widely eloquent as possible. The sheer, unarranged multiplicity of the novelty store returns as a sign of the infinite novelty implicit in the world.

One further implication of a series of this kind, though, is that it does not need the crisis of revolution in order to refresh itself and continue.

Implicit in Wittgenstein's essentially linguistic model of convention is the idea that new usage does not just probe the limits of convention but extends them, and that in extending them can actually establish new conventions. The aesthetic version of this process is often highlighted in Cavell's work: "The discovery of a new possibility is the discovery of a new medium."[160] For Cavell, all media exist within the orbit of art in general, so that the creation of a new medium does not alter but further confirms the outer boundaries of the aesthetic itself. This, he says, is the significance of "series in modern painting and sculpture," which he sees as more or less the same as "cycles in movies" and the search for an individual "'sound' in jazz and rock."[161] In other words, the new medium never really changes an art whose essential nature has already been determined. Since Cavell joins Greenberg in emphasizing the way that vanguard art always confirms the limits of art by progressively defining them, new media must actually help to advance the general process by which the boundaries of art get closer every year. Aesthetic progress, in this model, has the odd effect of steadily reducing the space within which art can move.

If, on the other hand, a new medium is a new convention and thus, in some sense, a new form of art, then it seems that art can proliferate itself indefinitely, without any need for a convulsive return to basic principles. This is more or less what Krauss suggests in her recent work, in which she takes Cavell's notion of a new medium to the next level by finding new media that seem to attain the status of new paradigms. There are eight such instances, in her account of art since the 1960s, in which the exploration of a particular technical support has gone far enough to become a new medium, which offers to future art the sort of logical support associated with a paradigm.[162] It is a little hard to see why there are just eight new media and no more, why these particular artists and not others have managed to establish within their idiosyncratic styles new systems of rules powerful enough to constitute another medium. And Krauss is even harsher than Greenberg in "shouting 'fake' and 'fraud'" at the art she defines as kitsch, which seems mainly to be installation art.[163] The sins of novelty art seem much the same for her as they were for Greenberg: trying to operate without rules, as if there are no walls, and as if art, or any human activity, could exist outside a paradigm.

In one of his classic pieces of art/criticism, Robert Smithson mounted an argument against the idea that art depends on the necessary confines of convention, which was also an argument specifically with Fried and Greenberg. He finds in Fried's review of a Morris Louis exhibition a phobic description of "the abyss that . . . *would* open up if innumerable conventions both of art and practical life did not restrict the consequences of our act within narrow bounds." To this he responds, "The 'innumerable conventions' do not exist for certain artists who *do* exist within a physical 'abyss.'"[164] Despite the drama of this pronouncement, Smithson does not actually believe that artists can work with a completely undifferentiated plenum. Like Fried, he thinks of art as generating "a set of conditions" within which it can and must work.[165] For him, though, it is in the nature of conditions to generate further conditions, new ones that extend in an essentially unpredictable way, so that art need not occupy itself endlessly with etching its boundaries in sharper and sharper lines. The set of combinations that constitutes novelty according to this model can elaborate itself in truly unpredictable ways and never hit the limit that brings on revolution.

The status of revolution is perhaps the defining paradox in the 1960s debate about the nature of novelty, the modernist tradition of the new, and the status of the newest art. The advocates of "permanent revolution" are the more conservative critics who resist the most recent developments in the arts. This makes sense only because they first returned revolution itself to an older meaning, so that it could signify a kind of restoration. Thus modernism for them steadily undoes the alienation of modernity, and novelty reconfirms the lost authority of tradition as such. Art that did not do this exposed itself as new in name only, dully repetitive within a series that never amounted to anything because it never ended. This purely metaphorical and aesthetic version of revolution had nothing to do with the actual politics of the 1960s, which did sometimes play a role in the advanced art of the time. But artists producing it, who might have been expected to make revolution a standard part of their rhetoric, for the most part did not. Of course, the actual politics of this time was sufficiently complex that revolution could seem routine, a confirmation of the economics of planned obsolescence and interminable innovation. Within the debate about novelty, though, revolution simply did not seem necessary, since the generative possibilities of the ordinary paradigms were endless. In any case, once revolution had been defined by critics such as Fried as a permanent state, then resistance to it could actually look progressive. The decade thus saw projects such as Mierle Ukeles' "Maintenance Art," which advertised itself as attending to what happens "after the revolution." To the art of development, change, revolution, "the new," Ukeles counterposed the art of maintenance, keeping "the dust off the pure individual creation," maintaining the new.[166] There is obviously a kind of politics in this deliberate avoidance of glamour, one that may seem a world away from the hectic publicity around Warhol's work. However, insofar as both works stake everything on the sheer extension of a repetitive series, and draw their sense of the new exclusively from that, they represent what was truly different in the art of their time.

CONCLUSION

Perhaps the most basic conclusion to be drawn from a history of the new is that it has had a history at all—that novelty is not just a modern concern but a timeless problem. How newness comes into the world, it turns out, is one of those ancient mysteries that have nagged at people ever since they began to think. What has changed over the centuries is the motive behind the question. Lucretius disdained the demand for novelty itself just as much as Plato had, and the purpose of the Epicurean system was not to make a claim for innovation or even change, but just to explain why the world is not a static and undifferentiated continuum. This desire to account for the apparent facts of experience, in the face of a primal certainty that neither matter nor energy can be created or destroyed, produced the first and most basic accounts of how newness manages to get into the world. Nothing said since then has departed very far from these early solutions.

Both the excessive value that modernity often attaches to the new and the critical sense of it as empty and pointless depend on a simplified notion of novelty as creation *ex nihilo*, the dismissal of which was in fact the very first step in philosophical understanding. In fact, much of what appears so contradictory in the modern appetite for new things may be traced to tensions within the concept of novelty, to conflicts among the different kinds of novelty passed down to us by tradition. Though the authority of science and technology has generally convinced us that invention is a dispersed, incremental, and eminently social process, more a matter of adjustment and recombination than of creation *ex nihilo*, we still tend to demand of it those thunderclaps of change characteristic of the revolutionary model. The peculiarly peristaltic rhythms of modern publicity—avid consumption followed by disappointed satiety—may be conditioned by this confusion over the nature of the new, which would not cause such mood swings if it were actually expected to come in tiny increments. On the other hand, feelings of frustration and even betrayal that arise whenever some new idea or development turns out to have been old all along would not sting so severely if it were generally accepted that many new things are revolutionary only in the original sense of that term.

Thus the argument between Greenberg and the neo-avant-garde, which seemed to be about the desirability of artistic innovation itself, was actually a contest between two different models of novelty: one incremental and progressive, the other revolutionary, in the classic sense of a return to basics. The meteoric rise and fall of cybernetics, which proposed itself as a general science of innovation, can be traced to the uncertain relationship within it of the same two models, once the recursive return of noise to the system began to look like the betrayal of innovation and not a different phase of it. The fact that Kuhn has been thought of as both a dangerous relativist and a repressive traditionalist certainly has to do with the difficult balance he tried to work out between innovation and tradition, but it also has to do with the complexity of his ideas about innovation itself. Even Kuhn's normal science, dedicated as it is to preservation of the paradigm, brings about its own kind of novelty, as scientific revolutions bring the new back into the fold of normal science. Though the heat of these intellectual debates may come from the unexamined feeling that newness must be a simple thing to be advanced or betrayed, their content depends on differences within the concept of the new itself.

One of the most durable of these disputes is about aesthetic modernism, whose devotion to the new once seemed part of a general insurrection against the *ancien régime* and now is usually considered a kind of hoax. Eminent critics as different as Frank Kermode, Paul de Man, and Fredric Jameson agree that novelty is one of the most useless and shallow pretensions of a movement that was especially well supplied with them.[1] How can writers and artists base their claims on the new when it is so clear that there is nothing new, so that the old will inevitably emerge to debunk their works? Why would writers and artists stake their all on the new when it is so clear that the new instantly becomes old, so that the future durability of art is sacrificed to a momentary demand? Though modernism, as a movement and as a collection of works, has turned out to be more durable than the postmodernism that was supposed to replace it, the problem signified by the prefix has not gone away, and the tension between the modern as a particular period style and the modern as a recurring historical moment remains. As the particular innovations of modernist art drop further back into the past, they fall further out of sync with the purely temporal newness of the present day, so that the very term *modern* comes to seem a mocking self-contradiction.

Considered in context, though, aesthetic modernism turns out to be less an exceptional, egregious case than one part of a general modern investigation of the new. The need to formulate novelty was an imperative that modern artists and writers shared with the sciences of their time, as they shared most of the formulas it seemed possible to use. Examined at all closely, modernist interest in the new also turns out to be remarkably complex, with little relationship to the radical creation *ex nihilo* that is often the straw man in the critiques. The general use of Make It New as the slogan for this kind of radical novelty turns out to be based on a misunderstanding and misapplication of the history and meaning of that phrase. And beyond that simple phrase there turns out to be, among modern writers and artists, a startling welter of ideas about the new, ranging back and forth between incremental recombination and recurrent revolution. Though modernism as such seems inextricably connected to a demand for novelty in its purest and most abstract state, many modernists restricted their attempts to the relatively new, and many admitted—or even insisted—that what seems new is really only the old come back again. What Arendt called the pathos of the new, that always disappointed quest for a completely new beginning, was itself old by the beginning of the twentieth century, and though the feeling was still there, ideas about novelty had become so complex, after Darwin and modern physics, that even the most heartfelt demands could hardly be simple or naïve.

In fact, what makes aesthetic modernism distinct within the general modern project on the new, and what may give it a certain priority within that project, is its constitutional self-consciousness about the symbolic. One of the most striking things about the history of novelty is the growing power of language as a model. In evolutionary terms, of course, language is just as much a mystery as consciousness, and it was also put aside by Darwin as a beginning too momentous for natural selection to explain. On the other hand, evolution has often been understood as if it were a language, and its usefulness in this respect is one of the reasons why language has steadily increased in prestige over the years as a model of the new in general. But the real reason for the continued prestige of the linguistic model is its demonstrated ability to change and grow and thus to become new itself. This model, which began with the pre-Socratics as a simple combinatory, and which was still in the heyday of information theory little more than a cipher, became in the later work of Wittgenstein a flexible and open-ended system powerful enough to motivate original thinking about the new in a number of disciplines. All the difference is made by the inclusion of the social, since usage does have the power to generate new meanings, whereas the alphabet by itself can generate only new combinations.

What this means, though, is that novelty, which was once linked inextricably to the individual, to originality, and which has often been defined in terms of a tension with the social, actually seems more feasible as a social phenomenon. If Darwin is right, as later thinkers from Maxwell to Kuhn clearly thought he was, then variation is one of the natural consequences of development in any complex system. Thus Luhmann can argue that even original genius is an effect of the social, of the innumerable interactions of a complex society, which will tend to produce some few bits of the unprecedented just as surely as they reproduce the given.[2]

Is it just a bit too convenient to believe that large social systems, which we can hardly avoid in any case, will give us the new along with the sameness that is their most obvious effect? To be sure, this has always been one article of faith about modern social systems—they throw off anomalies as a matter of course. But to think in terms limited to modern social systems is to ignore the fact that the sociality at work in language, as Wittgenstein sees it, is temporal as well as spatial. The rules of language, he says, always include an implicit *and so on*, which is meant not to summarize but to extend the set of possible statements. What is said today will certainly constrain what can be said in the future, but not in any absolute sense, for the generative rules of language are apparently open-ended enough even to allow for their own alteration.

Any truly generative convention, from DNA to the rules of grammar, must come equipped with some version of this *and so on*. Even if the extension of it into the future is automatic, though, its expansion is not. In the case of DNA, for instance, biologists have shown that future novelty requires the interpretation of the genetic message within the context of development and environment. Future changes in language obviously require the contributions of future speakers speaking in unprecedented situations. But so long as such extensions are not forestalled, then the possibility of novelty exists—and so it is the indefinite postponement of the end that finally justifies our belief in beginnings.

ACKNOWLEDGMENTS

Early versions of some of the material that went into chapters 5 and 6 were delivered as talks at Johns Hopkins University and at the 2010 Modernist Studies Association conference in Victoria, British Columbia. I am grateful to those who attended and discussed these papers. Some parts of chapters 5 and 6 were read in a previous form by Mark Seltzer and Ronald Bush, and I want to express my gratitude for their forebearance and good sense. I am also indebted to the readers for the University of Chicago Press, who made many useful suggestions, without which the final text of this book would have been much less satisfactory.

NOTES

INTRODUCTION

1. Elizabeth E. Guffey, *Retro: The Culture of Revival* (London: Reaktion, 2006), 148.

2. Nancy Holt, ed., *The Writing of Robert Smithson* (New York: New York University Press, 1979), 51, 49. See also Guffey, *Retro*, 85.

3. Manuel De Landa, *Philosophy and Simulation: The Emergence of Synthetic Reason* (London: Continuum, 2011).

4. See, for example, Sam Gillespie, *The Mathematics of Novelty: Alain Badiou's Minimalist Metaphysics* (Melbourne: Re Press, 2008), and Simon O'Sullivan and Stephen Zepke, eds., *Deleuze, Guattari and the Production of the New* (London: Continuum, 2008).

5. Alberto Toscano, "In Praise of Negativism," in O'Sullivan and Zepke, *Deleuze, Guattari*, 56–59.

6. Joseph E. Schumpeter, *Capitalism, Socialism, and Democracy* (1950), 117; quoted in Everett M. Rogers, *Diffusion of Innovations*, 5th ed. (New York: Free Press, 2003), 136.

7. Rogers, *Diffusion of Innovations*, 110.

8. Ibid., 11.

9. Elizabeth Grosz, *The Nick of Time: Politics, Evolution, and the Untimely* (Durham, NC: Duke University Press, 2004), 37.

10. David W. Galenson, *Painting outside the Lines: Patterns of Creativity in Modern Art* (Cambridge, MA: Harvard University Press, 2001), 42.

11. Ibid., 32.

12. Ibid., 42.

13. Nick Lane, *Life Ascending: The Ten Great Inventions of Evolution* (New York: Norton, 2009).

14. Joel Cracraft, "The Origin of Evolutionary Novelties: Pattern and Process at Different Hierarchical Levels," in *Evolutionary Innovations*, ed. Matthew H. Nitecki (Chicago: University of Chicago Press, 1990), 24.

15. Jed Rasula, "Make It New," *Modernism/Modernity* 7 (2010): 713–33.

16. Ibid., 713.

17. Terry Eagleton, "Fast Forward," *Times Literary Supplement*, March 25, 2011, 3.

18. Stanley Cavell, *Must We Mean What We Say?* (Cambridge: Cambridge University Press, 2002), 185.

19. Michael Wellbourne, "Meno's Paradox," *Philosophy* 61 (1986): 229–43.

20. Thomas S. Kuhn, *The Structure of Scientific Revolutions*, 4th ed. (Chicago: University of Chicago Press, 2012), 129.

21. Peter Bürger, *Theory of the Avant-Garde*, trans. Michael Shaw (Minneapolis: University of Minnesota Press, 1984), 58.

CHAPTER ONE

1. Salman Rushdie, *The Satanic Verses* (New York: Viking, 1988), 8. Homi Bhabha's discussion of this question also made it central to discussions of postcolonialism: *The Location of Culture* (London: Routledge, 1994), 224.

2. William James, *Writings 1902–1910*, ed. Bruce Kuklick (New York: Library of America, 1987), 1049.

3. Reinhart Koselleck, *Futures Past: On the Semantics of Historical Time*, trans. Keith Tribe (Cambridge, MA: MIT Press, 1985), 203, 238; Antoine Compagnon, *The Five Paradoxes of Modernity*, trans. Franklin Philip (New York: Columbia University Press, 1994), 4; Peter Osborne, *The Politics of Time: Modernity and Avant-Garde* (London: Verso, 1995), 9–20. For an argument against the new as the exclusive justification of the modern, see Hans Blumenberg, *The Legitimacy of the Modern Age*, trans. Robert M. Wallace (Cambridge, MA: MIT Press, 1985), especially 99.

4. Maria de Grazia, "The Modern Divide: From Either Side," *Journal of Medieval and Early Modern Studies* 37 (2007): 454; Niklas Luhmann, *Art as a Social System*, trans. Eva M. Knodt (Stanford, CA: Stanford University Press, 2000), 200.

5. Blumenberg, *Legitimacy of the Modern Age*, 184; de Grazia, "The Modern Divide," 457; Compagnon, *Five Paradoxes of Modernity*, 5.

6. George Boas, "Historical Periods," *Journal of Aesthetics and Art Criticism* 11 (1953): 253–54; quoted in Erwin Panofsky, *Renaissance and Renascences in Western Art* (New York: Harper & Row, 1969), 1. The ellipsis is Panofsky's. See his discussion of this point, 1–2.

7. For a more complete discussion, see chapter 6.

8. Panofsky, *Renaissance and Renascences in Western Art*, 2; Paul de Man, *Blindness and Insight: Essays in the Rhetoric of Contemporary Criticism*, 2nd ed. (Minneapolis: University of Minnesota Press, 1983), 151, 157.

9. As Frank Kermode puts it, "Schism is meaningless without reference to some prior condition; the absolutely New is simply unintelligible, even as novelty." *The Sense of an Ending: Studies in the Theory of Fiction* (1966; reprint, Oxford: Oxford University Press, 2000), 116.

10. Josiah Royce, "The Reality of the Temporal," *International Journal of Ethics* 20 (1910): 267. On the other hand, Hermann Minkowski insists that "it is completely natural that I recognize what I see again, just as it is completely natural that I find new what I have before my eyes for the first time, that is, that I have the notion of 'never or not yet seen' in its presence." See the selection from Minkowski's *Lived Time* in *The Human Experience of Time: The Development of Its Philosophic Meaning*, ed. Charles Sherover (Evanston, IL: Northwestern University Press, 2001), 505.

11. Hannah Arendt, *The Human Condition* (Chicago: University of Chicago Press, 1958), 249.

12. Karl Jaspers, *Descartes und die Philosophie* (Berlin: de Gruyter, 1966), 57. See Charles Whitney, *Francis Bacon and Modernity* (New Haven, CT: Yale University Press, 1986), 102.

13. Hannah Arendt, *On Revolution* (New York: Viking, 1965), 27.

14. Theodor Adorno, *Aesthetic Theory*, trans. C. Lenhardt (New York: Routledge & Kegan Paul, 1984), 47.

15. Ibid., 30.

16. Ibid.

17. Ibid., 339.

18. Luhmann, *Art as a Social System*, 199.

19. Maarten Van Dyck, "The Paradox of Conceptual Novelty and Galileo's Use of Experiments," *Philosophy of Science* 72 (December 2005): 864–75.

20. For a detailed analysis and dismissal of this idea, see Morris R. Cohen and Ernest Nagel, *An Introduction to Logic*, 2nd ed. (Indianapolis: Hackett, 1993), 173–80.

21. Adorno, *Aesthetic Theory*, 31.

22. Compagnon, *Five Paradoxes of Modernity*, 60.

23. Ibid., 59.

24. Hans-Georg Gadamer, *The Beginning of Philosophy*, trans. Rod Coltman (New York: Continuum, 1998), 115.

25. Ludwig Wittgenstein, *Tractatus Logico-Philosophicus*, trans. D. F. Pears and B. F. McGuinness (Atlantic Highlands, NJ: Humanities Press, 1961), 6.

26. James, *Writings 1902–1910*, 1081–83. For the views of a British pragmatist on the same issue, see F. C. S. Schiller, "Creation, Emergence, Novelty," *Proceedings of the Aristotelian Society*, n.s. 31 (1930–31): 25–36.

27. Wittgenstein, *Tractatus Logico-Philosophicus*, 63.

28. Ibid., 6.

29. Ibid., 8.

30. Ibid., 5.

31. A. H. Coxon, *The Fragments of Parmenides: A Critical Text with Introduction and Translation, the Ancient Testimonia and a Commentary*, rev. ed. (Las Vegas: Parmenides, 2009), 64.

32. Gadamer, *Beginning of Philosophy*, 117–18.

33. Bertrand Russell, *Principles of Mathematics* (Cambridge: Cambridge University Press, 1903), 449.

34. See the account of Parmenides in Bertrand Russell's *History of Western Philosophy* (New York: Simon & Schuster, 1972), 49.

35. *The Complete Works of Aristotle*, ed. Jonathan Barnes (Princeton, NJ: Princeton University Press, 1984), 1:519. For Parmenides' priority in this respect, see Alexander P. D. Mourelatos, "Pre-Socratic Origins of the Principle That There Are No Origins from Nothing," *Journal of Philosophy* 78 (1981): 649–65.

36. R. J. Hankinson, "Parmenides and the Metaphysics of Changelessness," in *Presocratic Philosophy: Essays in Honor of Alexander Mourelatos*, ed. Victor Caston and Daniel W. Graham (Aldershot: Ashgate, 2002), 79; Mourelatos, "Pre-Socratic Origins," 651–52.

37. Mourelatos, "Pre-Socratic Origins," 652.

38. Simplicius, *Commentary on Aristotle's "On the Heavens,"* in *The First Philosophers: The Presocratics and Sophists*, trans. Robin Waterfield (Oxford: Oxford University Press, 2000), 86.

39. Gadamer, *Beginning of Philosophy*, 120; Jaap Mansfeld, "Aëtius, Aristotle and Others on Coming-to-Be and Passing-Away," in Caston and Graham, *Presocratic Philosophy*, 274–75.

40. Karl Popper calls it "the first hypothetico-deductive theory of the world." Karl R. Popper, *The World of Parmenides: Essays on the Presocratic Enlightenment* (London: Routledge, 1998), 17.

41. Waterfield, *First Philosophers*, 52.

42. Popper, *World of Parmenides*, 148.

43. B. Jowett, trans., *The Dialogues of Plato* (New York: Oxford University Press, 1892), 4:244; Charles H. Kahn, "Parmenides and Plato," in Caston and Graham, *Presocratic Philosophy*, 82–83.

44. Plato, *Timaeus*; quoted in Catherine Wilson, *Epicureanism at the Origins of Modernity* (Oxford: Clarendon Press, 2008), 45.

45. Coxon, *Fragments of Parmenides*, 27–28.

46. Jowett, *Dialogues of Plato*, 3:457.

47. Ibid., 3:112.

48. Ibid., 3:112, 181.

49. Coxon, *Fragments of Parmenides*, 118.

50. Christian Wildberg, "*On Generation and Corruption* I. 7: Aristotle on *Poiein* and *Paschein*," in *Aristotle: On Generation and Corruption, Book I, Symposium Aristotelicum*, ed. Frans de Haas and Jaap Mansfeld (Oxford: Clarendon Press, 2004), 219.

51. Barnes, *Complete Works of Aristotle*, 1:513.

52. From the *Physics*; quoted in Christopher Shields, *Aristotle* (London: Routledge, 2007), 55.

53. Sarah Brodie, "*On Generation and Corruption* I. 4: Distinguishing Alteration—Substantial Change, Elemental Change, and First Matter in *GC*," in de Haas and Mansfeld, *Aristotle: On Generation and Corruption*, 125; Lynn S. Joy, "Scientific Explanation from Formal Causes to Laws of Nature," in *The Cambridge History of Science*, ed. Katharine Park and Lorraine Daston (Cambridge: Cambridge University Press, 2006), 3:97–99.

54. From the *Physics*; quoted in Shields, *Aristotle*, 55.

55. Mansfeld, "Aëtius, Aristotle and Others," 285; Richard Sorabji, *Time, Creation and the Continuum: Theories in Antiquity and the Early Middle Ages* (Ithaca, NY: Cornell University Press, 1983), 246–48.

56. For a discussion of the responses to Zeno by Russell, James, and Whitehead, and a refutation based on modern physics, see Adolf Grünbaum, "Modern Science and Zeno's Paradoxes of Motion," in *The Philosophy of Time*, ed. Richard M. Gale (Atlantic Highlands, NJ: Humanities Press; Sussex: Harvester Press, 1968), 422–501.

57. Empedocles, in Waterfield, *First Philosophers*, 148.

58. Ibid.

59. Coxon, *Fragments of Parmenides*, 23.

60. Aristotle, *On Generation and Corruption*, in Waterfield, *First Philosophers*, 150.

61. Mircea Eliade, *Cosmos and History: The Myth of the Eternal Return*, trans. Willard R. Trask (New York: Harper & Row, 1959).

62. Sorabji, *Time, Creation and the Continuum*, 182–86.

63. Jowett, *Dialogues of Plato*, 3:473.

64. Waterfield, *First Philosophers*, 164; Popper, *World of Parmenides*, 17–18.

65. Lucretius, *On the Nature of Things*, trans. Martin Ferguson Smith (Indianapolis: Hackett, 2001), 7. See also Ferguson Smith's introduction, xxv.

66. Lucretius, *On the Nature of Things*, 43.

67. Ibid., 30.

68. Gordon Campbell, *Lucretius on Creation and Evolution: A Commentary on "De Rerum Natura" Book Five, Lines 772–1104* (Oxford: Oxford University Press, 2003), 165–66.

69. Lucretius, *On the Nature of Things*, 141.

70. Ibid., 41.

71. Blumenberg, *Legitimacy of the Modern Age*, 169.

72. Waterfield, *First Philosophers*, 182.

73. Sorabji, *Time, Creation and the Continuum*, 366.

74. Mansfeld, "Aëtius, Aristotle and Others," 276.

75. Blumenberg, *Legitimacy of the Modern Age*, 581–82.

76. Arendt, *On Revolution*, 213.

77. Carolyn R. Miller, "The Aristotelian Topos: Hunting for Novelty," in *Rereading Aristotle's Rhetoric*, ed. Alan G. Gross and Arthur E. Walzer (Carbondale: Southern Illinois University Press, 2000), 141.

78. Patricia Curd, "The Metaphysics of Physics: Mixture and Separation in Empedocles and Anaxagoras," in Caston and Graham, *Presocratic Philosophy*, 155.

79. Ibid., 156.

80. Duncan F. Kennedy, *Rethinking Reality: Lucretius and the Textualization of Nature* (Ann Arbor: University of Michigan Press, 2002), 86–87.

81. Lucretius, *On the Nature of Things*, 8.

82. Ibid., 25.

83. Myles Burnyeat, *The "Theaetetus" of Plato* (Indianapolis: Hackett, 1990), 340.

84. Jowett, *Dialogues of Plato*, 4:268.

85. Ibid.

86. For a compact discussion of the unacceptable consequences arising from

either alternative, see Timothy Chappell, *Reading Plato's "Theaetetus"* (Indianapolis: Hackett, 2004), 219.

87. Burnyeat, *"Theaetetus" of Plato*, 152.

88. For example, in the *Timaeus*, in which he disputes the notion that the four elements might be "the first principles and letters or elements of the whole, when they cannot reasonably be compared by a man of any sense even to syllables or first compounds" (Jowett, *Dialogues of Plato*, 3:468). See Burnyeat, *"Theaetetus" of Plato*, 216.

89. James, *Writings 1902–1910*, 715–16.

90. Wittgenstein himself suggested the relationship between the *Tractatus* and the *Theaetetus*. See *Philosophical Investigations*, trans. G. E. M. Anscombe (New York: Macmillan, 1968), 21. See also the discussion in Burnyeat, *"Theaetetus" of Plato*, 149–64.

CHAPTER TWO

1. N. Joseph Torchia, OP, *Creation ex Nihilo and the Theology of St. Augustine: The Anti-Manichean Polemic and Beyond* (New York: Peter Lang, 1999).

2. Richard Sorabji, *Time, Creation and the Continuum* (Ithaca, NY: Cornell University Press, 1983), 194.

3. Paul Copan, "Is *Creatio ex Nihilo* A Post-Biblical Invention? An Examination of Gerhard May's Proposal," *Trinity Journal* 17 (1996): 77–93.

4. Hans Blumenberg, *The Legitimacy of the Modern Age*, trans. Robert M. Wallace (Cambridge, MA: MIT Press, 1985), 132–33.

5. Hanna Arendt, *On Revolution* (New York: Viking, 1965), 20.

6. Sorabji, *Time, Creation and the Continuum*, 302–3.

7. G. R. Evans, *Old Arts and New Theology: The Beginnings of Theology as an Academic Discipline* (Oxford: Clarendon Press, 1980), 184.

8. Blumenberg, *Legitimacy of the Modern Age*, 532–33.

9. Gerhart B. Ladner, *The Idea of Reform: Its Impact on Christian Thought and Action in the Age of the Fathers* (Cambridge, MA: Harvard University Press, 1959), 82.

10. Ibid., 59.

11. Ibid., 134.

12. Ibid., 157.

13. Evans, *Old Arts and New Theology*, 167–68.

14. James S. Preus, "Theological Legitimation for Innovation in the Middle Ages," *Viator* 3 (1972): 5.

15. Erasmus, *Collected Works* 8:149–53; quoted in Joseph M. Levine, *The Autonomy of History* (Chicago: University of Chicago Press, 1999), 28.

16. Antoine Compagnon, *The Five Paradoxes of Modernity*, trans. Franklin Philip (New York: Columbia University Press, 1994), 7.

17. Preus, "Theological Legitimation," 13.

18. Karl F. Morrison, *The Mimetic Tradition of Reform in the West* (Princeton, NJ: Princeton University Press, 1982), 41.

19. Ladner, *Idea of Reform*, 16.

20. Preus, "Theological Legitimation," 20–21.

21. Erwin Panofsky, *Renaissance and Renascences in Western Art* (New York: Harper & Row, 1969), 38. See also Ladner, *Idea of Reform*, 20–21.

22. Panofsky, *Renaissance and Renascences in Western Art*, 18–21.

23. Ibid., 34–35.

24. Ibid., 113.

25. E. J. Hobsbawm, "Revolution," in *Revolution in History*, ed. Roy Porter and Mikuláš Teich (Cambridge: Cambridge University Press, 1986), 8.

26. Arendt, *On Revolution*, 21.

27. I. Bernard Cohen, *Revolution in Science* (Cambridge, MA: Belknap Press of Harvard University Press, 1985), 66, quoting an unnamed dictionary of 1611.

28. Ibid., 57; Arendt, *On Revolution*, 35.

29. Reinhart Koselleck, *Futures Past: On the Semantics of Historical Time*, trans. Keith Tribe (Cambridge, MA: MIT Press, 1985), 44.

30. Martin Malia, *History's Locomotives: Revolutions and the Making of the Modern World* (New Haven, CT: Yale University Press, 2006), 289.

31. Cohen, *Revolution in Science*, 57–58, 64.

32. Koselleck, *Futures Past*, 41.

33. M. I. Finley, "Revolution in Antiquity," in Porter and Teich, *Revolution and History*, 50; Cohen, *Revolution in Science*, 54–55; Malia, *History's Locomotives*, 299–300.

34. Cohen, *Revolution in Science*, 55.

35. Finley, "Revolution in Antiquity," 49–50; Cohen, *Revolution in Science*, 178–79.

36. Malia, *History's Locomotives*, 144.

37. Cohen, *Revolution in Science*, 71; Arendt, *On Revolution*, 36.

38. Malia, *History's Locomotives*, 6; Cohen, *Revolution in Science*, 65, 208; Arendt, *On Revolution*, 37.

39. From Thomas Paine, *The Rights of Man*; quoted in Cohen, *Revolution in Science*, xi.

40. Malia, *History's Locomotives*, 4.

41. Ibid., 146; Cohen, *Revolution in Science*, 64.

42. Malia, *History's Locomotives*, 163.

43. Arendt, *On Revolution*, 37–39.

44. Koselleck, *Futures Past*, 46.

45. Malia, *History's Locomotives*, 256.

46. Cohen, *Revolution in Science*, 274.

47. Pierre-Joseph Proudhon, quoted in Arendt, *On Revolution*, 44.

48. Ibid., 207.

49. Cohen, *Revolution in Science*, 262–69.

50. See, for example, Katharine Park and Lorraine Daston, "Introduction: The Age of the New," in *The Cambridge History of Science: Early Modern Science*, ed. Katharine Park and Lorraine Daston (Cambridge: Cambridge University Press, 2006), 12–13.

51. Cohen, *Revolution in Science*, 22, 277–78, 380, 574.

52. Steven Shapin, *The Scientific Revolution* (Chicago: University of Chicago Press, 1996), 1.

53. Cohen, *Revolution in Science*, 230.

54. Ibid., 158, 214–16.

55. Ibid., 216.

56. Charles Whitney, *Francis Bacon and Modernity* (New Haven, CT: Yale University Press, 1986), 15, 31, 110.

57. Shapin, *Scientific Revolution*, 139. See also Roy Porter, "The Scientific Revolution: A Spoke in the Wheel?" in Porter and Teich, *Revolution in History*, 299.

58. For specific appeals linking the new science to the Renaissance and the Reformation, see Theo Verbeek, "Tradition and Novelty: Descartes and Some Cartesians," in *The Rise of Modern Philosophy*, ed. Tom Sorell (Oxford: Clarendon Press, 1993), 184–85.

59. Whitney, *Francis Bacon and Modernity*, 95.

60. Julian Martin, "Francis Bacon, Authority, and the Moderns," in Sorell, *Rise of Modern Philosophy*, 74; Cohen, *Revolution in Science*, 142.

61. Cohen devotes quite a few pages to showing that Kant did not call for or identify a "Copernican revolution" in science, though he did intend to effect a complete revolution himself (*Revolution in Science*, 247). See also Whitney, *Francis Bacon and Modernity*, 101.

62. Thomas S. Kuhn, *The Structure of Scientific Revolutions*, 4th ed. (Chicago: University of Chicago Press, 2012), 203.

63. Ibid., 53.

64. Daniel Garber, "Physics and Foundations," in Park and Daston, *Cambridge History of Science: Early Modern Science*, 31.

65. Shapin, *Scientific Revolution*, 74.

66. John Henry, *The Scientific Revolution and the Origins of Modern Science*, 2nd ed. (London: Palgrave, 2002), 17; Shapin, *Scientific Revolution*, 67.

67. Peter Alexander, *Ideas, Qualities and Corpuscles: Locke and Boyle on the External World* (Cambridge: Cambridge University Press, 1985), 50, 53; David C. Lindberg, "Conceptions of the Scientific Revolution," in *Reappraisals of the Scientific Revolution*, ed. David C. Lindberg and Robert S. Westman (Cambridge: Cambridge University Press, 1990), 2.

68. Shapin, *Scientific Revolution*, 75.

69. John Cottingham, "Cartesian Metaphysics, Modern Philosophy," in Sorell, *Rise of Modern Philosophy*, 147.

70. For Patrizzi, see Ann Blair, "Natural Philosophy," in Park and Daston, *Cambridge History of Science: Early Modern Science*, 376–77.

71. Francis Bacon, *Novum Organum*; quoted in Cohen, *Revolution in Science*, 150.

72. Francis Bacon, *New Organon*; quoted in Lindberg, "Conceptions of the Scientific Revolution," 4.

73. Ibid., 8.

74. Randall Collins, *The Sociology of Philosophies: A Global Theory of Intellectual Change* (Cambridge, MA: Belknap Press of Harvard University Press, 1998), 849. See also Garber, "Physics and Foundations," 45.

75. Shapin, *Scientific Revolution*, 58.

76. Ibid., 30, 36. See the discussion in Collins, *Sociology of Philosophies*, 536.

77. Blair, "Natural Philosophy," 375; Alfred North Whitehead, *Science and the Modern World* (New York: Macmillan, 1944), 145.

78. Catherine Wilson, *Epicureanism at the Origins of Modernity* (Oxford: Clarendon Press, 2008), 227. See also Lynn S. Joy, "Scientific Explanation from Formal Causes to Laws of Nature," in Park and Daston, *Cambridge History of Science: Early Modern Science*, 79, and Alexander, *Ideas, Qualities and Corpuscles*, 60–61.

79. Wilson, *Epicureanism at the Origins of Modernity*, 53. See also Garber, "Physics and Foundations," 49.

80. Wilson, *Epicureanism at the Origins of Modernity*, 159.

81. Margaret J. Osler, "Ancient, Moderns, and the History of Philosophy: Gassendi's Epicurean Project," in Sorell, *Rise of Modern Philosophy*, 129–43.

82. Wilson quotes the chemist Daniel Sennert's *Epitome naturalis scientiae* (1600) to the effect that "I wonder the Doctrine of Atomes should be traduced as Novelty" when "All the Learnedest Philosophers have acknowledged that there are such Atomes, not to speak of *Empedocles, Democritus, Epicurus*" (*Epicureanism at the Origins of Modernity*, 39).

83. Ibid., 100.

84. Descartes, *Discourse on Method*; quoted in Cottingham, "Cartesian Metaphysics, Modern Philosophy," 156.

85. Ibid., 165.

86. Henry, *Scientific Revolution and the Origins of Modern Science*, 72–73.

87. Isaac Newton, *Principia Mathematica* (1713); quoted in Garber, "Physics and Foundations," 55.

88. Wilson, *Epicureanism at the Origins of Modernity*, 53.

89. Garber, "Physics and Foundations," 24.

90. Ibid., 49; Alexander, *Ideas, Qualities and Corpuscles*, 62; Wilson, *Epicureanism at the Origins of Modernity*, 55, 244–45.

91. Garber, "Physics and Foundations," 48; Blair, "Natural Philosophy," 396; Shapin, *Scientific Revolution*, 47.

92. Isaac Newton, *Opticks*, ed. I. B. Cohen, 4th ed. (New York: Dover, 1952), 400; quoted in Wilson, *Epicureanism at the Origins of Modernity*, 32.

93. Robert Boyle, *The Origin of Forms and Qualities*; quoted in Alexander, *Ideas, Qualities and Corpuscles*, 83.

94. Ibid., 60–61; Wilson, *Epicureanism at the Origins of Modernity*, 22–23.

95. Wilson, *Epicureanism at the Origins of Modernity*, 59–60.

96. Joy, "Scientific Explanation from Formal Causes to Laws of Nature," 71.

97. Garber, "Physics and Foundations," 51; Blair, "Natural Philosophy," 396; Henry, *Scientific Revolution and the Origins of Modern Science*, 70.

98. Wilson, *Epicureanism at the Origins of Modernity*, 83, 107; Elliott Sober, *Evidence and Evolution: The Logic behind the Science* (Cambridge: Cambridge University Press, 2008), 122–25.

99. Osler, "Ancient, Moderns, and the History of Philosophy," 140–42.

100. Shapin, *Scientific Revolution*, 143.

101. Lucretius, *On the Nature of Things*, trans. Martin Ferguson Smith (Indianapolis: Hackett, 2001), 18; Wilson, *Epicureanism at the Origins of Modernity*, 86–87.

102. Cohen, *Revolution in Science*, 153–54; Henry, *Scientific Revolution and the Origins of Modern Science*, 71–72.

103. Wilson, *Epicureanism at the Origins of Modernity*, 98, 226.

104. Galileo, quoted in Shapin, *Scientific Revolution*, 69; Cohen, *Revolution in Science*, 140.

105. Francis Bacon, *Novum Organum*; quoted in Whitney, *Francis Bacon and Modernity*, 107.

106. Robert Boyle, *About the Excellency and Grounds of the Mechanical Hypothesis*; quoted in Alexander, *Ideas, Qualities and Corpuscles*, 63.

107. Gottfried Leibniz, *Conversation du marquis de pianese et du pere emery eremite* (ca. 1680); quoted in Wilson, *Epicureanism at the Origins of Modernity*, 102.

108. Ian Hacking, *The Emergence of Probability*, 2nd ed. (Cambridge: Cambridge University Press, 2006), 89.

109. Bertrand Russell, *The Problems of Philosophy* (1912; reprint, Oxford: Oxford University Press, 1959), 90.

110. Robert Friedel, *A Culture of Improvement: Technology and the Western Millennium* (Cambridge, MA: MIT Press, 2007).

CHAPTER THREE

1. Salman Rushdie, *The Satanic Verses* (New York: Viking, 1988), 251.

2. Ibid.

3. Ibid., 5.

4. Ibid., 418.

5. John C. Greene, *Science, Ideology, and World View: Essays in the History of Evolutionary Ideas* (Berkeley: University of California Press, 1981), 166.

6. Elizabeth Grosz, *The Nick of Time: Politics, Evolution, and the Untimely* (Durham, NC: Duke University Press, 2004), 9.

7. Armin P. Moczek, "On the Origins of Novelty in Development and Evolution," *BioEssays* 30 (2008): 432–47; quotation is from p. 432.

8. Gerd B. Müller, "Epigenetic Innovation," in *Evolution: The Extended Synthesis*, ed. Massimo Pigliucci and Gerd B. Müller (Cambridge, MA: MIT Press, 2010), 308.

9. Mary Jane West-Eberhard, *Developmental Plasticity and Evolution* (Oxford: Oxford University Press, 2003), 505.

10. "Thus evolution is all-pervasive. Galaxies, chemical elements, religions, language, and political systems all evolve." Douglas J. Futuyama, *Evolutionary Biology* (Sunderland, MA: Sinauer, 1979), 7.

11. For examples relevant to literature, see William Flesch, *Comeuppance: Costly Signaling, Altruistic Punishment, and Other Biological Components of Fiction* (Cambridge, MA: Harvard University Press, 2009), and Brian Boyd, *On the Origin of Stories: Evolution, Cognition, and Fiction* (Cambridge, MA: Harvard University Press, 2009). In *Art as a Social System*, first published in German in 1995, Niklas Luhmann treats evolution as an "untried theory" as far as the social sciences are concerned. Insofar as most applications of the term outside biology are mainly analogical, Luhmann must be right, but the existence of works like those just listed suggests that he is no longer alone in attempting a strict application of evolutionary theory outside biology. Niklas Luhmann, *Art as a Social System*, trans. Eva M. Knodt (Stanford, CA: Stanford University Press, 2000), 214.

12. Matthew H. Nitecki, ed., *Evolutionary Innovations* (Chicago: University of Chicago Press, 1990), 4.

13. Aristotle, *On the Soul*; quoted in David J. Depew and Bruce H. Weber, *Darwinism Evolving: Systems Dynamics and the Genealogy of Natural Selection* (Cambridge, MA: MIT Press, 1995), 37.

14. Immanuel Kant, *Critique of Teleological Judgement* (1790), trans. J. C. Meredith (Oxford: Oxford University Press, 1928), 31; quoted in Michael Ruse, *Defining Darwin: Essays in the History and Philosophy of Evolutionary Biology* (Amherst, NY: Prometheus, 2009), 40.

15. Note the definition offered by Depew and Weber: "A system is alive if and only if it exhibits the structures and behavior of informed, self-replicating, dissipative autocatalytic cycles" (*Darwinism Evolving*, 467).

16. François Jacob, *The Logic of Life: A History of Heredity*, trans. Betty E. Spillmann (New York: Pantheon, 1982), 57, 73.

17. Olivier Rieppel, "Atomism, Epigenesis, Preformation and Pre-Existence: A Clarification of Terms and Consequences," *Biological Journal of the Linnean Society* 28 (1986): 331–33.

18. Depew and Weber, *Darwinism Evolving*, 35–42. For a description of Darwin's opinion of Aristotle and a discussion of the relationship between their views, see Allan Gotthelf, "Darwin on Aristotle," *Journal of the History of Biology* 32 (1999): 3–30.

19. Robert J. Richards, *The Meaning of Evolution: The Morphological Construction and Ideological Reconstruction of Darwin's Theory* (Chicago: University of Chicago Press, 1992), 6–7. See also Rieppel, "Atomism, Epigenesis, Preformation and Pre-Existence," 333–34.

20. For a useful philosophical discussion of preformationism and epigenesis as the Scylla and Charybdis of evolutionary theory, see Jason Scott Robert, *Embryology, Epigenesis, and Evolution: Taking Development Seriously* (Cambridge: Cambridge University Press, 2004), 35–41.

21. Depew and Weber, *Darwinism Evolving*, 36; Robin Waterfield, *The First Philosophers: The Presocratics and Sophists* (Oxford: Oxford University Press, 2000), 134.

22. Lucretius, *On the Nature of Things*, trans. Martin Ferguson Smith (Indianapolis: Hackett, 2001), 133.

23. Gordon Campbell, *Lucretius on Creation and Evolution: A Commentary on "De Rerum Natura" Book Five, Lines 772-1104* (Oxford: Oxford University Press, 2003), 58, 98-99, 108.

24. E. S. Russell, *Form and Function: A Contribution to the History of Animal Morphology* (New York: Dutton, 1917), v.

25. Rieppel, "Atomism, Epigenesis, Preformation and Pre-Existence," 336; Jacob, *Logic of Life*, 73.

26. Campbell, *Lucretius on Creation and Evolution*, 107.

27. Nicolas Malebranche, *Recherche de la vérité*; quoted in Jacob, *Logic of Life*, 60.

28. Russell, *Form and Function*, 114; Peter J. Bowler, *Evolution: The History of an Idea*, rev. ed. (Berkeley: University of California Press, 1989), 57-58.

29. Campbell, *Lucretius on Creation and Evolution*, 133-34; Richards, *Meaning of Evolution*, 7.

30. Richards, *Meaning of Evolution*, 7.

31. Jacob, *Logic of Life*, 57.

32. Stephen Jay Gould, *The Structure of Evolutionary Theory* (Cambridge, MA: Belknap Press of Harvard University Press, 2002), 160-61.

33. Ernst Mayr, *The Growth of Biological Thought: Diversity, Evolution, and Inheritance* (Cambridge, MA: Harvard University Press, 1982), 327.

34. William Whewell, *The Philosophy of the Inductive Sciences*; quoted in David J. Depew, "The Rhetoric of the *Origin of Species*," in *The Cambridge Companion to the "Origin of Species*," ed. Michael Ruse and Robert J. Richards (Cambridge: Cambridge University Press, 2009), 241.

35. Richards, *Meaning of Evolution*, 15.

36. Ibid., 28, 47; Russell, *Form and Function*, 92; Gregory A. Wray, "Evolution and Development," in *Evolution: The First Four Billion Years*, ed. Michael Ruse and Joseph Travis (Cambridge, MA: Belknap Press of Harvard University Press, 2009), 209-10.

37. Bowler, *Evolution*, 33-34; Mayr, *Growth of Biological Thought*, 406.

38. Bowler, *Evolution*, 115-16; Jacob, *Logic of Life*, 156; Jean Gayon, "Georges Cuvier," in Ruse and Travis, *Evolution*, 500-501, 699.

39. Lucretius, *On the Nature of Things*, 37.

40. Gould, *Structure of Evolutionary Theory*, 488-89. The same term had been used by Buffon. See Mayr, *Growth of Biological Thought*, 374.

41. Ruse, *Defining Darwin*, 41.

42. Depew and Weber, *Darwinism Evolving*, 34, 45; Pietro Corsi, "Etienne Geoffroy Saint-Hilaire," in Ruse and Travis, *Evolution*, 607.

43. Richard Owen, quoted in Gould, *Structure of Evolutionary Theory*, 327. For a

précis of Owen's position on the origin of species and on evolution in general, see Nicolaas A. Rupke, "Richard Owen," in Ruse and Travis, *Evolution*, 795–98.

44. Depew and Weber, *Darwinism Evolving*, 45. Note Gould's caution that Cuvier did not say that extinctions and replacements were total (*Structure of Evolutionary Theory*, 483).

45. Depew and Weber, *Darwinism Evolving*, 45–47; Gould, *Structure of Evolutionary Theory*, 180.

46. Janet Browne, *Charles Darwin: Voyaging* (New York: Knopf, 1995), 512–15.

47. Charles Darwin, *The Annotated "Origin": A Facsimile Edition of "On the Origin of Species"* (Cambridge.MA: Harvard University Press, 2009), 312. This edition is a facsimile of the 1859 edition of the *Origin*. The passage can be found in *The Origin of Species: A Variorum Text*, ed. Morse Peckham (2006; reprint, Philadelphia: University of Pennsylvania Press, 1959), on 521, where it is clear that Darwin left the phrasing unchanged through later editions.

48. Jacob, *Logic of Life*, 190.

49. Darwin, *Annotated "Origin,"* 312.

50. Timothy Shanahan, *The Evolution of Darwinism: Selection, Adaptation, and Progress in Evolutionary Biology* (Cambridge: Cambridge University Press, 2004), 21.

51. William Ogle, private correspondence, 1882; quoted in Depew and Weber, *Darwinism Evolving*, 43. For a discussion of the context of this letter, see Gotthelf, "Darwin on Aristotle."

52. J. M'Cann, "Anti-Darwinism" (1869); quoted in Charles Darwin, *The Descent of Man* (New York: Appleton, 1872), 61.

53. Elliott Sober, *Evidence and Evolution: The Logic Behind the Science* (Cambridge: Cambridge University Press, 2008), 116, 124–25. See also Campbell, *Lucretius on Creation and Evolution*, 6, and John Beatty, "Reconsidering the Importance of Chance Variation," in Pigliucci and Müller, *Evolution*, 22–24.

54. Jacques Monod, *Chance and Necessity: An Essay on the Natural Philosophy of Modern Biology*, trans. Austryn Wainhouse (New York: Vintage, 1972), especially 111–12; Mayr, *Growth of Biological Thought*, 86, 502; Gould, *Structure of Evolutionary Theory*, 30, 1027. See also Jacob, *Logic of Life*, 167, and M. J. S. Hodge, "Natural Selection as a Causal, Empirical, and Probabilistic Theory," in *The Probabilistic Revolution*, ed. Lorenz Krüger, Lorraine J. Daston, and Michael Heidelberger (Cambridge, MA: MIT Press, 1987), 2:233–70.

55. Alfred Russell Wallace, *Darwinism* (London: Macmillan, 1889), 99; quoted in John R. G. Turner, "Random Genetic Drift, R. A. Fisher, and the Oxford School of Ecological Genetics," in Krüger et al., *Probabilistic Revolution*, 2:316.

56. Darwin himself resisted Wallace's notion that variation should be seen as a kind of constant in nature, an "inherent and necessary contingency, under all circumstances" (*Annotated Origin*, 43; see the *Variorum*, 117–18, for the slight changes made to this passage in later editions), as he resisted Joseph Hooker's suggestion

that it would be better to see it as an "innate principle" in nature. See Robert Olby, "Variation and Inheritance," in Ruse and Richards, *Cambridge Companion to the "Origin of Species,"* 35–36. But he also criticized former scientists who had refused to see variation as a consistent *vera causa*, a true cause operating in nature much like gravity (Darwin, *Annotated Origin*, 482; *Variorum*, 750).

57. See the discussion of Darwin's "debt to both poles of the dichotomy" of formalism and functionalism in Gould, *Structure of Evolutionary Theory*, 330–32.

58. Ibid., 254–55.

59. Ibid., 257–60.

60. Though Darwin was not comfortable with the idea of "innate variability of unknown cause" (Olby, "Variation and Inheritance," 43), he was certain that there would always be "abundant variability" for natural selection to work on (David Kohn, "Darwin's Keystone: The Principle of Divergence," in Ruse and Richards, *Cambridge Companion to the "Origin of Species,"* 91).

61. Russell, *Form and Function*, 241.

62. Gould, *Structure of Evolutionary Theory*, 294.

63. Darwin, *Annotated Origin*, 194; *Variorum*, 361.

64. Charles Darwin, *The Variation of Plants and Animals under Domestication* (1868; reprint, Cambridge: Cambridge University Press, 2010), 233.

65. Mayr, *Growth of Biological Thought*, 509.

66. Ernst Mayr, *Evolution and the Diversity of Life: Selected Essays* (Cambridge, MA: Harvard University Press, 1976), 89.

67. Darwin, *Variorum*, 269. This is a statement that first appeared in the third edition of the *Origin* (1861).

68. Tim Lewens, *Darwin* (London: Routledge, 2007), 61.

69. Darwin, *Annotated "Origin,"* 471; *Variorum*, 735.

70. Jacob, *Logic of Life*, 153.

71. Mayr, *Evolution and the Diversity of Life*, 91.

72. Darwin, *Descent of Man*, 35.

73. William James, "Great Men and Their Environment," in *The Will to Believe and Other Essays in Popular Philosophy* (London: Longmans, Green, 1896), 221. The essay was originally published in the *Atlantic Monthly* as "Great Men, Great Thoughts, and the Environment" in 1880.

74. Ibid., 238.

75. See Philip R. Wiener, *Evolution and the Founders of Pragmatism* (Cambridge, MA: Harvard University Press, 1949), especially 101, 103, and Robert J. Richards, *Darwin and the Emergence of Evolutionary Theories of Mind and Behavior* (Chicago: University of Chicago Press, 1987), 427, 436, 440.

76. James, "Great Men and Their Environment," 247.

77. William James, *Some Problems of Philosophy*, in *Writings 1901–1910*, ed. Bruce Kuklick (New York: Library of America, 1987), 1057.

78. Shanahan, *Evolution of Darwinism*, 120; Gould, *Structure of Evolutionary Theory*, 14, 139, 158, 381.

79. Russell, *Form and Function*, 312.

80. Gould, *Structure of Evolutionary Theory*, 364; Mayr, *Evolution and the Diversity of Life*, 92; Gerd B. Müller and Günter P. Wagner, "Novelty in Evolution: Restructuring the Concept," *Annual Review of Ecological Systems* 22 (1991): 229–30.

81. Marjorie Grene and David Depew, *The Philosophy of Biology: An Episodic History* (Cambridge: Cambridge University Press, 2004), 235; Gould, *Structure of Evolutionary Theory*, 342–44.

82. Mayr, *Evolution and the Diversity of Life*, 93; Mayr, *Growth of Biological Thought*, 548; Jan Sapp, *Beyond the Gene: Cytoplasmic Inheritance and the Struggle for Authority in Genetics* (New York: Oxford University Press, 1987), 21–22.

83. William Bateson, "Heredity and Variation in Modern Lights," in Haeckel, Thomson, Weismann, and others, *Evolution in Modern Thought* (New York: Boni and Liveright, 1920), 103.

84. Bowler, *Evolution*, 276–77; Gould, *Structure of Evolutionary Theory*, 431.

85. Hugo de Vries, *Species and Varieties: Their Origin by Mutation* (1905); quoted in Grene and Depew, *Philosophy of Biology*, 249, and Gould, *Structure of Evolutionary Theory*, 427.

86. Darwin, *Annotated "Origin,"* 471; *Variorum*, 735; Gould, *Structure of Evolutionary Theory*, 151; Mayr, *Growth of Biological Thought*, 259.

87. Wiener, *Evolution and the Founders of Pragmatism*, 101; Henri Bergson, *Creative Evolution*, trans. Arthur Mitchell (New York: Holt, 1911), 63.

88. De Vries did believe in a kind of "species selection" as a struggle between mutations, though not in the kind of individual selection that Darwin had defined, which de Vries dismissed as a struggle between "fluctuations." See Gould, *Structure of Evolutionary Theory*, 447.

89. Hugo de Vries, *Espèces et Variétés*; quoted in Jacob, *Logic of Life*, 222.

90. Hugo de Vries, *The Mutation Theory*, trans. J. B. Farmer and A. D. Darbishire (Chicago: Open Court, 1909), 4, 32.

91. Scientific understanding of mutation and the evolution of new genes has become much more complex, just in the past few years. For a survey and discussion of the various ways in which genetic material can be duplicated, repurposed, recombined, and altered to give rise to new genes, see Henrik Kaessman, "Origins, Evolution, and Phenotypic Impact of New Genes," *Genomic Research* 20 (2010): 1313–26.

92. Gould, *Structure of Evolutionary Theory*, 426.

93. Mayr, *Evolution and the Diversity of Life*, 92. See Gould's *Structure of Evolutionary Theory* in general for an epic account of the arguments for saltationism.

94. Julian Huxley, *Evolution: The Modern Synthesis* (New York: Harper and Brothers, 1943), 28.

95. Julian Huxley, *The Individual in the Animal Kingdom* (Cambridge: Cambridge

University Press, 1912), vii; Ruse, *Defining Darwin*, 125. For the influence of Bergson on other biologists of Huxley's generation, see Michael Ruse, "Henri Bergson," in Ruse and Travis, *Evolution*, 446; Mayr, *Evolution and the Diversity of Life*, 357; Vassiliki Betty Smocovitis, *Unifying Biology: The Evolutionary Synthesis and Evolutionary Biology* (Princeton, NJ: Princeton University Press, 1996), 111.

96. Bergson, *Creative Evolution*, 56.

97. John Mullarkey, *Bergson and Philosophy* (Edinburgh: Edinburgh University Press, 1999), 72, 65.

98. Bergson, *Creative Evolution*, 28.

99. Ibid., 249; Mullarkey, *Bergson and Philosophy*, 128.

100. Bergson, *Creative Evolution*, 89.

101. Ibid., 92.

102. Mullarkey, *Bergson and Philosophy*, 139.

103. Richards, *Darwin and the Emergence of Evolutionary Theories*, 332. Morgan had also been a pupil of T. H. Huxley. See ibid., 375.

104. C. Lloyd Morgan, *Emergent Evolution* (New York: Holt, 1926), 3, 12.

105. David Blitz, *Emergent Evolution: Qualitative Novelty and the Levels of Reality* (Dordrecht: Kluwer, 1992), 77.

106. Morgan, *Emergent Evolution*, 64–66.

107. H. S. Jennings, "Diverse Doctrines of Evolution, Their Relation to the Practice of Science and of Life," *Science* 65 (1927): 19–25. For an account of Jennings's dissatisfaction with natural selection and turn to emergent evolution, see Sapp, *Beyond the Gene*, 91–92.

108. Philip Clayton, *Mind and Emergence: From Quantum to Consciousness* (Oxford: Oxford University Press, 2004), 67, 75.

109. Terrence W. Deacon, "Multilevel Selection in a Complex Adaptive System: The Problem of Language Origins," in *Evolution and Learning: The Baldwin Effect Reconsidered*, ed. Bruce H. Weber and David J. Depew (Cambridge, MA: MIT Press, 2003), 85.

110. Richards, *Meaning of Evolution*, 5; Bowler, *Evolution*, 9.

111. Richards, *Meaning of Evolution*, 5.

112. Bergson, *Creative Evolution*, 239.

113. Gould, *Structure of Evolutionary Theory*, 1216–17.

114. Gillian Beer, *Darwin's Plots: Evolutionary Narrative in Darwin, George Eliot and Nineteenth-Century Fiction*, 2nd ed. (Cambridge: Cambridge University Press, 2000), 39.

CHAPTER FOUR

1. C. S. Peirce, "The Doctrine of Necessity Examined," originally published in the *Monist*, 1892; quoted from *Philosophical Writings of Peirce*, ed. Justus Buchler (New York: Dover, 1955), 318.

2. Ibid., 319.

3. Ibid., 337.

4. Ibid., 334, 335.

5. Ibid., 336.

6. Ibid., 164.

7. Ibid., 324.

8. Ibid.; Ian Hacking, *The Taming of Chance* (Cambridge: Cambridge University Press, 1990), 11.

9. R. A. Fisher, quoted in Gerd Gigerenzer et al., *The Empire of Chance: How Probability Changed Science and Everyday Life* (Cambridge: Cambridge University Press, 1989), 60.

10. Jan von Plato, "Probabilistic Physics the Classical Way," in *The Probabilistic Revolution*, ed. Lorenz Krüger, Gerd Gigerenzer, and Mary S. Morgan (Cambridge, MA: MIT Press, 1987), 2:380.

11. David Hume, *An Enquiry concerning Human Understanding*, ed. Peter Millican (Oxford: Oxford University Press, 2007), 80; see also Gigerenzer et al., *Empire of Chance*, 9–10.

12. Lorraine J. Daston, "The Domestication of Risk," in Krüger, Gigerenzer, and Morgan, *Probabilistic Revolution*, 1:238–40.

13. Gigerenzer et al., *Empire of Chance*, 29–30.

14. Ibid., 11–12.

15. Hacking, *Taming of Chance*, 95; Gigerenzer et al., *Empire of Chance*, 39–40.

16. Hacking, *Taming of Chance*, 102.

17. Gigerenzer et al., *Empire of Chance*, 142.

18. Hacking, *Taming of Chance*, 73, 108.

19. Ibid., 107. Quetelet originally conceived of the average man as a fiction, and he postulated a great many average beings, depending on different contexts and circumstances. Over time, though, both Quetelet's ideas about the average and the popular version of them became simplified. See Stephen J. Stigler, *The History of Statistics: The Measurement of Uncertainty before 1900* (Cambridge, MA: Harvard University Press, 1986), 170.

20. Gigerenzer et al., *Empire of Chance*, 29–30.

21. Buchler, *Philosophical Writings of Peirce*, 325.

22. Quentin Meillassoux, *After Finitude: An Essay on the Necessity of Contingency*, trans. Ray Brassier (London: Continuum, 2008), 98.

23. Elliott Sober, *Evidence and Evolution: The Logic behind the Science* (Cambridge: Cambridge University Press, 2008), 13.

24. Ibid., 104–5.

25. Gigerenzer et al., *Empire of Chance*, 136.

26. Hacking, *Taming of Chance*, 107; Stephen Jay Gould, *The Structure of Evolutionary Theory* (Cambridge, MA: Belknap Press of Harvard University Press, 2002), 595.

27. M. J. S. Hodge, "Natural Selection as a Causal, Empirical, and Probabilis-

tic Theory," in Krüger, Gigerenzer, and Morgan, *Probabilistic Revolution*, 2:265; John R. G. Turner, "Random Genetic Drift, R. A. Fisher, and the Oxford School of Ecological Genetics," in Krüger, Gigerenzer, and Morgan, *Probabilistic Revolution*, 2:325.

28. R. A. Fisher, *Creative Aspects of Natural Law* (Cambridge: Cambridge University Press, 1950), 4.

29. Gigerenzer et al., *Empire of Chance*, 160; Turner, "Random Genetic Drift," 2:318–19.

30. Peter Atkins, *The Laws of Thermodynamics: A Very Short Introduction* (Oxford: Oxford University Press, 2010), 8, 23, 29.

31. Gigerenzer et al., *Empire of Chance*, 62.

32. Atkins, *Laws of Thermodynamics*, 51.

33. David J. Depew and Bruce Weber, *Darwinism Evolving: Systems Dynamics and the Genealogy of Natural Selection* (Cambridge, MA: MIT Press, 1995), 261.

34. Lawrence Sklar, *Physics and Chance: Philosophical Issues in the Foundations of Statistical Mechanics* (Cambridge: Cambridge University Press, 1993), 41–42.

35. Ibid., 297–300.

36. Ibid., 38–39.

37. W. D. Niven, ed., *The Scientific Papers of James Clerk Maxwell* (Cambridge: Cambridge University Press, 1890), 2:253.

38. Understood in this way, statistical mechanics would be classical mechanics "applied under conditions of less than perfect information." Bas van Fraassen, *The Scientific Image* (Oxford: Oxford University Press, 1980), 164.

39. Buchler, *Philosophical Writings of Peirce*, 364–74.

40. J. C. Maxwell, "Science and Free Will" (1873), in *The Life of James Clerk Maxwell*, ed. Lewis Campbell and William Garnett (London: Macmillan, 1882), 444.

41. Sklar, *Physics and Chance*, 103–8.

42. Van Fraassen, *Scientific Image*, 188.

43. Maria Carla Galavotti, "Probability," in *The Routledge Companion to the Philosophy of Science*, ed. Stathis Psillos and Martin Curd (New York: Routledge, 2008), 419.

44. Sklar, *Physics and Chance*, 369.

45. Ibid., 420; Barry Loewer, "Determinism and Chance," *Studies in the History and Philosophy of Modern Physics* 32 (2001): 609–20. For a useful discussion from a nontechnical point of view, see Mary Ann Doane, *The Emergence of Cinematic Time: Modernity, Contingency, the Archive* (Cambridge, MA: Harvard University Press, 2002), 96–100.

46. David Z. Albert, *Time and Chance* (Cambridge, MA: Harvard University Press, 2000), 103; Loewer, "Determinism and Chance," 611.

47. Lorenz Krüger, "The Slow Rise of Probabilism," in Krüger, Gigerenzer, and Morgan, *Probabilistic Revolution*, 1:80. Gigerenzer et al., *Empire of Chance*, 185.

48. Maxwell, "Science and Free Will," 442.

49. Sober, *Evidence and Evolution*, 116–17. For Herschel's use of this episode against Darwin, see 124.

50. Gigerenzer et al., *Empire of Chance*, 133.

51. Sigmund Freud, *The Interpretation of Dreams*; quoted in Friedrich Kittler, *Optical Media*, trans. Anthony Enns (Cambridge: Polity Press, 2010), 111.

52. Looked at from another point of view, "all of probability theory might be seen with some justice as a form of information theory." Pieter Adriaans and Johan van Benthem, "Introduction: Information Is What Information Does," in *Philosophy of Information*, ed. Pieter Adriaans and Johan van Benthem (Amsterdam: Elsevier, 2008), 5.

53. Norbert Wiener, *Cybernetics, or Control and Communication in the Animal and the Machine* (New York: John Wiley & Sons; Paris: Hermann, 1948), 150.

54. John R. Pierce, *An Introduction to Information Theory: Symbols, Signals and Noise*, 2nd ed. (New York: Dover, 1980), 35–39.

55. R. V. L. Hartley, "Transmission of Information," *Bell System Technical Journal* (1928): 535.

56. Flo Conway and Jim Siegelman, *Dark Hero of the Information Age: In Search of Norbert Wiener, the Father of Cybernetics* (New York: Basic Books, 2005), 189.

57. Pierce, *Introduction to Information Theory*, 43.

58. Heinz von Foerster, unpublished interview; quoted in Conway and Siegelman, *Dark Hero of the Information Age*, 189.

59. Yehoshua Bar-Hillel and Rudolf Carnap, "Semantic Information," *British Journal for the Philosophy of Science* 4 (August 1953): 147–57.

60. Galavotti, "Probability," 421–22. It was Carnap who first formalized the difference between probability as objective frequency and probability as subjective chance. See Adriaans and van Benthem, introduction to *Philosophy of Information*, 10.

61. Warren Weaver, "Recent Contributions to the Mathematical Theory of Communication," in *The Mathematical Theory of Communication*, by Claude Shannon and Warren Weaver (Urbana: University of Illinois Press, 1949), 100.

62. Shannon and Weaver, *Mathematical Theory of Communication*, 20.

63. Bernd-Olaf Küppers, "Information and Communication in Living Matter," in *Information and the Nature of Reality: From Physics to Metaphysics*, ed. Paul Davies and Niels Henrik Gregersen (Cambridge: Cambridge University Press, 2010), 179.

64. Shannon and Weaver, *Mathematical Theory of Communication*, 26.

65. Jeffrey S. Wicken, *Evolution, Thermodynamics, and Information: Extending the Darwinian Program* (New York: Oxford University Press, 1987), 24. See also Weaver's bluff dismissal of the apparently "bizarre" fact that information and uncertainty are matched in Shannon's theory ("Recent Contributions to the Mathematical Theory of Communication," 116).

66. Luciano Floridi, "Information," in *The Blackwell Guide to the Philosophy of Computing and Information* (Oxford: Blackwell, 2004), 52.

67. P. R. Masani, *Norbert Wiener 1894–1964* (Basel: Birkhäuser Verlag, 1990), 153; Pierce, *Introduction to Information Theory*, 24.

68. Atkins, *Laws of Thermodynamics*, 48.

69. Ibid., 53.

70. Paul Davies, "Universe from Bit," in Davies and Gregersen, *Information and the Nature of Reality*, 78; Jeffrey S. Wicken, "Thermodynamics, Evolution, and Emergence: Ingredients for a New Synthesis," in *Entropy, Information, and Evolution: New Perspectives on Physical and Biological Evolution*, ed. Bruce H. Weber, David J. Depew, and James D. Smith (Cambridge, MA: MIT Press, 1988), 147.

71. Thomas A. Cover and Joy A. Thomas, *Elements of Information Theory*, 2nd ed. (Hoboken, NJ: John Wiley & Sons, 2006), 11, 54.

72. Pierce, *Introduction to Information Theory*, 21.

73. John von Neumann, quoted, without further reference, in A. Golan, "Information and Entropy Econometrics—Editor's View," *Journal of Econometrics* 107 (2002): 1–15. See also Wicken, *Evolution, Thermodynamics, and Information*, 24.

74. Pierce, *Introduction to Information Theory*, 21–23; Wicken, *Evolution, Thermodynamics, and Information*, 24.

75. Norbert Wiener, *Collected Works with Commentaries*, ed. P. Masani (Cambridge: MIT Press, 1985), 4:226.

76. Lily E. Kay, *Who Wrote the Book of Life? A History of the Genetic Code* (Stanford, CA: Stanford University Press, 2000), 94.

77. Shannon and Weaver, *Mathematical Theory of Communication*, 99.

78. Ibid., 3.

79. Terrence W. Deacon, "What Is Missing from Theories of Information?," in Davies and Gregersen, *Information and the Nature of Reality*, 158. There have been a number of attempts to extend Shannon's mathematical model so that it might also account for semantic content. See Fred Dretske, "Epistemology and Information," in Adriaans and van Benthem, *Philosophy of Information*, 32.

80. Shannon and Weaver, *Mathematical Theory of Communication*, 96–98.

81. Ibid., 114.

82. Ibid., 117.

83. Shannon did in fact do some work along these lines. See Pierce, *Introduction to Information Theory*, 88.

84. Deacon, "What Is Missing from Theories of Information?," 148.

85. Ibid., 147. See also Luciano Floridi, "Trends in the Philosophy of Information," in Adriaans and van Benthem, *Philosophy of Information*, 117.

86. Eric Steinhart, "The Physics of Information," in Floridi, *Blackwell Guide to the Philosophy of Information*, 178–85.

87. Seth Lloyd, "The Computational Universe," in Davies and Gregersen, *Information and the Nature of Reality*, 98.

88. John Maynard Smith and Eörs Szathmáry, *The Major Transitions in Evolution* (Oxford: W. H. Freeman, 1995), 309.

89. John Collier, "The Dynamics of Biological Order," in Weber, Depew, and Smith, *Entropy, Information, and Evolution*, 236.

90. Küppers, "Information and Communication in Living Matter," 180–81.

91. Ibid., 181.

92. F. H. C. Crick, J. S. Griffith, and L. E. Orgel, "Codes without Commas," *Proceedings of the National Academy of Sciences* 43 (1957): 420.

93. Crick admitted this, but did not repent, "since 'genetic code' sounds a lot more intriguing than 'genetic cipher.'" See Kay, *Who Wrote the Book of Life?*, 151–52. For Crick's original paper on the problem, see F. H. Crick et al., "General Nature of the Genetic Code for Proteins," *Nature* 192 (1961): 1227–32.

94. See Crick, in Kay, *Who Wrote the Book of Life?*, 174.

95. F. H. C. Crick, "On Protein Synthesis," *Symposia of the Society for Experimental Biology* 12 (1958): 153.

96. François Jacob, *The Logic of Life: A History of Heredity*, trans. Betty E. Spillmann (New York: Pantheon, 1982), 275.

97. Jacques Monod, *Chance and Necessity: An Essay on the Natural Philosophy of Modern Biology*, trans. Austryn Wainhouse (New York: Vintage, 1972), 104.

98. Evelyn Fox Keller, *The Century of the Gene* (Cambridge, MA: Harvard University Press, 2000), 111.

99. Ernst Mayr, *Evolution and the Diversity of Life: Selected Essays* (Cambridge, MA: Harvard University Press, 1976), 35.

100. Quoted in Kay, *Who Wrote the Book of Life?*, 126.

101. John Maynard Smith, "The Concept of Information in Biology," *Philosophy of Science* 67 (June 2000): 178–79.

102. Kay, *Who Wrote the Book of Life?*, 307.

103. Richard Dawkins, *The Blind Watchmaker* (1986); quoted in Susan Oyama, *Evolution's Eye: A Systems View of the Biology-Culture Divide* (Durham, NC: Duke University Press, 2000), 51.

104. Jacob, *Logic of Life*, 289.

105. John Maynard Smith, *Shaping Life: Genes, Embryos and Evolution* (New Haven: Yale University Press, 1999), 19–20.

106. Jacob, *Logic of Life*, 292.

107. Maynard Smith, *Shaping Life*, 19.

108. Francisco Ayala, "Molecular Evolution," in *Evolution: The First Four Billion Years*, ed. Michael Ruse and Joseph Travis (Cambridge, MA: Belknap Press of Harvard University Press, 2009), 133–36.

109. Jesper Hoffmayer, "Genes, Development, and Semiosis," in *Genes in Development: Re-Reading the Molecular Paradigm*, ed. Eva M. Neumann-Held and Cristoph Rehmann-Sutter (Durham, NC: Duke University Press, 2006), 167. See also Jason Scott Robert, *Embryology, Epigenesis, and Evolution: Taking Development Seriously* (Cambridge: Cambridge University Press, 2004), 43–54.

110. David L. Hull, Rodney E. Langman, and Sigrid S. Glenn, "A General Account

of Selection: Biology, Immunology, and Behavior," in *Science and Selection: Essays on Biological Evolution and the Philosophy of Science*, by David L. Hull (Cambridge: Cambridge University Press, 2001), 59.

111. Jacob, *Logic of Life*, 2.

112. Quoted in Kay, *Who Wrote the Book of Life?*, 17.

113. Kay, *Who Wrote the Book of Life?*, 178, 294.

114. Paul E. Griffiths and Eva M. Neumann-Held, "The Many Faces of the Gene," *BioScience* 49 (1999): 659; Kay, *Who Wrote the Book of Life?*, 2. As Kay points out, Shannon himself resisted the application of information theory terminology to genetics, and even such committed proponents as Jacques Monod had their doubts (ibid., 99, 210). See also the discussion in Alex Rosenberg and Daniel W. McShea, *Philosophy of Biology: A Contemporary Introduction* (New York: Routledge, 2008), 175–77.

115. H. F. Nijhout, "Metaphors and the Role of Genes in Development," *BioEssays* 12 (1990): 442; Kay, *Who Wrote the Book of Life?*, 69, 186, 328.

116. Evelyn Fox Keller, *Refiguring Life: Metaphors of Twentieth-Century Biology* (New York: Columbia University Press, 1995), 23, 99.

117. Kay, *Who Wrote the Book of Life?*, 214–16.

118. Griffiths and Neumann-Held, "Many Faces of the Gene," 656. See also Robert, *Embryology, Epigenesis, and Evolution*, 48–54.

119. Gerd B. Müller, "Epigenetic Innovation," in *Evolution—The Extended Synthesis*, ed. Massimo Pigliucci and Gerd B. Müller (Cambridge, MA: MIT Press, 2010), 310.

120. Stuart A. Newman and Gerd B. Müller, "Genes and Form," in Neumann-Held and Rehmann-Sutter, *Genes in Development*, 41.

121. Mary Jane West-Eberhard, *Developmental Plasticity and Evolution* (Oxford: Oxford University Press, 2003), 331. For a good discussion of current positions in developmental biology from an independent point of view, see Robert, *Embryology, Epigenesis, and Evolution*, 109–30.

122. West-Eberhard, *Developmental Plasticity and Evolution*, 15; Kay, *Who Wrote the Book of Life?*, 140. It is worth noting that this is a position adopted by Maynard Smith in *Shaping Life*.

123. Müller, "Epigenetic Innovation," 322. See also John Collier, "Information in Biological Systems," in Adriaans and van Benthem, *Philosophy of Information*, 781. Collier's essay (764–87) is an evenhanded account of the controversies surrounding information theory in the discipline of biology.

124. West-Eberhard, *Developmental Plasticity and Evolution*, 90.

125. Ibid., 144.

126. For another such argument from a different discipline, see Dwight Read, David Lane, and Sander van der Leeuw, "The Innovation Innovation," in *Complexity Perspectives in Innovation and Social Change*, ed. D. Lane et al. (Dordrecht: Springer, 2009), 43–84.

127. West-Eberhard, *Developmental Plasticity and Evolution*, 340.

128. Ibid., 348.

129. Ibid., 159.

130. Hans Blumenberg, *The Legitimacy of the Modern Age*, trans. Robert M. Wallace (Cambridge, MA: MIT Press, 1983), 169–70.

CHAPTER FIVE

1. Thomas Kuhn, *The Structure of Scientific Revolutions*, 4th ed. (Chicago: University of Chicago Press, 2012), 136.

2. Ibid., 207.

3. Steffano Gattei, *Thomas Kuhn's "Linguistic Turn" and the Legacy of Logical Empiricism* (Aldershot: Ashgate, 2008), 2.

4. The first criticisms of Kuhn's book, including Margaret Masterman's classic critique of the paradigm, and Kuhn's response, are included in Imre Lakatos and Alan Musgrave, eds., *Criticism and the Growth of Knowledge* (Cambridge: Cambridge University Press, 1970). For a useful history of the concept of the paradigm before Kuhn, see Paul Hoyningen-Huene, *Reconstructing Scientific Revolutions: Thomas Kuhn's Philosophy of Science* (Chicago: University of Chicago Press, 1993), 132–33. Similarities between Kuhn's paradigm and the episteme of Michel Foucault, who both referred to Kuhn and denied his influence, are discussed by Giorgio Agamben in *The Signature of All Things: On Method*, trans. Luca D'Isanto (New York: Zone Books, 2009), 9–16.

5. Kuhn, *Structure of Scientific Revolutions*, 63, 85, 97, 111, 113.

6. Ibid., 93.

7. Ibid., 44. For a useful discussion of Kuhn's relationship to Wittgenstein, see Gattei, *Thomas Kuhn's "Linguistic Turn,"* especially 18–19 and 202–3.

8. Thomas S. Kuhn, *The Road since Structure*, ed. James Conant and John Haugeland (Chicago: University of Chicago Press, 2000), 36, 92.

9. Kuhn, *Structure of Scientific Revolutions*, 111.

10. Ibid., 111, 192.

11. Ibid., 129. See Joseph Rouse, "Kuhn's Philosophy of Scientific Practice," in *Thomas Kuhn*, ed. Thomas Nickles (Cambridge: Cambridge University Press, 2003), 112.

12. Kuhn, *Structure of Scientific Revolutions*, 126.

13. For a discussion of what he calls "the *Meno* paradox" in relation to Kuhn, see Thomas Nickles, "Normal Science: From Logic to Case-Based and Model-Based Reasoning," in Nickles, *Thomas Kuhn*, 148–49. Agamben addresses this problem by focusing on the sense of *paradigm* in which it simply means a useful example. For him, argument by means of paradigms is neither deductive nor inductive but exemplary, and thus it escapes the closure described as "the *Meno* paradox." See Agamben, *Signature of All Things*, 23–31.

14. Stephen Mumford, "Metaphysics," in *The Routledge Companion to the Philosophy of Science*, ed. Stathis Psillos and Martin Curd (London: Routledge, 2008), 29.

15. See Kuhn, *Road since Structure*, 14.

16. Kuhn, *Structure of Scientific Revolutions*, 5.

17. Ibid., 24, 34–35.

18. Randall Collins, *The Sociology of Philosophies: A Global Theory of Intellectual Change* (Cambridge, MA: Harvard University Press, 1998), 31. For an older view, one reprinted in the year that *The Structure of Scientific Revolutions* appeared, see Abbott Payson Usher, *A History of Mechanical Inventions*, rev. ed. (Cambridge, MA: Harvard University Press, 1962) (originally published 1929).

19. Kuhn, *Structure of Scientific Revolutions*, 2.

20. Ibid., 79.

21. Ibid., 5.

22. Hoyningen-Huene, who has produced the most detailed paraphrase of Kuhn's book, skates past the anomaly in three pages, though even these few pages are mostly devoted to the reception and interpretation of anomalies and not their essential nature. See Hoyningen-Huene, *Reconstructing Scientific Revolutions*, 230–32.

23. Ian Hacking, introductory essay in Kuhn, *Structure of Scientific Revolutions*, xxvi.

24. Kuhn, *Structure of Scientific Revolutions*, 126–27.

25. Ibid., 52.

26. Hacking, introductory essay in ibid., xi–xii.

27. Ibid., 92–95.

28. Ibid., 110–11.

29. K. B. Wray, "Kuhnian Revolutions Revisited," *Synthese* 158 (2007): 66. See also Gattei, *Thomas Kuhn's "Linguistic Turn,"* 31–32, 108–9.

30. Kuhn, *Structure of Scientific Revolutions*, 122.

31. Ibid., 157.

32. Ibid., 93, 160.

33. Ibid., 170, 172.

34. Ibid., 173.

35. There is some controversy in the literature about the extent to which this is true. See Paul Hoyningen-Huene and Thomas C. Reydon, "Discussion: Kuhn's Evolutionary Analogy in *The Structure of Scientific Revolutions* and *The Road Since Structure*," *Philosophy of Science* 77 (2010): 468–76. See also Thomas Nickles, "The Strange Story of Scientific Method," in J. Maheus and T. Nickles, *Models of Creativity and Discovery* (Dordrecht: Springer, 2009), 186.

36. Kuhn, *Structure of Scientific Revolutions*, 64.

37. Thomas S. Kuhn, *The Essential Tension: Selected Studies in Scientific Tradition and Change* (Chicago: University of Chicago Press, 1977), 234.

38. See Hoyningen-Huene, *Reconstructing Scientific Revolutions*, 196, and Nickles, "Normal Science," 153–54.

39. Kuhn, *Essential Tension*, 237.

40. Gattei, *Thomas Kuhn's "Linguistic Turn,"* 196, 204.

41. Vasso Kindi, "Novelty and Revolution in Art and Science: The Connection between Kuhn and Cavell," *Perspectives on Science* 18 (2010): 301.

42. As Jacob puts it: "Although reproduction is an accurate mechanism, although it almost always leads to the formation of an identical organism, yet it inexorably produces from time to time something different: this narrow margin of flexibility is sufficient to ensure the variations needed for evolution." François Jacob, *The Logic of Life: A History of Heredity*, trans. Betty E. Spillman (New York: Pantheon, 1982), 130.

43. One of Kuhn's most interesting statements in this respect is included in the 1969 postscript added to the second edition of *The Structure of Scientific Revolutions*. There he says that "ways of seeing" that have "withstood the tests of group use are worth transmitting from generation to generation" (Kuhn, *Structure of Scientific Revolutions*, 195). This seems a full version of the process he calls "natural selection" on 146.

44. Kuhn, *Road since Structure*, 98.

45. Probably the most influential indictment of cybernetics is Peter Galison, "The Ontology of the Enemy: Norbert Wiener and the Cybernetic Vision," *Critical Inquiry* 21 (1998): 228–66.

46. P. R. Masani, *Norbert Wiener, 1984–1964* (Basel: Birkhäuser Verlag, 1990), 39; Steve J. Heims, *John von Neumann and Norbert Wiener: From Mathematics to the Technologies of Life and Death* (Cambridge, MA: MIT Press, 1980), 9.

47. William James, *Some Problems of Philosophy*, in *Writings 1902–1910*, ed. Bruce Kuklick (New York: Library of America, 1987), 1058–59.

48. Bruce Kuklick, *The Rise of American Philosophy* (New Haven, CT: Yale University Press, 1977), 332; Robert D. Richardson, *William James: In the Maelstrom of American Modernism* (Boston: Houghton Mifflin, 2006), 424–27.

49. Josiah Royce, "The Reality of the Temporal," *International Journal of Ethics* 20 (1910): 262–64.

50. Ibid., 264.

51. Ibid., 270.

52. For a description of the dissertation and an account of Russell's reaction to it, see I. Grattan-Guinness, "Wiener on the Logics of Russell and Schroeder," *Annals of Science* 32 (1975): 103–32.

53. See Bertrand Russell, *The Problems of Philosophy* (New York: Holt, 1912), 224.

54. For Eliot's response, see *The Letters of T. S. Eliot*, ed. Valerie Eliot (San Diego: Harcourt Brace Jovanovich, 1988), 1:79–81.

55. Norbert Wiener, "Relativism," *Journal of Philosophy, Psychology, and Scientific Methods* 11 (1914): 575. Also available in Norbert Wiener, *Collected Works with Commentaries*, ed. P. Masani (Cambridge, MA: MIT Press, 1985), 4:64.

56. Wiener, "Relativism," 575.

57. Ibid., 568.

58. Ibid., 577.

59. Norbert Wiener, "The Highest Good," *Journal of Philosophy, Psychology, and Scientific Methods* 11 (1914): 512–20.

60. Norbert Wiener, "The Relation of Space and Geometry to Experience," *Monist* 32 (1922): 12–60, 200–247, 364–94. Also available in *Collected Works* 1:87–214.

61. Norbert Wiener, *Cybernetics, or Control and Communication in the Animal and the Machine* (New York: John Wiley & Sons; Paris: Hermann, 1948), 48.

62. Thomas S. Kuhn, *Black-Body Theory and the Quantum Discontinuity, 1894–1912* (New York: Oxford University Press, 1978), 28.

63. Ibid., 27.

64. Ibid., 185.

65. Wiener, *Cybernetics*, 49.

66. Ibid.

67. In *Cybernetics* and elsewhere, Wiener makes the connection to Bergson explicit. See 49. See also Masani, *Norbert Wiener, 1984–1964*, 57–58.

68. Norbert Wiener, *I Am a Mathematician*; quoted in Masani, *Norbert Wiener, 1984–1964*, 80.

69. Wiener, *Cybernetics*, 43.

70. Norbert Wiener, *Cybernetics, or Control and Communication in the Animal and the Machine*, 2nd ed. (Cambridge, MA: MIT Press, 1961), 179. (The second edition of *Cybernetics* includes the original 1948 edition and two additional chapters.)

71. For a useful discussion, see Wiener, "Time, Communications, and the Nervous System," in *Collected Works*, 4:228.

72. Masani, *Norbert Wiener, 1984–1964*, 143.

73. Ibid., 153.

74. Wiener, *Cybernetics* (1st ed.), 18.

75. Wiener, "The Mathematics of Self-Organizing Science," in *Collected Works*, 4:279.

76. Masani, *Norbert Wiener, 1984–1964*, 257.

77. Flo Conway and Jim Siegelman, *Dark Hero of the Information Age: In Search of Norbert Wiener, the Father of Cybernetics* (New York: Basic Books, 2005), 148.

78. Wiener, "Homeostasis in the Individual and Society," in *Collected Works*, 4:380.

79. Wiener, *Cybernetics* (1st ed.), 47.

80. Ibid., 187.

81. Norbert Wiener, *The Human Use of Human Beings* (Boston: Houghton Mifflin, 1950), 15.

82. Wiener, *Cybernetics* (1st ed.), 186. See also Heims, *John von Neumann and Norbert Wiener*, 311, and Masani, *Norbert Wiener, 1984–1964*, 283–84.

83. Conway and Siegelman, *Dark Hero of the Information Age*, 289. Steve Joshua Heims, introduction to Norbert Wiener, *Invention: The Care and Feeding of Ideas* (Cambridge, MA: MIT Press, 1993), xii.

84. Conway and Siegelman, *Dark Hero of the Information Age*, 289. Heims, introduction to Wiener, *Invention*, xiii.

85. Wiener, *Invention*, 7.

86. Ibid.

87. Ibid.

88. Ibid., 8.

89. Ibid., 9.

90. Ibid., 15.

91. Ibid., 122.

92. Heims, *Von Neumann and Wiener*, 119.

93. Wiener, *Invention*, 18–19.

94. Ibid., 44.

95. Robert Friedel, *A Culture of Improvement: Technology and the Western Millennium* (Cambridge, MA: MIT Press, 2007), 405. See also Bas C. van Fraassen, *Scientific Representation: Paradoxes of Perspective* (Oxford: Clarendon Press, 2008), 94–101.

96. Wiener, *Invention*, 91.

97. Friedel, *Culture of Improvement*, 300. See also Usher, *A History of Mechanical Inventions*, 353.

98. Wiener, *Invention*, 96.

99. Ibid., 64.

100. Ibid., 65.

101. Ibid., 65, 66, 79, 83.

102. Ibid., 87.

103. Ibid., 100.

104. Ibid., 101.

105. Norbert Wiener, *The Tempter* (New York: Random House, 1959), ii and 6.

106. Ibid., 97.

107. Ibid., 157.

108. Ibid., 183.

109. Ibid., 190.

110. Ibid., 93.

111. Ibid., 93–94.

112. Ibid., 94.

113. Ibid., 113.

114. Ibid., 132.

115. Ibid., 93.

116. Wiener, *Cybernetics* (1st ed.), 190.

117. Wiener, *Tempter*, 128.

118. For a well-balanced discussion of Wiener and cybernetics in relation to "liberal humanism," see N. Katherine Hayles, *How We Became Posthuman* (Chicago: University of Chicago Press, 1999), 84–112.

119. Charles Olson, "The Kingfishers" (1949); quoted in Steve Joshua Heims, *The Cybernetics Group* (Cambridge, MA: MIT Press, 1991), 271.

120. *The Writings of Robert Smithson*, ed. Nancy Holt (New York: New York University Press, 1979), 33. For a reference to "communications theory," see 15.

CHAPTER SIX

1. Arthur C. Danto, "The Artworld," *Journal of Philosophy* 61 (1964): 580.

2. Arthur C. Danto, "Response to Hans Belting," in *Action, Art, History: Engagements with Arthur C. Danto*, ed. Daniel Herwitz and Michael Kelly (New York: Columbia University Press, 2007), 144.

3. Danto, "The Artworld," 573.

4. Ibid.

5. Ibid., 577. Danto does not mention Kuhn in the essay itself, but he acknowledged much later having had Kuhn in mind when writing it. See Caroline A. Jones, "The Modernist Paradigm: The Artworld and Thomas Kuhn," *Critical Inquiry* 26 (2000): 501. Danto mentions Kuhn in *Narration and Knowledge* (New York: Columbia University Press, 2007), xi–xii, and *After the End of Art* (Princeton, NJ: Princeton University Press, 1997), 29–30.

6. Danto, "The Artworld," 573.

7. Josiah Royce, "The Reality of the Temporal," *International Journal of Ethics* 20 (1910): 267.

8. Theodor Adorno, *Aesthetic Theory*, trans. C. Lenhardt (New York: Routledge & Kegan Paul, 1984), 47. See J. M. Bernstein, *Against Voluptuous Bodies: Late Modernism and the Meaning of Painting* (Stanford, CA: Stanford University Press, 2006), 209.

9. Niklas Luhmann, *Art as a Social System*, trans. Eva M. Knodt (Stanford, CA: Stanford University Press, 2000), 199–202.

10. For Samuel Johnson, see James Engell, "Johnson on Novelty and Originality," *Modern Philology* 75 (2009): 273–79. For Joseph Addison, see Clarence DeWitt Thorpe, "Addison and Some of His Predecessors on 'Novelty,'" *PMLA* 52 (1937): 1114–29.

11. Luhmann, *Art as a Social System*, 201.

12. Alain Badiou, *The Century*, trans. Albert Toscano (New York: Polity, 2007), 134.

13. Odilon Redon, "Suggestive Art," in *Manifesto: A Century of Isms*, ed. Mary Ann Caws (Lincoln: University of Nebraska Press, 2001), 52.

14. For a catalogue of such comments, see David W. Galenson, *Painting outside the Lines: Patterns of Creativity in Modern Art* (Cambridge, MA: Harvard University Press, 2001), 32–33.

15. Kasimir Malevich, "Suprematism," in Caws, *Manifesto*, 405.

16. Jackson Pollock, quoted in Galenson, *Painting outside the Lines*, 47.

17. See the excerpts from Nordau (1883) and Hitler (1937) in *Modernism: An Anthology of Sources and Documents*, ed. Vassiliki Kolocotroni, Jane Goldman, and Olga Taxidou (Chicago: University of Chicago Press, 1998), 26, 561.

18. Amédée Ozenfant, "The Art of Living" (1927–28), in Caws, *Manifesto*, 443.

19. Antoine Compagnon, *The Five Paradoxes of Modernity*, trans. Franklin Philip (New York: Columbia University Press, 1994), 57. Compagnon's examples are Manet and Cézanne.

20. Franz Marc, "Der Blaue Reiter" (1912), in Caws, *Manifesto*, 277.

21. Kolocotroni, Goldman, and Taxidou, *Modernism*, 107. See Compagnon, *Five Paradoxes of Modernity*, xv, and Ulrich Lehmann, *Tigersprung: Fashion in Modernity* (Cambridge, MA: MIT Press, 2002), 9, 21–22.

22. Robert Graves and Laura Riding, *A Survey of Modernist Poetry* (New York: Haskell House, 1928), 117. The British edition of this text appeared in 1926.

23. Rosalind E. Krauss, *The Originality of the Avant-Garde and Other Modernist Myths* (Cambridge, MA: MIT Press, 1986).

24. Paul de Man, *Blindness and Insight: Essays in the Rhetoric of Contemporary Criticism*, 2nd ed. (Minneapolis: University of Minnesota Press, 1983), 148, 161. See also the argument in Frank Kermode, *The Sense of an Ending: Studies in the Theory of Fiction* (1966; reprint, Oxford: Oxford University Press, 2000), 116.

25. See Compagnon, *Five Paradoxes of Modernity*, 59–60.

26. Bruno Latour, *We Have Never Been Modern*, trans. Catherine Porter (Cambridge, MA: Harvard University Press, 1993), 69.

27. Randall Collins, *The Sociology of Philosophies: A Global Theory of Intellectual Change* (Cambridge, MA: Harvard University Press, 1998), 80.

28. Guillaume Apollinaire, from *The Cubist Painters* (1913), in Kolocotroni, Goldman, and Taxidou, *Modernism*, 263; David Burliuk et al., "Slap in the Face of Public Taste," (1912), in Caws, *Manifesto*, 230.

29. El Lissitzky, "Topography of Typography" (1923), in Caws, *Manifesto*, 394.

30. Umberto Boccioni et al., "Manifesto of the Futurist Painters" (1910), in Caws, *Manifesto*, 183.

31. Guillaume Apollinaire, "The New Painting" (1912), in Caws, *Manifesto*, 123.

32. F. T. Marinetti, "The Founding and Manifesto of Futurism" (1909), in Kolocotroni, Goldman, and Taxidou, *Modernism*, 250.

33. Wassily Kandinsky, "The Problem of Form" (1912), in Kolocotroni, Goldman, and Taxidou, *Modernism*, 270. See Compagnon, *Five Paradoxes of Modernity*, 66.

34. Tristan Tzara, "Dada Manifesto" (1918), in Kolocotroni, Goldman, and Taxidou, *Modernism*, 277.

35. Hans Richter, "Towards a New World Plasticism" (1927), in Caws, *Manifesto*, 433.

36. Eugene Jolas, "Suggestions for a New Magic" (1927), in Kolocotroni, Goldman, and Taxidou, *Modernism*, 312.

37. Umberto Boccioni, "Technical Manifesto of Futurist Sculpture" (1912), in Caws, *Manifesto*, 178.

38. Mikhail Larionov and Natalya Goncharova, "Rayonists and Futurists" (1913), in Caws, *Manifesto*, 240.

39. See Badiou, *Century*, 8, and Jed Rasula, "Make It New," *Modernism/Modernity* 17 (2010): 715.

40. C. Day Lewis, from *A Hope for Poetry* (1934), in Kolocotroni, Goldman, and Taxidou, *Modernism*, 490.

41. Vladimir Tatlin, "The Initiative Individual Artist in the Creativity of the Collective" (1919), in Caws, *Manifesto*, 401.

42. Clive Bell, "The English Group" (1912), in Kolocotroni, Goldman, and Taxidou, *Modernism*, 193.

43. Robert Motherwell, *Collected Writings*, ed. Stephanie Terenzio (New York: Oxford University Press, 1992), 35; quoted in Galenson, *Painting outside the Lines*, 33.

44. The most prominent proponent of the positive side of this argument is T. J. Clark. See especially *Farewell to an Idea* (New Haven, CT: Yale University Press, 1999).

45. Karl Marx, *The Communist Manifesto*, in *Selected Writings*, ed. David McLellan (Oxford: Oxford University Press, 1985), 224.

46. Richard Wagner, "Art and Revolution" (1849), in Kolocotroni, Goldman, and Taxidou, *Modernism*, 8.

47. Badiou, *Century*, 65.

48. Ibid., 29.

49. Stanley Cavell, "Impressions of Revolution," *Musical Quarterly* 85 (20001): 262.

50. Latour, *We Have Never Been Modern*, 126.

51. Ibid., 70–71.

52. Badiou, *Century*, 136.

53. Emile Zola, "Naturalism on the Stage" (1880), in Kolocotroni, Goldman, and Taxidou, *Modernism*, 171. For a similar idea, of the First World War as the culmination of a process of evolution, see Rasula, "Make It New," 721.

54. For a usefully specific account of Zola's debt to different versions of the theory of evolution, see David Baguley, "Zola and Darwin: a Reassessment," in *The Evolution of Literature: Legacies of Darwin in European Cultures*, ed. Nicholas Saul and Simon J. James (Amsterdam: Rodopi, 2011), 201–12.

55. Jean Moréas, "The Symbolist Manifesto" (1886), in Caws, *Manifesto*, 50.

56. Joaquín Torres García, "Art-Evolution" (1917), in Caws, *Manifesto*, 374.

57. Pierre Reverdy, "On Cubism" (1917), in Caws, *Manifesto*, 139. Reverdy speaks of cubism as "the art in evolution of our time" (138).

58. Kandinsky, "Problem of Form," in Kolocotroni, Goldman, and Taxidou, *Modernism*, 271.

59. Ezra Pound, "Postscript," in Remy de Gourmont, *The Natural Philosophy of Love*, trans. Ezra Pound (New York: Boni & Liveright, 1922), 208.

60. Le Corbusier and Amédée Ozenfant, "Purism" (1920), in Caws, *Manifesto*, 439, 441.

61. Guillaume Apollinaire, "Parade" (1917), in Kolocotroni, Goldman, and Taxidou, *Modernism*, 213.

62. Boccioni, "Technical Manifesto of Futurist Sculpture," in Caws, *Manifesto*, 182.

63. Walter Pater, *The Renaissance: Studies in Art and Poetry*, ed. Donald L. Hill (Berkeley: University of California Press, 1980), 189.

64. Zola, "Naturalism on the Stage," in Kolocotroni, Goldman, and Taxidou, *Modernism*, 170.

65. Graves and Riding, *Survey of Modernist Poetry*, 125.

66. John Dos Passos, "The Writer as Technician" (1935), in Kolocotroni, Goldman, and Taxidou, *Modernism*, 545.

67. Salvador Dali, "Photography, Pure Creation of the Mind" (1927), in Caws, *Manifesto*, 483.

68. Vicente Huidobro, "We Must Create" (1922), in Caws, *Manifesto*, 379.

69. Ibid.

70. Fernand Léger, "The Aesthetic of the Machine" (1924), in Caws, *Manifesto*, 506.

71. Naum Gabo and Antoine Pevsner, "The Realistic Manifesto" (1920), in Caws, *Manifesto*, 399.

72. James Abbott McNeill Whistler, "The Ten O'Clock" (1885), in Caws, *Manifesto*, 7.

73. Guillaume Apollinaire, "Cubism Differs" (1913), in Caws, *Manifesto*, 124.

74. Theo van Doesburg, "Towards a Constructive Poetry" (1923), in Caws, *Manifesto*, 424.

75. Whistler, "The Ten O'Clock," in Caws, *Manifesto*, 13.

76. Luigi Russolo, "The Art of Noise" (1913), in Caws, *Manifesto*, 210.

77. Piet Mondrian, "Neoplasticism in Painting" (1917–1918), in Caws, *Manifesto*, 426.

78. Ferdinand Hodler, "Parallelism" (1900), in Caws, *Manifesto*, 54.

79. Kandinsky, "Problem of Form," in Kolocotroni, Goldman, and Taxidou, *Modernism*, 270.

80. Luhmann, *Art as a Social System*, 223.

81. Kasimir Malevich, "Suprematism" (1927), in Caws, *Manifesto*, 407.

82. Vladimir Mayakovsky, "The Relationship between Contemporary Theatre and Cinema and Art," in *The Film Factory: Russian and Soviet Cinema in Documents*, ed. Richard Taylor and Ian Christie (Cambridge, MA: Harvard University Press, 1988), 37; quoted in Rasula, "Make It New," 725.

83. Georg Lukacs, "Realism in the Balance," in *Aesthetics and Politics*, ed. Ronald Taylor (London: Verso, 1980), 54.

84. Dali, "Photography," in Caws, *Manifesto*, 482.

85. Luhmann, *Art as a Social System*, 225.

86. Ibid., 214.

87. Peter Gay, *Modernism: The Lure of Heresy* (New York: Norton, 2008), 46, 106.

88. Richard Rorty, "Philosophy as a New Kind of Writing," *New Literary History* 10 (1978): 153; Frank Lentricchia, "Lyric in the Culture of Capitalism," *American Literary History* 1 (1989): 73; Jackson Lears, "Uneasy Courtship: Modern Art and Mod-

ern Advertising," *American Quarterly* 39 (1987): 138; Fredric Jameson, "Reification and Utopia in Mass Culture," *Social Text* 1 (1979): 136. Damrosch is in fact quoting another participant, in statements made at a conference. David Damrosch, *Meetings of the Mind* (Princeton, NJ: Princeton University Press, 2000), 16.

89. For Chinese names and terms, the most current transliteration will be given, with Pound's version or versions in parentheses.

90. James Legge, *The Life and Teachings of Confucius* (Philadelphia: Lippincott, 1867), 268. Though the exact anecdote, including the bathtub, may not appear elsewhere, the principle behind the anecdote does. The treatment of T'ang in the *Shu Jing*, the original history work on which the *T'ung-Chien Kang-Mu* is based, includes this observation: "When a sovereign's virtue is daily being renewed he is cherished throughout the myriad regions; when his mind is full only of himself he is abandoned by the nine branches of his kindred." Clae Waltham, *Shu Ching: Book of History; A Modernized Edition of the Translations of James Legge* (Chicago: Gateway, 1971), 71. This earlier version of the T'ang story makes it clear that what needs to be renewed is the virtue of the sovereign, a fact that was also important to Pound but that tended to drop out as he simplified his translation.

91. See Hugh Kenner's discussion of Chu Hsi in *The Pound Era* (Berkeley: University of California Press, 1971), 231.

92. A. David Moody, *Ezra Pound: Poet* (Oxford: Oxford University Press, 2007), 238; Mary Paterson Cheadle, *Ezra Pound's Confucian Translations* (Ann Arbor: University of Michigan Press, 1997), 10.

93. Cheadle, *Ezra Pound's Confucian Translations*, 23.

94. Ezra Pound, *Ta Hio: The Great Learning, Newly Rendered into the American Language* (Seattle: University of Washington Chapbooks, 1928), 10.

95. M. G. Pauthier, *Confucius et Mencius: Les quatres livres de philosophie morale et politique de la Chine* (Paris: Charpentier, Libraire-Éditeur, 1858), 44.

96. Legge, *Life and Teachings of Confucius*, 268.

97. Pound, *Ta Hio*, 12.

98. Ibid.

99. On this point, see Douglas Mao, *Solid Objects: Modernism and the Test of Production* (Princeton, NJ: Princeton University Press, 1998), 279n23.

100. Legge, *Life and Teachings of Confucius*, 268.

101. Pound, *Ta Hio*, 12.

102. Ibid.

103. Ovid, *Metamorphoses*; quoted in F. R. Ankersmit, *Historical Representation* (Stanford, CA: Stanford University Press, 2005), 116.

104. Norman J. Girardot, *The Victorian Translation of China: James Legge's Oriental Pilgrimage* (Berkeley: University of California Press, 2002), 40–41, 236.

105. Gerhart B. Ladner, *The Idea of Reform: Its Impact on Christian Thought and Action in the Age of the Fathers* (Cambridge, MA: Harvard University Press, 1959), 44–45.

106. Jacob Burckhardt, *The Civilization of the Renaissance in Italy* (New York: Modern Library, 1954), 130.

107. Ladner, *Idea of Reform*, 20–21.

108. Ezra Pound, *Jefferson and/or Mussolini* (1935; reprint, New York: Liveright, 1970), 112.

109. Ibid., 113.

110. Cheadle, *Ezra Pound's Confucian Translations*, 39. In the mid-50s, Pound asked Achilles Fang for help in finding a brush-stroked version of *xin* (hsin) that clearly depicted the axe and what he saw as a tree and some piled wood. See *Ezra Pound's Chinese Friends: Stories in Letters*, ed. Zhaoming Qian (Oxford: Oxford University Press, 2008), 148.

111. Pound, *Jefferson and/or Mussolini*, 113; Cheadle, *Ezra Pound's Confucian Translations*, 80–84.

112. *Ezra Pound's Poetry and Prose: Contributions to Periodicals*, ed. Lea Baechler, A. Walton Litz, and James Longenbach (New York: Garland, 1991), 1:199.

113. T. S. Eliot, letter, June 18, 1934; quoted in Humphrey Carpenter, *A Serious Character: The Life of Ezra Pound* (Boston: Houghton Mifflin, 1988), 526.

114. K. John, "The Eternal Schoolboy," *New Statesman and Nation* 8 (November 3, 1934): 630–32; Babette Deutsch, "Indomitable Ezra Pound," *New York Herald Tribune Book Review*, June 2, 1935, 18.

115. Hugh Kenner, "The Rose in the Steel Dust," *Hudson Review* 3 (1950): 81. The discussion reappears in Kenner's *The Poetry of Ezra Pound* (London: Faber, 1951), 234. Kenner does not further identify his source here, but the reference to *The Great Digest* makes it clear that he is referring to Pound's more recent translation of the *Da Xue* (Confucius, *The Great Digest & Unwobbling Pivot*, trans. and commentary by Ezra Pound [New York: New Directions, 1951]), because the earlier translation had been called *The Great Learning*. There were not very many reviews of *The Great Digest*. None of those consulted for this study call attention to the bathtub anecdote or the slogan. See, for example, Kathleen Raine, "There Is No Trifling," *New Republic* 126 (March 24, 1952): 17, 22, and Anthony West, "Unwobbling Pivot," *New Yorker* 28 (May 31, 1952): 98.

116. Kenner, "Rose," 81.

117. Ibid.

118. Philip Rahv, "Fiction and the Criticism of Fiction," *Kenyon Review* 18 (1956): 284.

119. Northrop Frye, "The Realistic Oriole: A Study of Wallace Stevens," *Hudson Review* 10 (1957): 370.

120. Roy Harvey Pearce, "Toward an American Epic," *Hudson Review* 12 (1959): 362.

121. Marvin Mudrick, review, *Hudson Review* 19 (1966): 311.

122. R. H. Pearce, "Art in Culture," *American Quarterly* 11 (1959): 79; Richard Ellmann, "Ez and Old Billyum," *Kenyon Review* 28 (1966): 474.

123. Gay, *Modernism*, 4; Alfred Appel Jr., *Jazz Modernism: From Ellington to Armstrong to Matisse and Joyce* (New York: Knopf, 2002), 27.

CHAPTER SEVEN

1. Harold Rosenberg, *The Tradition of the New* (1959; reprint, New York: McGraw-Hill, 1965), 9.

2. Lionel Trilling, "On the Modern Element in Modern Literature," *Partisan Review* 28 (January–February 1961): 17.

3. As Fredric Jameson points out, modernism can't explain why its aesthetic products should remain interesting, since it can't even have recourse to the classical standard of timeless value. The self-defeating nature of the new is therefore one reason, according to Jameson, to reject the innovation model of modernism, at least as a freestanding explanation. Fredric Jameson, *A Singular Modernity* (London: Verso, 2002), 126.

4. Caroline A. Jones, "The Modernist Paradigm: The Artworld and Thomas Kuhn," *Critical Inquiry* 26 (2000): 497.

5. Jonathan Edwards, quoted in Michael Fried, *Art and Objecthood: Essays and Reviews* (Chicago: University of Chicago Press, 1998), 148.

6. For analyses and critical responses, see Rosalind E. Krauss, *The Optical Unconscious* (Cambridge, MA: MIT Press, 1994), 6–7; Hal Foster, *The Return of the Real* (Cambridge, MA: MIT Press, 1996), 52; Pamela A. Lee, *Chronophobia: On Time in the Art of the 1960s* (Cambridge, MA: MIT Press, 2004), 49.

7. Fried, *Art and Objecthood*, 99.

8. For one discussion of this particular nexus, see Stephen W. Melville, *Philosophy beside Itself: On Deconstruction and Modernism* (Minneapolis: University of Minnesota Press, 1986), 3–33.

9. As Jameson points out, the very term *modernism* was relatively infrequent until the 1960s (*Singular Modernity*, 100). For Bürger on the neo-avant-garde, see his *Theory of the Avant-Garde*, trans. Michael Shaw (Minneapolis: University of Minnesota Press, 1984), 58–63.

10. For a good representation of the first few decades of this debate, one conditioned very largely by the issues of autonomy and political commitment, see Francis Frascina, ed., *Pollock and After: The Critical Debate*, 2nd ed. (London: Routledge, 2000).

11. Rosalind Krauss, "1960b," in *Art since 1900*, ed. Hal Foster et al., 2nd ed. (New York: Thames and Hudson, 2011), 2:477.

12. Clement Greenberg, *The Collected Essays and Criticism*, ed. John O'Brien (Chicago: University of Chicago Press: 1986–93), 1:133.

13. "The best new art will always surprise you somehow; if it didn't, it would not be new and it would not be the best." Clement Greenberg, *Homemade Esthetics: Observations on Art and Taste* (Oxford: Oxford University Press, 1999), 39.

14. Greenberg, *Collected Essays and Criticism*, 4:208.

15. Ibid., 1:14.

16. See Thierry de Duve, *Clement Greenberg between the Lines*, trans. Brian Holmes (Paris: Editions Dis Voir, n.d.), 81.

17. Greenberg, *Collected Essays and Criticism*, 3:11.

18. Ibid., 4:109.

19. Ibid., 3:82.

20. Ibid., 3:83.

21. Ibid., 3:90.

22. Ibid., 1:80, 133.

23. Ibid., 2:319.

24. Greenberg, *Homemade Esthetics*, 54. See similar statements in the "debate" included in de Duve, *Clement Greenberg between the Lines*, 125–26.

25. J. M. Bernstein, *Against Voluptuous Bodies: Late Modernism and the Meaning of Painting* (Stanford, CA: Stanford University Press, 2006), 203.

26. Greenberg, *Collected Essays and Criticism*, 2:48, 143; 4:5, 10.

27. Ibid., 4:143.

28. For a brief discussion of Greenberg in relation to "historical returns" in art history, see Foster, *Return of the Real*, x.

29. Greenberg, *Collected Essays and Criticism*, 2:255.

30. Ibid., 3:83.

31. De Duve, *Clement Greenberg between the Lines*, 66.

32. Greenberg, *Collected Essays and Criticism*, 2:248.

33. Ibid., 4:83.

34. Ibid., 3:34.

35. Ibid., 3:217.

36. Greenberg, *Homemade Esthetics*, 52.

37. Krauss, "1960b," 2:479; Greenberg, *Collected Essays and Criticism*, 2:325.

38. Caroline A. Jones, *Eyesight Alone: Clement Greenberg's Modernism and the Bureaucratization of the Senses* (Chicago: University of Chicago Press, 2005), 108–12.

39. Greenberg, *Collected Essays and Criticism*, 3:82, 142.

40. Ibid., 2:15.

41. Stanley Cavell, *The World Viewed: Reflections on the Ontology of Film*, enlarged ed. (Cambridge, MA: Harvard University Press, 1979), xxv.

42. Stanley Cavell, *Must We Mean What We Say?*, updated ed. (Cambridge: Cambridge University Press, 2002), 184.

43. Stanley Cavell, "Crossing Paths," in *Action, Art, History: Engagements with Arthur C. Danto*, ed. Daniel Herwitz and Michael Kelly (New York: Columbia University Press, 2007), 25.

44. Cavell, *Must We Mean What We Say?*, xiv.

45. Ibid., 42.

46. Thomas S. Kuhn, *The Structure of Scientific Revolutions*, 4th ed. (Chicago: University of Chicago Press, 2012), xlv. For discussions of this relationship, see Jones,

"Modernist Paradigm," 508, and Vasso Kindi, "Novelty and Revolution in Art and Science: The Connection between Kuhn and Cavell," *Perspectives on Science* 18 (2010): 284–86.

47. Stanley Cavell, *Little Did I Know* (Stanford, CA: Stanford University Press, 2010), 354–55. For a comment on these problems, see Cavell, *Must We Mean What We Say?*, 53.

48. Stanley Cavell, *The Claim of Reason: Wittgenstein, Skepticism, Morality, and Tragedy* (New York: Oxford University Press, 1979), 25. See also Sandra Laugier, "Introduction to the French Edition of *Must We Mean What We Say?*," *Critical Inquiry* 37 (2010): 639.

49. Cavell, *Must We Mean What We Say?*, 61.

50. Ludwig Wittgenstein, *Philosophical Investigations*, trans. G. E. M. Anscombe, P. M. S. Hacker, and Joachim Schulte (Chichester: Wiley-Blackwell, 2009). See, for example, 94. For another of the many instances of the phrase in Cavell's work, see Cavell, *Claim of Reason*, 184.

51. Stephen Mulhall, *Stanley Cavell: Philosophy's Recounting of the Ordinary* (Oxford: Oxford University Press, 1994), 103. See also Diarmuid Costello, "On the Very Idea of a 'Specific' Medium: Michael Fried and Stanley Cavell on Painting and Photography as Arts," *Critical Inquiry* 34 (2008): 290–91.

52. Greenberg, *Collected Essays and Criticism*, 3:84.

53. Wittgenstein, *Philosophical Investigations*, 25.

54. Ibid., 33.

55. Ibid., 83–84.

56. See ibid., 86.

57. Ibid., 209.

58. Cavell, *Claim of Reason*, 185, 189. See Mulhall, *Stanley Cavell*, 83.

59. Cavell, *Must We Mean What We Say?*, xxxvi.

60. Ibid., 201.

61. See Cavell, *The World Viewed*, 106, and *Claim of Reason*, 96; Mulhall, *Stanley Cavell*, 70; and Bernstein, *Against Voluptuous Bodies*, 92.

62. Greenberg, *Collected Essays and Criticism*, 1:6.

63. Stanley Cavell, "Impressions of Revolution," *Musical Quarterly* 85 (2001): 267, 272.

64. Mulhall, *Stanley Cavell*, 166. Cavell, *Must We Mean What We Say?*, 84, 86.

65. Cavell, "Impressions of Revolution," 264–65.

66. Cavell, *Must We Mean What We Say?*, 73.

67. Cavell, *World Viewed*, 110. Kindi, "Novelty and Revolution in Art and Science," 287, 291, 293. Kindi argues on 290 that this sense of return to tradition is absent from Kuhn, but the argument here is that this is precisely what makes Cavell's model resemble Kuhn's so closely.

68. Cavell, *Must We Mean What We Say?*, 189.

69. Ibid., 219.

70. Cavell, *World Viewed*, 72. See Mulhall, *Stanley Cavell*, 31, and Bernstein, *Against Voluptuous Bodies*, 93.

71. Cavell, *Must We Mean What We Say?*, 206.

72. Ibid., 203.

73. Ibid., 222.

74. Cavell, *World Viewed*, 15. Mulhall addresses the feeling that Cavell's vision of modernism may be simply conservative in *Stanley Cavell*, 163–64.

75. Krauss, *Optical Unconscious*, 248, 309.

76. Costello, "On the Very Idea of a 'Specific' Medium," 290–91; Jones, "Modernist Paradigm," 523.

77. Fried, *Art and Objecthood*, 33.

78. Ibid., 15.

79. Cavell, *Must We Mean What We Say?*, xv, 203, 217, 220.

80. Jones, "Modernist Paradigm," 488, 510, 512. See also Fried's response to this article, "Response to Caroline A. Jones," *Critical Inquiry* 27 (2001): 703–5.

81. Fried, *Art and Objecthood*, 30–31.

82. Ibid., 132.

83. Ibid., 262, 264.

84. Ibid., 147.

85. Ibid., 61. See also Michael Fried, "How Modernism Works: A Response to T. J. Clark," *Critical Inquiry* 9 (1982): 223, 231.

86. Fried, *Art and Objecthood*, 258.

87. Ibid., 149.

88. Ibid., 234.

89. Of the many responses to Fried's work, one of the most useful in this context is Stephen Mulhall, "Crimes and Deeds of Glory: Michael Fried's Modernism," *British Journal of Aesthetics* 41 (2001): 1–23.

90. Fried, *Art and Objecthood*, 17, 34.

91. Ibid., 218.

92. See Kindi, "Novelty and Revolution in Art and Science," for a number of important points: the history of the term *perpetual revolution*, extending back to Proudhon; and Kuhn's opposition to the idea (295). In "Music Discomposed," published three years after "Modernist Painting and Formal Criticism," Cavell uses the more conventional term *permanent revolution* (*Must We Mean What We Say?*, 205). See also Melville, *Philosophy beside Itself*, 31.

93. Rosalind E. Krauss, *Under Blue Cup* (Cambridge, MA: MIT Press, 2011), 7, 17.

94. Ibid., 99.

95. Foster, *Return of the Real*, x.

96. Giorgio Agamben, *The Signature of All Things: On Method*, trans. Luca D'Isanto (New York: Zone Books, 2009), 27.

97. Roland Barthes, *The Neutral*, trans. Rosalind E. Krauss and Denis Hollier (New York: Columbia University Press, 2005), 27, 42.

98. See Jones, "Modernist Paradigm," 489, 498.

99. Greenberg, *Collected Essays and Criticism*, 4:262, 302.

100. See the debate with Greenberg in de Duve, *Clement Greenberg between the Lines*, 125-26.

101. Greenberg, *Collected Essays and Criticism*, 1:102.

102. Ibid., 54. See Bernstein, *Against Voluptuous Bodies*, 232.

103. Greenberg, *Collected Essays and Criticism*, 1:101.

104. Ibid., 2:145. See de Duve, *Clement Greenberg between the Lines*, 81.

105. Cavell, *Must We Mean What We Say?*, xxxvi. See Mulhall, *Stanley Cavell*, xi.

106. Greenberg, *Collected Essays and Criticism*, 1:12.

107. Ibid., 4:288. See Arthur C. Danto, *After the End of Art* (Princeton, NJ: Princeton University Press, 1997), 104-5.

108. Cavell, *Must We Mean What We Say?*, 221-22. See Gordon C. F. Bearn, "Staging Authenticity: A Critique of Cavell's Modernism," *Philosophy and Literature* 24 (2000): 304.

109. Michael B. Miller, *The Bon Marché: Bourgeois Culture and the Department Store, 1869-1920* (Princeton, NJ: Princeton University Press, 1981), 25.

110. Rachel Bowlby, *Just Looking: Consumer Culture in Dreiser, Gissing and Zola* (New York: Methuen, 1985), 67.

111. Anne M. Wagner, "Reading *Minimal Art*," in *Minimal Art: A Critical Anthology*, ed. Gregory Battcock (1968; reprint, Berkeley: University of California Press, 1995), 10.

112. Joseph Kosuth, "1975," in *Conceptual Art: A Critical Anthology*, ed. Alexander Alberro and Blake Stimson (Cambridge, MA: MIT Press, 1999), 336.

113. Charles Harrison, "Notes toward Art Work," in Alberro and Stimson, *Conceptual Art*, 205.

114. Daniel Buren, quoted in Max Kozloff, "The Trouble with Art-as-Idea," in Alberro and Stimson, *Conceptual Art*, 274.

115. Sol LeWitt, "Paragraphs on Conceptual Art," in Alberro and Stimson, *Conceptual Art*, 15, and quoted in Anne Rorimer, *New Art in the 60s and 70s: Redefining Reality* (London: Thames & Hudson, 2001), 158.

116. Rorimer, *New Art in the 60s and 70s*, 135. See also Alberro and Stimson, *Conceptual Art*, 184. For a similar statement from Mel Bochner, see Rorimer, *New Art in the 60s and 70s*, 182.

117. Lucy Lippard, *Six Years: The Dematerialization of the Art Object* (New York: Praeger, 1973), 263.

118. Ian Burn, "The Art Market: Affluence and Degradation," in Alberro and Stimson, *Conceptual Art*, 324.

119. From *The Writings of Robert Smithson*, ed. Nancy Holt (New York: New York University Press, 1979), 51.

120. Quoted in Arthur C. Danto, *Andy Warhol* (New Haven, CT: Yale University Press, 2009), 81.

121. Andy Warhol, quoted in ibid., 84.

122. Tony Scherman and David Dalton, *Pop: The Genius of Andy Warhol* (New York: Harper, 2009), 109, 155.

123. Andy Warhol, quoted in Wayne Koestenbaum, *Andy Warhol* (London: Weidenfeld & Nicolson, 2001), 139.

124. Andy Warhol, *The Philosophy of Andy Warhol: From A to B and Back Again* (New York: Harcourt Brace Jovanovich, 1975), 82; quoted in Foster, *Return of the Real*, 72.

125. Andy Warhol, quoted in Charles F. Stuckey, "Warhol: Backwards and For-wards," *Flash Art* 101 (January/February 1981): 142.

126. From Benjamin H. D. Buchloh, "An Interview with Andy Warhol," in *Andy Warhol*, ed. Annette Michelson (Cambridge, MA: MIT Press, 2001), 124.

127. E. C. Goossen, "Two Exhibitions," in Battcock, *Minimal Art*, 168.

128. Barbara Rose, "ABC Art," in Battcock, *Minimal Art*, 274. For the rumored art-ist who worked entirely by telephone, see Michael Benedikt, "Sculpture as Architec-ture," in ibid., 88.

129. Daniel Buren, "Beware," in Alberro and Stimson, *Conceptual Art*, 153.

130. James Rosenquist, quoted in Foster et al., *Art since 1900*, 2:485.

131. Carl Andre, Robert Barry, Lawrence Weiner, discussion; Daniel Buren, "Is Teaching Art Necessary," *Galerie des Artes* (September 1968), quoted in Lippard, *Six Years*, 40, 52.

132. Foster, *Return of the Real*, 25.

133. Burn, "The Art Market," 324.

134. Scherman and Dalton, *Pop*, 129, 141.

135. Toby Mussman, "Literalness and the Infinite," in Battcock, *Minimal Art*, 237.

136. Wagner, "Reading *Minimal Art*," 3.

137. Scherman and Dalton, *Pop*, 197.

138. *The Critical Response to Andy Warhol*, ed. Alan R. Pratt (Westport, CT: Green-wood Press, 1997), 28–34.

139. Warhol, *Philosophy*, 148.

140. Henry Geldzahler, "Andy Warhol," *Art International* 8 (April 1964): 3.

141. Danto, *Andy Warhol*, 143.

142. Rosalind E. Krauss, "Carnal Knowledge," in Michelson, *Andy Warhol*, 117.

143. Hugh J. Silverman, "Andy Warhol: Chiasmatic Visibility," in *Impossible Pres-ences: Surface and Screen in the Photogenic Era*, ed. Terry Smith (Chicago: University of Chicago Press, 2001), 197.

144. Arthur Danto, "The Artworld," *Journal of Philosophy* 61 (October 15, 1964): 572.

145. Danto, "Artworld," 573, and *Andy Warhol*, 28. For another elaboration of Danto's position, see Arthur C. Danto, *Beyond the Brillo Box: The Visual Arts in Post-Historical Perspective* (New York: Farrar Straus Giroux, 1992), 3–12. For a critique of the general tendency to interpret Warhol's work in philosophical or political con-

texts, exclusive of its visual appearance, see Paul Mattick, "The Andy Warhol of Philosophy and the Philosophy of Andy Warhol," *Critical Inquiry* 24 (Summer 1998): 965–87.

146. Kosuth, "1975," 166.

147. Ibid., 164.

148. Ibid., 164–65.

149. For the first of these, see Burn, "The Art Market," 189. For the second, see the manifestos of the Art & Language group in ibid.

150. Rosalind Krauss, "1957b," in Foster et al., *Art since 1900*, 2:436.

151. See, for example, Yves Alain Bois, "1961," in Foster et al., *Art since 1900*, 2:493.

152. John Klein, "The Dispersal of the Modernist Series," *Oxford Art Journal* 21 (1998): 132.

153. Smithson, *Writings*, 12.

154. Mel Bochner, "The Serial Attitude," in Alberro and Stimson, *Conceptual Art*, 25.

155. Krauss, *Originality of the Avant-Garde*, 253. See also LeWitt's "Paragraphs on Conceptual Art," 13.

156. Wittgenstein, *Philosophical Investigations*, 89.

157. John Baldessari, *John Baldessari: Works 1966–81* (Eindhoven, Netherlands: Stedelijk Van Abbemuseum, 1981), 49; quoted in Rorimer, *New Art in the 60s and 70s*, 134.

158. Rorimer, *New Art in the 60s and 70s*, 139.

159. Douglas Huebler, *Variable Piece No. 70 (in process)—Global* (1971); quoted in ibid., 140.

160. Cavell, *World Viewed*, 32.

161. Ibid., 103.

162. Krauss, *Under Blue Cup*, 19.

163. Ibid., 69.

164. Smithson, *Writings*, 84.

165. Ibid., 85.

166. Lippard, *Six Years*, 220.

CONCLUSION

1. Frank Kermode, *The Sense of an Ending: Studies in the Theory of Fiction* (1966; reprint, Oxford: Oxford University Press, 2000); Paul de Man, *Blindness and Insight: Essays in the Rhetoric of Contemporary Criticism,* 2nd ed. (Minneapolis: University of Minnesota Press, 1983); Fredric Jameson, *A Singular Modernity* (London: Verso, 2002).

2. Niklas Luhmann, *Art as a Social System,* trans. Eva M. Knodt (Stanford, CA: Stanford University Press, 2000), 223.

INDEX